CHOISIR
LE BONHEUR

Données de catalogage avant publication (Canada)

Foisy, Roger, 1936-

Choisir le bonheur: les merveilleuses possibilités de votre subconscient

Publ. antérieurement sous le titre: Les merveilleuses possibilités de votre subconscient. Montréal: La Presse, 1973.

ISBN 2-89455-001-4

1. Bonheur. 2. Succès. 3. Inconscient. I. Titre. II. Titre: Les merveilleuses possibilités de votre subconscient.

BJ1612.F63   1995   158'.1   C95-940280-2

© Guy Saint-Jean Éditeur Inc. 1995

Illustration de la page couverture: Jean-Guy Meister
Conception graphique de la page couverture: Christiane Séguin

Dépôt légal 1er trimestre 1995
Bibliothèques nationales du Québec et du Canada
ISBN 2-89455-001-4

DISTRIBUTION ET DIFFUSION

SUISSE
Transat s.a.
Rte des Jeunes, 4 ter
Case postale 125
1211 Genève 26,
Suisse
342.77.40

BELGIQUE
Diffusion Vander s.a.
321 Avenue des Volontaires
B-1150 Bruxelles,
Belgique
(2) 762.98.04

AMÉRIQUE
Diffusion Prologue Inc.
1650, boul. Lionel-Bertrand
Boisbriand (Québec)
Canada J7H 1N7
(514) 434-0306

FRANCE (Distribution)
Distique S.A.
5, rue du Maréchal Leclerc
28600 Luisant
France
37.30.57.00

(Diffusion)
C.E.D. Diffusion
72, Quai des Carrières
94220 Charenton
France
(1) 43.96.46.36

GUY SAINT-JEAN ÉDITEUR INC.
674, Place Publique, bureau 200B
Laval (Québec) Canada H7X 1G1
(514) 689-6402

Imprimé et relié au Canada

Roger Foisy, N.D., Ph.D.
de l'Académie des Sciences de New York

CHOISIR LE BONHEUR

Guy Saint-Jean
ÉDITEUR

Note: dans ce livre, le masculin, pris dans son sens large, désigne autant les femmes que les hommes.

TABLE DES MATIÈRES

Retournons à l'école... du bonheur !!!

Vous a-t-on déjà enseigné les lois du bonheur ?

Nombre de professionnels me confient tous les jours, lors de consultations, que bien qu'ils aient étudié aux quatre coins du monde, aucune université ou institution supérieure ne leur a enseigné les véritables lois pratiques du bonheur. La même situation prévaut dans les écoles primaires et secondaires. On n'offre jamais de cours de bonheur. Pourquoi ? Parce qu'on ne peut enseigner ce qu'on ne connaît pas.

Le bonheur est une science

Le bonheur obéit à des lois naturelles, tout comme la météorologie. Le météorologue consciencieux sait que le climat d'un lieu donné résulte d'un « engrenage » de lois naturelles. Un jour ensoleillé, une semaine pluvieuse, une tempête de neige ou de fréquentes périodes nuageuses ne sont pas l'effet du hasard. Les phénomènes météorologiques dépendent de bien des facteurs qui, réunis, convergent vers un résultat certain. La variation de la pression atmosphérique, la force et la direction des vents, l'humidité de l'air, la température, la nébulosité, voilà autant d'éléments qui, agissant les uns sur les autres, peuvent influencer ou modifier les conditions du temps.

Notre bonheur réagit ainsi. Il est une science qui découle d'une série de facteurs. Nous devons prendre conscience de ces éléments si nous voulons être heureux. Celui qui attend, celui qui demeure passif face au bonheur, en se disant: « Il viendra bien un jour... à tel ou tel moment, ce sera mon tour... », celui-là risque d'attendre longtemps. Le bonheur ne nous sourit pas simplement parce qu'il est normal qu'il y ait un peu de bonheur sur terre.

Nous savons très bien que s'il n'y a aucun nuage dans le ciel, il ne tombera pas une seule goutte de pluie, celle-ci relevant de phénomènes déterminés, obligatoires. C'est également le cas du bonheur. Mais où pouvons-nous découvrir ces phénomènes ? En nous !... Seulement en nous... Toujours en nous.

Personnellement, je passe ma vie à aider les gens qui viennent me consulter à mettre en pratique les lois naturelles de la santé et du bonheur. Ceux qui apprennent à se connaître, ceux qui mettent en pratique les lois naturelles du bonheur finissent toujours par être heureux. Il s'agit d'être scientifique.

Notre maison de bonheur

Celui qui désire construire une maison sait qu'il devra suivre un ordre logique au cours des différentes phases de la construction s'il veut obtenir de bons résultats. Il ne commence pas par délayer le plâtre qui couvrira les murs. Il n'ouvre pas une boîte de peinture, ne sort pas immédiatement des pinceaux. Le constructeur est plus scientifique. Il sait qu'il doit tout d'abord établir les fondations et élever la charpente s'il ne veut pas être déçu. Une maison bâtie au hasard risque de s'écrouler rapidement.

Notre maison de bonheur doit, elle aussi, reposer sur une base solide. Sa charpente doit être à toute épreuve. Nous sommes responsables non seulement de l'édification de notre bonheur, mais aussi de sa longévité.

Le devoir d'être heureux

Pourquoi certains se concentrent-ils sur les incidents déplaisants de leur existence et en oublient-ils les bons moments ? La vie sur terre ne serait-elle pas plus agréable si parents et éducateurs avaient insisté constamment sur le devoir d'être heureux plutôt que sur le bonheur du devoir ?

Retournons tous à l'école !

Il n'est pas trop tard. Quel que soit notre âge, retournons à l'école... mais à l'école du bonheur, cette fois. Apprenons-y à neutraliser tous les ennemis de notre bonheur, tels que nos peurs, nos rancunes, notre égoïsme, nos soucis, notre pessimisme. Comment ? En développant l'habitude de penser positivement avec confiance, enthousiasme et bonne humeur.

Vivement, qu'on enseigne dans nos écoles, dans nos collèges et dans nos universités la science du bonheur !... afin que soient connues les lois naturelles qui le régissent; ainsi, nous saurons comment prévenir et neutraliser le manque de confiance, l'anxiété, la timidité et nous pourrons enfin développer l'esprit d'initiative, l'audace, la confiance, la compassion dont plusieurs ont tant besoin. Existe-t-il une science ou un art plus utile que celui de notre bonheur ? Comment « pratiquer » notre bonheur ? J'ai bien dit « pratiquer », puisqu'*une once de pratique vaut mieux qu'une tonne de théorie.*

Pourquoi ne pas nous entraîner de façon à ce que le bonheur devienne pour nous aussi naturel que la marche ? Ne le considérons pas comme possible, mais plutôt comme essentiel. Il est aussi simple de s'habituer à voir le bon côté des choses qu'à considérer le mauvais. Tout n'est qu'une question d'habitude, notre bonheur aussi.

Que recherchez-vous dans la vie ?

Si l'on vous demandait ce que vous recherchez le plus ardemment dans votre vie, que répondriez-vous ? Le bonheur, sans aucun doute.

D'ailleurs nous recherchons tous le bonheur, souvent sans même nous en douter. N'essayons-nous pas tous plus ou moins d'améliorer notre condition, d'être plus heureux ?

Entre nous, le bonheur peut-il cohabiter avec des pensées tristes, soucieuses, pessimistes, rancunières, agressives ? Nous ne récoltons que ce que nous semons ! C'est une loi universelle. Ceux qui se répètent constamment que l'homme est mauvais, qu'ils sont et resteront toujours malheureux, que la vie n'est qu'un long calvaire n'ont absolument pas à s'en faire pour leur avenir. Ils ne verront toujours que des hommes mauvais, ils demeureront dans leur malheur, la vie n'étalera devant eux que des ronces et des épines. Les jolies fleurs ne poussent pas sur les cailloux.

Le vrai bonheur est si simple que la plupart des gens ne le trouvent pas et, surtout, ne le reconnaissent pas.

Cherchons-nous le bonheur surtout dans les choses qui passent, dans les plaisirs matériels, si nécessaires qu'ils soient ? Si oui, nous faisons fausse route. Le bonheur est un état. C'est ce que nous sommes qui nous rend heureux plutôt que ce que nous possédons.

Retournons à l'école... du bonheur. Le but de ce livre est de nous enseigner, de nous aider à mettre en pratique les lois naturelles du bonheur.

Qui est notre meilleur ami ?

Dans la vie, lorsque nous avons une tâche importante à accomplir, nous demandons souvent l'aide d'un ami.

Si mon auto est défectueuse, je peux décider de la réparer moi-même. Comme je ne connais rien à la mécanique, avant de me mettre à l'œuvre, je demanderai conseil à un ami qui, lui, s'y entend. Pour atteindre le bonheur, nous devons agir de la même façon. Nous avons tous un ami qui ne demande qu'à nous aider. Cet ami est si fidèle qu'il ne juge aucunement nos gestes et nos pensées. A plus ou moins brève échéance, il nous aidera à réaliser nos désirs, que ceux-ci soient positifs ou négatifs.

Peut-être le cherchez-vous, cet ami ? Peut-être ne le connaissez-vous pas ? Pourtant il est là; il veille sans relâche sur vous, que vous dormiez ou que vous soyez parfaitement éveillés. Où est-il ? Qui est-il ? Comment s'appelle-t-il ? Il n'est pas loin, il habite en nous. Son nom ? Subconscient... notre subconscient !

Beaucoup de gens agissent comme si le subconscient n'était donné qu'à certains. Voilà l'erreur ! Nous possédons tous un subconscient. Lorsque nous disons qu'il est notre meilleur ami, nous avons raison en ce sens que c'est lui qui nous permet de réaliser tous nos désirs. A chaque instant, notre subconscient nous sert et, souvent, nous semblons l'ignorer. Grâce à lui, nous sommes heureux ou malheureux, selon notre façon de l'orienter.

Notre subconscient = une pellicule photographique

Notre subconscient ressemble à une pellicule photographique. Il imprime en lui tout ce que nous pensons pour nous en transmettre l'image plus tard. Si je prends une photo en pleine noirceur, il ne faudra pas m'étonner de ne trouver que du noir sur l'image qui en résultera.

Le même problème se pose si je photographie un soleil éclatant. Je n'obtiendrai alors qu'une photo blanche. Ainsi, si je veux photographier un objet, je veillerai à me placer dans les conditions idéales.

Certaines lois existent que je dois respecter si je désire une image parfaite. Pour réussir une bonne photo, il me faudra un éclairage adéquat. Je vérifierai également la précision de mon objectif. Si, au moment de photographier, je ne peux même pas différencier les traits de mon sujet, je ne peux m'attendre à obtenir une image précise. Je vérifierai aussi le cadrage. Je verrai à ce que mon modèle demeure bien dans le champ de vision de mon appareil. Si je veux photographier une fleur rouge et que je vise une échelle, j'obtiendrai une image de l'échelle et non de la fleur. Notre subconscient agit de la même façon. Il imprime en lui ce que nous pensons, voulons et désirons et il nous en transmet l'image exacte plus tard, qu'elle soit bonne ou mauvaise.

Quel est votre présent état d'esprit ?

Notre état d'esprit détermine l'aide que nous apportera notre subconscient. Pourquoi ? Parce que celui-ci s'imprègne de ce que nous lui apportons.

Prenons Jean. Il s'éveille le matin et, s'apercevant que son réveille-matin n'a pas sonné, il se laisse rapidement gagner par la mauvaise humeur.

Il est en retard d'une dizaine de minutes. Le voilà qui prend panique. Il se dit: « Une autre mauvaise journée en perspective... et moi qui ai de l'ouvrage comme un fou, aujourd'hui ! »

Il se lève en vitesse... et l'idée d'une mauvaise journée commence à faire son chemin dans son subconscient. Il s'énerve et, comme on s'en doute, tout se met de la partie pour le ralentir. Il brise un lacet, un bouton de sa chemise saute, il se coupe en se rasant, etc... Il continue à se répéter que tout va mal. Cette idée germe en son subconscient.

Jean déjeune en vitesse. Il ne mange presque pas. Il saute dans son auto, s'aperçoit que le niveau d'essence est au plus bas. Il arrête à une station-service, fait le plein. En proie à une excitation grandissante, il perd un temps fou. Il arrive au bureau avec vingt minutes de retard et se met au travail. Inutile d'aller plus loin. Au milieu de l'avant-midi, il aura mal à la tête, il fera tout de travers, sera de mauvaise humeur, etc...

L'histoire de Jean n'est pas unique. Vous est-elle arrivée aujourd'hui ? ou peut-être hier ? Beaucoup de gens se diront: « C'est une journée tout à fait normale. Nous avons de bonnes et de mauvaises journées, celle-là était mauvaise. » Ces personnes ont tort. Toutes nos journées peuvent être bonnes. C'est nous qui décidons.

Si Jean, en se levant, avait eu une attitude plus positive, toute sa journée se serait déroulée différemment. Peut-être serait-il arrivé en retard, peut-être aurait-il connu plus d'embûches qu'au cours d'une journée normale... mais, en se convainquant au départ qu'une bonne journée s'annonçait, les petits problèmes auraient eu des répercussions différentes et, par le fait même, auraient été plus faciles à résoudre. Il est certain que tout le monde rencontre quotidiennement de petits problèmes, mais chacun d'entre ceux-ci revêt la dimension que nous lui donnons.

Le lendemain de la veille

Un chef d'entreprise me racontait comment il devait partager le travail de ses employés. Il me disait: « Le lundi s'avère souvent une journée moins efficace que les autres. » Pourquoi ? « Parce que le lundi annonce un changement de vie, me répondit-il. La fin de semaine se termine le lundi. » Nous en avons conclu que le subconscient de ses employés influençait considérablement leur travail.

Une vieille tradition persiste chez plusieurs personnes: « l'humeur du lundi matin ». Combien de fois n'entendons-nous pas des gens dire: « Ah ! le lundi matin, le lendemain de la veille, ce n'est pas drôle ! Ça nous prend toute une journée pour nous replonger dans le bain ! » Ainsi, ils ont habitué leur subconscient à considérer cette journée comme spéciale... et cette journée devient effectivement plus difficile à traverser. Par contre, si nous nous convainquions de l'aspect ordinaire du lundi, si nous

15

nous persuadions de la possibilité de fournir, ce jour-là, le même rendement que pendant le reste de la semaine, cette journée ne constituerait plus un problème.

Notre subconscient détient une puissance merveilleuse: celle de nous aider en tout. Il rend possibles toutes nos pensées, qu'elles soient positives ou négatives.

Conscient et subconscient

Des milliers de livres décrivent les caractéristiques de notre mental. Nous pouvons simplifier le tout de la façon suivante: notre conscient est rationnel, objectif, volontaire et actif; tandis que notre subconscient se montre irrationnel, subjectif, involontaire et automatique.

Connaissez-vous ce géant ?

Aucun système de mesure sur terre ne pourrait nous permettre de calculer la force du géant qui dort en nous: notre subconscient.

Nous sommes véritablement des géants très puissants mais nous ignorons, la plupart du temps, nos véritables capacités. En chacun de nous attend une abondance supérieure à tout ce qui peut exister ici-bas. Cependant, nous effleurons à peine la surface de nos aptitudes et de nos pouvoirs. Aucun instrument créé par l'homme ne peut mesurer les véritables limites du potentiel humain, de notre subconscient.

Alors, pourquoi ne pas nous servir de ce géant ? Pourquoi ne pas apporter notre contribution à la

16

vie, au bonheur des autres, puisque notre rôle est unique et que personne d'autre que nous ne peut le remplir ? Pourquoi ne pas demander et donner davantage à la vie ?

Comment s'y prendre ?

Simplement en éveillant et en employant ce géant qui somnole en nous: notre subconscient. Confions-lui les petites charges, les lourdes épreuves, tout ce qui nous semble insurmontable.

Pendant des années, les gens se résignent à l'insuffisance dans tous les domaines de leur vie. En fait, tout ce qu'ils ont à faire est d'ouvrir les écluses de l'attitude positive et de l'effort soutenu qui libèrent la puissance de leur géant.

Croyons-nous que nous avons vraiment le pouvoir et le droit de choisir le bonheur et la réussite ? La décision finale appartient à chacun. Avec l'aide de notre puissant géant, nous pouvons nous sortir des circonstances qui nous ont jusqu'ici gênés ou arrêtés.

Qui va réveiller notre géant, notre subconscient ?

Personne d'autre que nous ! Prenons nos propres risques. Si nous voulons remuer le monde, remuons-nous d'abord. Prenons pleinement conscience de nos propres capacités et de nos talents. Fonçons. Haussons le plafond de nos buts et de nos réalisations.

Se connaître: voilà le plus pressant besoin de l'homme moderne. De nos jours, nous déplorons avec raison le gaspillage des ressources de la nature. Cependant, nous oublions trop souvent le gaspillage des possibilités et des talents inhérents à chacun de nous. Est-ce notre cas ?

Réfléchissons-y quelques instants.

Nous vouons-nous à découvrir et à mettre à l'épreuve la puissance et les possibilités de ce géant, de notre géant ? Osons-nous nous engager totalement dans cette découverte de nous-mêmes qui nous apportera joie et réussite ?

Nous pourrons vivre pleinement notre vie en découvrant la vérité sur nous-mêmes et sur le bonheur. Ainsi nous nous acheminerons vers une vie meilleure et plus satisfaisante.

Oserons-nous éveiller et employer ce géant qui dort en nous ?

Apprenons à faire de nouvelles grimaces

« On ne peut pas montrer à un vieux singe à faire de nouvelles grimaces ! », diront certains. Mais pourquoi pas ? Plus le singe vieillit, plus il devient difficile de changer ses habitudes. C'est là le seul problème et il est possible de le résoudre.

Le bonheur = une habitude

L'habitude relève de notre subconscient. Elle s'imprime en lui. Au départ, nous avons tout appris consciemment. C'est ainsi que nous avons commencé à marcher, à nager, à parler, à conduire correctement notre voiture. En répétant, en recommençant toujours les mêmes gestes, en réalisant certaines performances maintes et maintes fois, nous avons acquis une habitude. Au fur et à mesure que nous progressions, de réussite en réussite, notre subconscient a pris la relève. Maintenant, nous pouvons marcher, nager ou parler sans toujours devoir vérifier si nous sommes bien en mesure de le faire. Nous avons l'habitude et le geste devient automatique. Notre subconscient nous mène.

Nous sommes libres d'acquérir de bonnes ou de mauvaises habitudes. Notre subconscient ne fait aucun choix; c'est notre conscient qui se charge de trier le bon du mauvais. Si nous répétons les mêmes gestes, si nous entretenons les mêmes pensées négatives durant un certain temps, nous serons contraints, par la force de l'habitude établie dans notre subconscient, de poursuivre dans la même voie. Cette règle s'applique également sur le plan positif pour les bonnes habitudes.

Nous devons admettre que nous sommes sous l'emprise de certains conditionnements. Nous sommes conditionnés par le milieu dans lequel nous vivons, par notre culture, par notre passé, par l'éducation que nous avons reçue, etc... Nous vivons donc « enfoncés » dans nos habitudes. Nous ne nous contrôlons pas; ce sont nos habitudes qui nous dirigent.

Tout notre bonheur dépend en majeure partie de notre vie intérieure. Il découle des matériaux mentaux que constituent nos pensées, nos émotions et notre imagination. Notre bonheur se construit constamment à même le moment présent. Nous devons donc entretenir de saines habitudes.

« D'accord, me direz-vous, mais comment dois-je faire pour me débarrasser de mes mauvaises habitudes ? Avez-vous un moyen efficace ? » Oui. Ce plan s'élabore en sept étapes, simples mais essentielles.

1 — Nous devons absolument croire que nous pou-

vons nous débarrasser de notre mauvaise habitude.

Avant tout, il nous faut une foi absolue en notre capacité de contrôle personnel ; et si cette première condition est respectée, nous pouvons ensuite nous consacrer au développement de la qualité que nous désirons acquérir.

2 — Écrire une liste de tous les avantages que nous retirerons de l'acquisition de l'habitude positive opposée.

Il est très important de bien nous convaincre que cette habitude nous procurera des avantages véritables, sinon nous risquerions de laisser l'ancienne habitude envahir ce nouveau terrain.

3 — Dresser une liste de tout ce que nous sommes prêts à sacrifier, à payer pour nous débarrasser de notre mauvaise habitude.

On n'obtient rien pour rien. Tout se paie.

Cette liste tient lieu d'un contrat avec nous-mêmes. Par l'écriture, nous traçons clairement ce que nous sommes prêts à payer en efforts et en sacrifices pour changer notre habitude. Le tout s'imprègne dans notre subconscient et nous aide à réaliser notre désir.

4 — Trouver une activité quotidienne qui soit satisfaisante.

Il s'agit ici d'un jeu, d'une occupation ou d'un passe-temps qui servira à diminuer adéquatement la tension créée par notre changement d'habitude.

Certaines personnes, par exemple, cessent de fumer. La tension devenant trop forte, elles commencent à manger des sucreries pour compenser leur perte. Souvent, cela tient à un manque d'activité satisfaisante. D'autres, par contre, cessent de fumer et, pour accentuer le bien-être issu de leur nouvelle habitude, commencent à pratiquer un sport comme la course à pied. Elles débutent lentement et acquièrent graduellement une meilleure endurance cardio-vasculaire. En somme, avec une nouvelle habitude, elles font d'une pierre deux coups.

5 — Faire immédiatement les premiers pas.

Tout commencer aujourd'hui, maintenant. Ne pas élaborer le plan d'une nouvelle habitude pour plus tard. Passons à l'action aujourd'hui même. Comme le dit le vieux proverbe: « Ne pas remettre à demain ce que nous pouvons faire le jour même. »

6 — S'imaginer posséder déjà la nouvelle qualité.

Plusieurs fois par jour, nous devons penser que nous sommes devenus ce que nous désirions être, comme si nous avions véritablement acquis depuis longtemps notre nouvelle qualité.

Reprenons l'exemple de notre ex-fumeur. Un ami lui offre une cigarette. Il dit: « Non, merci. J'ai cessé de fumer depuis x temps. » C'est bien. Mais il se sent mieux s'il répond: « Non, merci. Je ne fume pas. » Il devient alors un non-fumeur comme s'il l'avait toujours été au lieu de demeurer un ancien fumeur. Il agit comme si rien ne l'avait marqué de son ancienne habitude.

7 — S'efforcer constamment de penser, de vivre avec joie et enthousiasme.

Par nos changements d'habitude, cherchons à voir la vie autrement. Tout est susceptible de nous apporter du bonheur. Le soleil est bon, la pluie s'avère excellente. A force de me dire: « Je suis heureux aujourd'hui. », j'acquerrai l'habitude d'être heureux.

Si nous consacrons vraiment notre énergie à suivre consciencieusement ces sept étapes, nous pouvons surmonter n'importe quelle habitude, peu importe notre âge. Toute notre vie se traduit en habitudes, même notre bonheur !

Les douze vitamines du bonheur

Qui ne souhaite vivre heureux ?

C'est un rêve que tout le monde caresse. Pour nous en convaincre, il nous suffit de voir les cartes de souhaits, dans les magasins. Toujours, en toutes occasions, on parle de bonheur, de joie, de prospérité, etc...

Combien de gens réalisent véritablement ces vœux ? Ils sont rares ! Pourquoi ? Parce que, pour atteindre une vie heureuse, il faut vivre intensément et toujours mettre en pratique tous les facteurs du bonheur en obéissant aux lois qui le régissent. Le bonheur, comme toute science, est régi par des lois naturelles.

Bien inconsciemment, certaines personnes appliquent un bon nombre des principales lois du bonheur. Et elles vivent heureuses.

D'autres gens, par contre, souvent à cause de leurs habitudes malsaines, deviennent de jour en jour plus malheureux. Ils demeurent pessimistes, critiquent tout, cherchent constamment la « petite bête noire », se découragent à la moindre contrariété et rejettent le moindre effort. En somme, ils vivent en dépression constante. Comme ils voudraient bien vivre heureux, ils se sentent alors dans l'obligation d'anesthésier leur état d'âme malheureux avec de l'alcool, des sucreries, des drogues et autres camouflages dénaturés qui ne font qu'accentuer leur état de dépression et leurs souffrances intérieures. Consciemment ou non, ils ignorent les lois naturelles du bonheur.

Tous les pouvoirs sont en nous, il suffit d'en prendre possession. Aiguillons notre vie vers le bonheur. Croyons fermement en lui. Misons sur la puissance de notre subconscient et nous serons heureux.

Nous savons tous que, pour être et demeurer en bonne santé, notre corps a besoin d'une très grande variété de vitamines: A, B, C, D, E, F, K, P, etc... Mais, pour être heureux, nous avons aussi besoin de vitamines. Ce sont des vitamines mentales, émotives et spirituelles.

Il y a douze vitamines du bonheur à prendre, à digérer, à assimiler, à expérimenter quotidiennement si nous souhaitons vraiment acquérir un bonheur durable.

Qui sommes-nous ?

A quoi pensons-nous la plupart du temps ?

Lorsque nous lisons notre journal, regardons la télévision, écoutons la radio, nous remarquons une certaine constance dans les sujets traités. On parle du chômage, de la pollution, de la violence; on brasse tous nos problèmes dans la même marmite ; on mêle nos soucis à toutes les sauces. En somme, on nous oriente vers tout ce qui ne tourne pas rond dans le monde et autour de nous.

Nous répétons-nous constamment: « Je suis malheureux. Je suis toujours malheureux. » ? La vie devient donc, trop souvent, un grand malheur tant individuel que collectif.

Il est certain qu'avec un tel état d'esprit négatif, nous ne réglerons rien au sort du monde. Bien au contraire, tout cela nous rendra de plus en plus malheureux.

Quand tout va pour le mieux, il nous est facile d'être heureux. Mais c'est plutôt quand tout semble vouloir contrecarrer nos plans, nos désirs que nous devons maintenir notre joie intérieure, notre enthousiasme et notre confiance. C'est en conservant la certitude de la stabilité de notre bonheur et de notre réussite que nous pouvons vaincre les mauvais augures.

Quel est votre choix ?

Certaines personnes diront: « On ne choisit pas d'être heureux. » Voilà l'erreur ! Le bonheur est véritablement un choix mental, émotif, spirituel. C'est une question d'entraînement, de conditionnement.

Un ami me racontait comment, en optant pour le bonheur, il l'obtint réellement. Il enseignait depuis cinq ans. Tout en étant conscient que l'enseignement ne lui convenait pas, il continuait à pratiquer cette profession pour de vagues raisons de sécurité financière. Un jour, sa femme lui donna un fils. Il décida alors de faire en sorte que cet enfant ait de lui l'image d'un père vraiment heureux. Il prit donc la décision de quitter l'enseignement quoi qu'il arrive et de vivre sa vie comme il l'entendait.

Depuis longtemps, il rêvait d'un autre métier: le journalisme. Il se mit alors à écrire et à présenter des articles. Alors qu'on avait toujours, jusqu'à présent, refusé ses textes, voici que, soudainement, la situation changea. « Au lieu d'écrire d'une façon hésitante, me confiait-il, j'écrivais ces articles avec la certitude qu'ils seraient publiés. » Il était convaincu de sa réussite. Il agissait comme si tout allait bien fonctionner. Il s'entraîna au bonheur, convaincu qu'il était et devenait ce qu'il pensait à longueur de journée.

Pensons-nous, agissons-nous, vivons-nous comme si nous étions heureux ? Conservons cette attitude et nous développerons ainsi l'habitude du bonheur. Nous penserons, ressentirons, réagirons, vivrons avec joie et enthousiasme. Nous serons heureux.

Le bonheur n'est pas le résultat de la chance, du hasard ou des circonstances extérieures.

Les infirmes sont-ils plus malheureux ?

Les docteurs Paul Cameron, de l'Université de Louisville, et D. Van Hoeck, de l'Université Wayne de Détroit, à la suite de leurs recherches scientifiques auprès des infirmes, ont conclu qu'en général ces derniers ne sont pas plus malheureux que les gens valides. Au contraire, la plupart sont aussi heureux. Toutes proportions gardées, on note moins de suicides chez les infirmes.

Oui, le bonheur est véritablement un *choix* mental, émotif, spirituel. Quel est votre choix ?

===

Notre première vitamine du bonheur:

Nous sommes et nous devenons ce que nous pensons à longueur de journée.

===

Vous adaptez-vous facilement ?

Si, par un froid de 20 degrés sous zéro, nous nous promenions en maillot de bain, nous risquerions d'en mourir. Si, aux jours les plus chauds de l'été, nous nous habillions comme en hiver, soigneusement emmitouflés des pieds à la tête, nous risquerions de suffoquer. Pourquoi ? Parce que nous ne saurions pas nous adapter.

Si nous désirons être heureux, il faut nous adapter à la température ambiante, à notre entourage, à la vie.

Savez-vous vous adapter aux gens que vous côtoyez ou vous sentez-vous mal à l'aise, face à plusieurs d'entre eux ?

Éprouvez-vous des difficultés d'adaptation devant des situations imprévues ou certains événements de la vie ?

Ordinairement, chacun de nous planifie son existence. Nous « prévoyons » l'emploi de notre temps, de notre argent. Nous choisissons des vêtements à notre goût. Nous assistons à des spectacles susceptibles de nous intéresser, etc... En somme, nous essayons de nous créer un mode de vie qui nous convienne.

Mais qu'arrive-t-il lorsqu'un événement vient dérégler nos habitudes ? Souvent, alors, nous « perdons les pédales », pour employer une expression populaire. Nous ne savons plus où donner de la tête. Nous sommes malheureux. Pourquoi ? Parce que nous ne savons pas nous adapter.

Pour vivre heureux et équilibrés, il faut s'adapter,

d'abord à nous-mêmes et aux autres, et ensuite à ce qui nous entoure.

Pour nous adapter, nous devons nous sentir à la hauteur de toute situation. C'est pourquoi il nous faut réaliser que le plus important n'est pas de changer ou de réformer les autres, mais plutôt de se changer et de se réformer soi-même. Nous avons tellement de travail à faire sur nous-mêmes que, si nous nous y mettons vraiment, il ne nous restera plus de temps et d'énergie pour essayer de changer et de réformer autrui.

Il est beaucoup plus facile de voir la paille dans l'œil de notre voisin que la poutre dans le nôtre. Grand nombre de gens se limitent volontairement, se rétrécissent, se contentent de la médiocrité et se condamnent eux-mêmes à l'échec par leurs attitudes négatives et leur constant dénigrement des autres. Ainsi, il ne leur reste plus l'énergie suffisante pour se changer eux-mêmes.

Quelle est la principale cause de l'échec du mariage ?

Selon le Dr Malcolm Floy, psychiatre de l'Hôpital St. James de Baltimore, le fait de vouloir changer son conjoint est la cause directe de 73% des problèmes matrimoniaux.

Beaucoup d'hommes et de femmes croient que le seul fait du mariage pourra corriger plusieurs défauts qu'ils avaient constatés chez leur conjoint avant leur union. Nombre d'entre eux n'attendent que le lendemain de leur mariage pour régler les problèmes de relation qu'ils éprouvent.

Le Dr Floy explique: « L'homme est soudain mis en confrontation avec toutes sortes de demandes de son épouse. Elle lui dit des choses comme « Pourquoi bois-tu tant ? » ou encore « Je n'aime pas la façon dont tu regardes les autres femmes. » Le mari se trouve alors très surpris, étant donné qu'il a exactement le comportement d'avant son mariage. » Le psychiatre de Baltimore suggère donc que toutes les différences fondamentales entre l'homme et la femme soient bien étudiées par eux avant le mariage et que chacun se change lui-même sans réformer l'autre.

Que manque-t-il le plus dans le monde ?

Des réformateurs sociaux, politiques, économiques, religieux, culturels ? Non. Ce qui manque le plus, ce sont des gens qui se réforment eux-mêmes: des « *auto-réformateurs* ».

Réformons-nous en nous rééduquant dans le sens de la confiance, de l'optimisme, de la pensée mentale positive, de l'enthousiasme, de la persévérance. Nous exercerons alors une influence positive sur les circonstances extérieures qui ne semblent pas dépendre de nous.

La plupart du temps, ce n'est pas sur les événements ou le milieu extérieur qu'il nous faut agir, mais plutôt sur nous-mêmes. C'est la grande leçon du bonheur. Le bonheur est en nous et non à l'extérieur. En sommes-nous convaincus ?

Il y a une loi que nous devons absolument observer pour être heureux: vivre et laisser vivre. Cela signifie: « Nous mêler de nos affaires ! »

Combien de fois ne voulons-nous pas changer les habitudes des gens qui nous entourent ? Nous décrétons souvent ce que chacun devrait faire pour que tout le monde soit heureux. Volontairement ou non, nous faisons ainsi notre petite morale. Nous donnons notre mini-leçon. Et notre interlocuteur nous dit: « Mais toi, tu ne fais pas ça ! » Alors nous nous défendons: « Moi, ce n'est pas pareil ! »

N'oublions pas ce vieux dicton: « Ce que nous sommes parle plus fort que ce que nous disons. »

La société se compose d'individus différents. Le moule de l'homme uniforme, parfait n'existe pas. Chacun éprouve des désirs différents de ceux de son prochain et, par le fait même, doit prendre une route personnelle pour les combler. Ainsi, nous devons vivre à notre façon et laisser les autres vivre à leur façon, sans les juger.

Les pieds du roi

Il y a plusieurs milliers d'années, un puissant roi décida de visiter à pied son royaume.

Comme, à l'époque, on ne portait pas de sandales, à maintes et maintes reprises, il s'écorcha les pieds et les orteils, tantôt sur une roche, tantôt sur des ronces. En retournant à son château, les pieds blessés et en proie à une grande colère, il ordonna à ses serviteurs de poser du tapis partout dans son royaume. De cette façon, il ne se blesserait plus les pieds. Le roi menaça de décapiter tous ceux qui n'obéissaient pas à cet ordre immédiatement.

On commença donc les travaux. Mais, très rapidement, on s'aperçut qu'il manquait du tapis et que la tâche s'avérait irréalisable. On se « fatigua donc les méninges » pour trouver une solution.

Un bon vieux paysan proposa qu'au lieu de poser du tapis dans tout le royaume, il serait plus simple de bien entourer les pieds du roi de ce même tapis. De là, dit la légende, nous vinrent les premiers souliers.

Notre roi put ainsi se promener à sa guise sans plus se blesser les pieds.

===

Notre deuxième vitamine du bonheur:

Il n'y a personne d'autre à changer ou à réformer que nous-mêmes.

===

Quel est votre but dans la vie ?

La majorité des gens n'ont aucun but précis ! C'est pourquoi ils se plaignent, se trouvent malchanceux et se demandent constamment: « Pourquoi les bonnes choses arrivent-elles toujours aux autres ? »... « Pourquoi lui et pas moi ? »... « Qu'est-ce qu'il a de plus que moi ? ». Peut-être n'a-t-il, au fond, qu'une seule chose: un but. Vous le trouvez chanceux ? Il a lui-même créé sa chance. Il s'est fixé un but.

Je ne crois pas à la chance, au hasard, à la malchance, aux miracles. Tout l'univers est contrôlé par des lois naturelles. La chance, le hasard, les miracles n'illustrent que des lois naturelles que les gens ignorent.

32

Rien n'est impossible

Ray Leizer perdit l'usage de ses deux mains à la suite de l'explosion d'une mine en Israël. Il vint aux États-Unis pour se faire soigner; le Dr Henry Kessler lui posa des mains artificielles reliées aux muscles de ses avant-bras.

Désirant réaliser son but le plus cher, Ray Leizer, en pratiquant six heures par jour, devint, si incroyable que cela puisse paraître, pianiste de concert.

Il se joignit à l'Orchestre Symphonique de Chicago et signa un alléchant contrat avec une importante compagnie de disques. Il a ainsi réalisé son but. L'impossible est devenu possible.

Comment commencer ?

Il faut commencer par avoir un but. C'est là toute la différence entre le succès et l'échec.

Il y a des gens qui ne réussissent jamais. Ils sont nonchalants. Souvent, nous sommes portés à les traiter de paresseux. La paresse n'est à la fin, pour plusieurs, qu'un manque de motivation. Quelqu'un qui n'a aucun but ne peut être motivé.

La motivation est l'aliment intérieur qui pousse l'homme à agir. Toute personne très motivée est active. Elle sait exactement où elle va. Elle a un but. Dans les arts, dans le monde des affaires et même dans le sport, l'homme motivé, celui qui marche vers un but et fait tout en son pouvoir pour l'atteindre, celui-là réussit. Dans tous les domaines, si nous étudions bien les gens qui ont réussi, nous découvrirons qu'ils ont toujours pris un plaisir très vif à se fixer des buts et à les réaliser. Avoir un but et vouloir l'atteindre est un indice d'équilibre et de bonheur.

Avons-nous un but précis ?

Savons-nous exactement ce que nous voulons dans la vie ?

Si, dans un pays étranger, je demande à un guide de me faire visiter en même temps cinq ou six lieux différents, il refusera certainement de m'aider, à moins que je ne fasse un choix précis. Notre subconscient est notre guide continuel. Nous devons imprimer en lui le but précis que nous voulons atteindre. Pour cela, conditionnons-le, entraînons-le. Pensons positivement, montrons-lui des images claires, des émotions nettes.

Trop de gens malheureux ne font qu'exister et végéter. Ils ne savent pas ce qu'ils veulent, où ils vont et, par le fait même, ils deviennent de plus en plus malheureux. Ils se sentent complètement inutiles. Sommes-nous de ceux-là ?

Une loi naturelle nous incite à nous améliorer continuellement ou à dépérir. Qui n'avance pas recule. Nous ne pouvons absolument pas nous améliorer si nous n'avons pas un but à atteindre.

Un but est essentiel à notre bonheur. Il est à celui-ci ce qu'est l'air au maintien de notre existence. Sans but, notre vie devient insipide. Le seul fait de se fixer un but précis est le point de départ de toute vie réussie et heureuse.

Comment découvrir notre but ?

Comment pouvons-nous nous définir un but si nous n'en avons pas présentement ?

34

Tout d'abord, écrivons. Que devons-nous écrire ? Tout ce que nous désirons, tout ce que nous aimerions réaliser. Rêvons « tout éveillés » pendant quelques instants, et osons écrire ce qui nous comblerait.

Ensuite, précisons nos projets les plus chers et attelons-nous à leur réalisation. Quand ? Maintenant. Posons tout de suite notre premier geste, si simple soit-il. Faisons immédiatement le premier pas. Déterminons nous-mêmes notre premier but et écrivons-le. Puis lisons-le à haute voix régulièrement tous les jours. Cela impressionne considérablement notre subconscient.

Subdivisons le ou les buts fixés en petites étapes courtes et faciles à réaliser. Fixons-nous une date limite. Écrivons ce que nous pouvons faire immédiatement. Déjà nous nous approcherons de notre but.

Lorsque nous faisons ce travail, nous imprégnons notre subconscient de notre désir le plus cher. Une fois qu'il est bien averti de ce que nous désirons, notre subconscient se met au travail et le gros de la bataille est gagné.

Notre troisième vitamine du bonheur:

Maintenons constamment un but dans notre vie.

Votre passé et votre avenir vous inquiètent-ils ?

Votre droit au bonheur

Dans le monde d'aujourd'hui, avons-nous réellement le droit d'être joyeux, de nous sentir heureux ? Ne sommes-nous pas alors inconscients et égoïstes quand il y a tant de guerres, de chômage, de souffrances, de violence et de maladie partout dans le monde ? De quoi aurais-je l'air si je souriais alors que tant de problèmes m'entourent ?

Une personne pessimiste et de mauvaise humeur ne solutionne aucun problème. Bien au contraire, ces attitudes compliquent la situation plutôt que de la résoudre.

Le moment le plus important !

« L'instant présent » est le moment le plus important de notre vie. Il est le seul moment que nous puissions pleinement « influencer ». Ce n'est qu'à l'intérieur même de cet « instant présent » que nous bâtissons notre avenir.

Demain, nous serons heureux ou malheureux selon ce que nous pensons, imaginons, ressentons aujourd'hui, ici et maintenant. Nous n'atteindrons réellement le bonheur qu'à travers notre façon d'observer les lois de la nature. Chaque moment présent doit être vécu intensément. Il nous faut tirer parti au maximum de l'« instant qui passe ». Dans une seconde il n'existera plus... un autre présent l'aura aussitôt remplacé.

Celui qui ressasse constamment ses conflits passés, gaspille le moment le plus important de sa vie: *son présent.* De même, celui qui n'entasse que des désirs futurs ne profite pas de l'instant le plus important de sa vie: *son présent.* Seul celui qui vit pleinement dans le présent peut maîtriser les trois temps: le passé, le présent et le futur. Il laisse le passé et l'avenir l'habiter, mais chacun à sa place respective. Dans son esprit, la place de choix n'est réservée qu'au présent, et à lui seul.

Le pont s'écroule

J'aimerais reprendre ici l'exemple du pont, mentionné dans un de mes livres[1]. Un pont ne peut supporter qu'un certain poids. Cependant, si tous les véhicules qui y sont déjà passés et tous ceux qui passeront à l'avenir sur ce pont s'y trouvaient à un moment précis, qu'arriverait-il? Il ne fait aucun doute que le pont s'écroulerait.

Notre bonheur est semblable à ce pont. Si nos erreurs passées et nos problèmes futurs s'accumulent constamment sur notre présent, tout notre équilibre psychique s'effondre. Dans ces conditions, nous ne pouvons être heureux.

Il se considérait comme fini !

Je me souviens de ce type, grand amateur d'automobiles, qui tenait une station-service. A cause d'un associé malhonnête, il dut un jour se déclarer en faillite. Étant bon mécanicien, il n'eut aucun mal à se trouver un emploi dans un autre garage. Mais il s'attardait continuellement à revoir son passé, à re-

---

1— Voir « Les maladies psychosomatiques », Éditions de l'Homme, Montréal 1971.

gretter ses erreurs, à maudire son ex-associé.

Il devint aigri et malheureux. Il entrait constamment en conflit avec son patron et même avec ses compagnons de travail. Comme nous nous en doutons, il perdit son emploi. A cause d'un échec passé, il se considérait comme un homme fini. Éventuellement, il le devint. Il vivait un présent désenchanté et de ce fait ne voyait qu'un avenir noir et dénué de toute espérance.

Seulement pour aujourd'hui !

Vivons donc de notre mieux seulement pour aujourd'hui. A chaque jour suffit ... son bonheur ! En ne vivant qu'une journée, qu'une heure à la fois, nos efforts nous semblent plus faciles.

Certains voudraient accomplir de grandes choses dans l'avenir. Mais, pour atteindre leur but, il leur importe surtout de réaliser aujourd'hui les actions les plus banales de leur vie d'une façon extraordinaire. En d'autres mots, vivre heureux aujourd'hui, quoi qu'il advienne.

Il nous faut poser une brique à la fois, en commençant par celle que l'on tient dans la main. Chaque moment est unique, « exclusif ». Ne nous éparpillons pas dans le passé et le futur. Regardons droit devant nous: le présent. Chaque journée représente une vie nouvelle. Elle peut réparer tout notre passé et préparer notre avenir.

Ainsi, donnons-nous tout entier à notre tâche présente, quelle qu'elle soit.

Vivons chaque journée comme si elle était la dernière, comme si toute notre vie ne dépendait que de l'heure présente.

38

Notre quatrième vitamine du bonheur:

Vivons intensément notre moment présent... le seul moment dont nous disposons pour être heureux.

La vitamine de la réussite !

Avez-vous confiance en vous-mêmes et en ce que vous faites ?

On considère le manque de confiance en soi comme la tare psychologique la plus répandue de nos jours. Au cours d'une enquête, on a demandé à plus de mille personnes quel était leur plus grand handicap. Quatre-vingt-dix pour cent d'entre elles ont répondu: "Le manque de confiance en moi."

Sans confiance, nous ne pourrons jamais atteindre notre but. C'est l'intensité de notre foi qui importe et qui détermine notre réussite.

L'athlète, pour réussir, doit absolument avoir confiance en chacun de ses gestes. Le champion sauteur, par exemple, étudie tous ses gestes, les perfectionne tellement que, au moment de son saut, il est certain de se dépasser. Il a foi en ce qu'il fait. Il a confiance en sa réussite. Sa confiance devient une force qui le propulse toujours plus haut.

Comme tous nos muscles, notre confiance peut se développer par des exercices efficaces et réguliers.

Certaines personnes orientent mal leur confiance.

39

Elles mettent toute leur foi dans la certitude de leur échec. Elles sont convaincues que leur moindre problème est incurable. Ainsi, leur négativisme a beau jeu et domine entièrement leur vie.

D'autres, par contre, ont une confiance positive. Elles croient à leur bonheur, à la vie, au trésor extraordinaire qu'elles découvrent quotidiennement en elles. Elles croient fermement à la puissance de leurs pensées, de leurs émotions et des images qu'elles entretiennent. Leur vie se transforme proportionnellement à leur foi.

Nous sommes tous des créateurs

L'imagination créatrice n'appartient qu'à l'homme. L'homme est plus qu'une créature passive; il est un créateur actif. Il possède le pouvoir de créer son bonheur comme il peut engendrer son malheur.

Un homme qui se répète constamment qu'il devient de plus en plus malheureux et malchanceux demeurera toujours déprimé et « misérable ». Il aura imprégné son subconscient de tous ses malheurs.

Notre subconscient ne tranche pas le négatif du positif. Il accepte tout ce que nous lui donnons. Il enregistre tout simplement nos pensées et nos désirs pour ensuite les exécuter sans discernement. Il s'exprimera soit par le bonheur et l'optimisme, soit par le malheur et le pessimisme. Il peut même nous pousser jusqu'à la dépression. Personne n'échappe à cette loi naturelle à laquelle nous sommes tous soumis.

Notre vie s'avère heureuse ou malheureuse selon la force ou la faiblesse de notre confiance. La confiance constitue la clé du bonheur et de la réussite. Avec elle, l'homme peut donner la pleine mesure de lui-même et goûter entièrement à tout le piquant de l'existence, étant délivré des soucis et des anxiétés qui terrassent ceux qui n'ont pas la foi.

La peur du ridicule et de l'échec

Le facteur déterminant du manque de confiance en soi est souvent la peur de l'échec. Pourquoi avons-nous peur d'échouer ? Nous craignons l'image que les autres se feront de nous après notre échec; nous craignons leurs critiques, leurs sarcasmes et le ridicule qui pourrait en résulter. L'opinion qu'ils ont de nous est plus importante à nos yeux que notre propre opinion de nous-mêmes.

Qu'est-ce que la confiance en soi ?

C'est la certitude d'être capable d'accomplir la tâche assignée, de se montrer à la hauteur de la situation.

Personne ne peut fournir son plein rendement, ni même s'épanouir totalement, s'il a l'esprit empoisonné par un sentiment d'infériorité, d'anxiété et de crainte. Avez-vous déjà remarqué que jamais nous n'entreprenons de plus grandes choses que celles que nous inspire notre confiance en nous-mêmes ? Nous n'accomplissons réellement que ce que nous nous croyons capables de faire. La foi quintuple nos capacités et sans elle nous ne pouvons rien.

Jeune, Beethoven n'avait aucun trait caractéristique, si l'on excepte sa croyance en la musique. Et ce n'est que grâce à sa foi en son talent qu'il devint

41

un des plus grands compositeurs que le monde de la musique ait connu.

Tout être ne bénéficiant que d'un talent, mais possédant une pleine confiance en lui-même, accomplit toujours plus de choses qu'un autre possédant vingt talents mais ne croyant pas en lui-même.

Un étudiant, qui avait pourtant bien réussi toutes ses études jusqu'au niveau supérieur, dut changer quatre fois de faculté à l'Université, en trois ans. Et, à chaque fois, il perdait de plus en plus confiance... jusqu'au jour où il prit conscience de son véritable problème: un manque total de confiance en soi.

Il suivit si bien mes conseils que, l'année suivante, il revint à l'Université, confiant, déterminé à réussir. Aujourd'hui, il exerce une profession qu'il aime et donne constamment le meilleur de lui-même. Il a confiance en lui et il est heureux.

Que faire pour améliorer notre confiance en nous-mêmes ?

1 — Maintenons dans notre esprit une image de nous-mêmes resplendissants de confiance. Cette image s'imprégnera dans notre subconscient et matérialisera dans notre vie cette confiance désirée.

2 — Apprenons par cœur les formules suivantes et répétons-les le plus souvent possible au cours de la journée:

« J'ai de plus en plus confiance en moi-même. »

« J'ose et je fonce de plus en plus. »

« Partout, avec tout le monde, je suis de plus en plus à l'aise. »

3 — Efforçons-nous d'accomplir ce que nous craignions le plus auparavant.

Découvrons toutes les ressources intérieures que nous possédons. Elles ne demandent qu'à s'affirmer au grand jour. Ainsi, nous développerons notre confiance en nous-mêmes jusqu'à ce que celle-ci devienne une habitude. Toutes nos autres qualités en seront fortifiées. Nous marcherons dans la vie avec du soleil plein le cœur.

Notre cinquième vitamine du bonheur:

Développons notre confiance en nous-mêmes et en notre réussite !

La vitamine-jeunesse

Êtes-vous jeunes ou vieux ?

L'âge chronologique n'a rien à voir avec la jeunesse ou la vieillesse. Un vieillard de quatre-vingt-quinze ans est parfois plus jeune qu'un homme de vingt-cinq ans.

Nous pouvons prendre un jeune homme de vingt ans en parfaite santé et, en le conditionnant négativement, en faire un vieillard en moins de cinq ans.

Certaines personnes vieillissent de dix ans par année. Comment s'y prennent-elles ? Elles se conditionnent, se convainquent inconsciemment de leur vieillesse. Elles se disent et se répètent constamment que toutes les activités physiques, mentales, intellectuelles et spirituelles sont inutiles et dangereuses. Ainsi, elles s'enlèvent elles-mêmes tout intérêt pour la vie, les gens et les choses. En somme, elles vieillissent prématurément.

Combien de fois n'avons-nous pas entendu ces remarques: « On n'a plus vingt ans ! », « On vieillit ! », « On n'a plus la force qu'on avait !», etc... ? Sans même s'en rendre compte, ces personnes se persuadent que leur jeunesse s'évade. Elles la perdent effectivement. Elles se vieillissent elles-mêmes.

Souvent, des gens vivent en bonne santé jusqu'au jour de leur retraite. Dès lors, ils tombent malades et meurent rapidement. Pourquoi ? Ils se sont convaincus qu'ils ne valaient plus rien.

L'optimisme, le sens de l'humour, l'amour, la bonne volonté, l'enthousiasme sont les qualités qui nous conservent jeunes; et, quel que soit notre âge, nous devons les cultiver si nous voulons demeurer physiquement et mentalement jeunes.

Maintenons toujours un intérêt soutenu pour quelque chose. Prenons toujours un grand plaisir à accomplir la moindre de nos activités. Si nous perdons le goût de vivre, il est certain que nous mourrons prématurément. N'arrêtons jamais d'apprendre, peu importe notre âge. Aimons la vie. Aimons notre travail. Aimons les gens qui nous entourent. Ainsi, nous resterons jeunes de cœur et d'esprit. Nous vivrons une véritable jeunesse.

Développons notre enthousiasme pour la vie. Il ne faut jamais oublier que nous recevons de la vie ce que nous lui apportons.

Notre subconscient ne vieillit jamais

Il demeure toujours ce réservoir inépuisable à même lequel chacune de nos actions va chercher la puissance nécessaire à sa réalisation.

Pour plusieurs, la vieillesse est le pire ennemi. Il n'y a pourtant rien de tragique à ajouter des années à notre âge. Bien au contraire, si nous sommes convaincus que nous ajoutons chaque jour une autre petite portion à notre bonheur, nous aurons de jour en jour une raison de plus d'être heureux. En fait nous avons, intérieurement, l'âge que nous désirons. Nous sommes aussi jeunes que nous le ressentons, le croyons, le pensons.

Ce dont nous avons peur se manifeste toujours dans notre vie. Balayons les craintes de notre cœur. N'ayons pas peur de vieillir prématurément. Chaque jour n'est pas une journée de moins à vivre, mais plutôt une expérience qui s'ajoute à notre vie. Avec ce principe, nous ne serons que plus jeunes et plus heureux.

Qu'est-ce que l'enthousiasme ?

L'enthousiasme, c'est l'épice de la vie, la bougie d'allumage de notre bonheur, la vitamine-jeunesse par excellence.

Voyons le monde avec le regard émerveillé et enthousiaste de l'enfant.

La plus formidable aventure

Un des grands secrets du bonheur et d'une jeunesse prolongée, c'est de considérer la vie comme « la plus formidable aventure ». A moins de rencontrer les surprises de la vie avec un esprit d'aventure, disons d'avance adieu au bonheur.

Quel est le dénominateur commun à tous les gens heureux ? Ils prennent tout de la vie comme une aventure. Ils en font... une aventure. Et vous, avez-vous découvert cet élixir du bonheur ?

Comment vieillir en demeurant jeunes ?

Si nous nous préoccupons trop de compter les années de notre âge, c'est que nous ne sommes pas assez occupés à vivre notre vie. L'oisiveté est la mère... de la vieillesse.

Pour vieillir heureux tout en demeurant jeunes, nous devons absolument:

1 — Développer en nous la joie de vivre et l'enthousiasme.

2 — Maintenir toujours un vif intérêt pour quelque chose. Ne pas se laisser aller à dire que rien ne vaut plus la peine. Tout peut être intéressant. L'intérêt est dans l'œil de celui qui regarde et non dans la chose elle-même.

3 — Continuer à apprendre quelque chose de nouveau. Tous les jours, faisons le bilan de ce que nous avons appris de nouveau.

4 — Aimer tous et tout. Celui qui aime demeure jeune et heureux.

5 — Considérer la vie comme la plus « formidable aventure ».

Notre sixième vitamine du bonheur:

La motivation et l'enthousiasme: clés de notre jeunesse, quel que soit notre âge.

Avez-vous des problèmes ?

Oui ? Tant mieux ! Plusieurs croient que les gens heureux n'ont aucun problème. Au contraire, tout le monde, sans exception, a ses problèmes. Nous sommes tous susceptibles de subir une défaite. Notre vie ne peut toujours marcher « comme sur des roulettes ». L'important est que nous sachions « rouler » sur n'importe quel terrain.

La vie est épicée d'une série de problèmes plus ou moins tragiques. Dès que nous en résolvons un, un autre se présente. L'optimiste, l'homme heureux, les considère comme des occasions constantes de se développer, d'apprendre. Il s'en sert comme d'un marchepied vers la réussite. Avec chaque victoire remportée sur un de nos problèmes, nous « croissons » en expérience, en sagesse et en bonheur. En triomphant avec une attitude positive, nous renforçons notre caractère, notre personnalité et nos chances de succès.

Prenons l'exemple de ces athlètes consciencieux qui, après une défaite, étudient le film de leur performance. Ils revoient chacun de leurs mouvements trouvent la faille. Ensuite, ils s'entraînent à combler cette lacune, à ne plus répéter la même erreur. Bref, la défaite qu'ils ont subie devient positive. En se basant sur l'expérience qu'ils en retirent, ils se transforment et s'améliorent.

Toute personne qui a connu le goût amer de la défaite apprécie davantage la joie stimulante de la victoire sur ses problèmes et sur les difficultés de la vie. Le bonheur est fait de courage, de persévérance, de confiance et de savoir-faire face aux difficultés.

Le mari d'une de mes patientes perdit son emploi de chauffeur d'autobus. Il n'aurait jamais osé laisser son travail, vu la sécurité qu'il y trouvait depuis 17 ans.

Pourquoi fut-il congédié? Un vieil inspecteur, agacé par ses agissements, observa que notre homme, toujours prêt à rendre service, ne se contentait pas de faire monter ses passagers aux arrêts réglementaires. De plus, l'inspecteur remarqua que notre chauffeur, d'une bonne humeur proverbiale, distribuait constamment taquineries et blagues à ses passagers.

Il n'en fallait pas plus pour qu'il soit congédié. Sur les instances de sa femme, il vint me voir, complètement découragé.

Il m'avoua qu'il ne pouvait gagner sa vie que comme chauffeur d'autobus, ne sachant rien faire d'autre. Il m'apprit aussi que son rêve le plus cher était d'ouvrir son propre commerce. Il n'avait jamais osé l'exécuter à cause de sa sécurité d'emploi.

Je l'encourageai à réaliser son rêve, en lui faisant comprendre que la sécurité ne se trouve pas dans un emploi, mais plutôt en « soi ».

A ce moment, avec le remboursement de sa contribution de 17 ans au fonds de retraite de la compagnie, il ouvrit un restaurant. Aujourd'hui, c'est un des restaurants les plus chics et les plus fréquentés de Montréal.

Chaque problème porte en lui la semence d'une plus grande possibilité de réussite et de bonheur.

Les citrons et la limonade

Pour plusieurs, le bonheur c'est une vie constamment ensoleillée. Ils oublient que le soleil ne brille constamment que dans le désert. Accepteriez-vous de vivre toujours en plein désert ?

Nous ne sommes pas seuls à devoir surmonter des problèmes. Les gens heureux doivent aussi surmonter des difficultés, des critiques, des revers et des problèmes de toutes sortes.

Prenons l'habitude de surmonter les obstacles, de résoudre nos problèmes, de corriger nos erreurs, de traverser les embûches avec optimisme. Ne nous faisons pas des problèmes avec un grain de sel. Au contraire, soyons de bons alpinistes, prenons plutôt les montagnes pour des grains de sel. En d'autres mots, convertissons les citrons de la vie en limonade. Quoi qu'il advienne, nous pouvons vaincre et surmonter les obstacles.

Comment pouvons-nous résoudre nos problèmes ?

En devenant un athlète consciencieux du bonheur. En étudiant le film de notre problème.

Premièrement: écrivons, analysons et définissons notre problème.

Deuxièmement: soyons convaincus que tout problème renferme une solution.

Troisièmement: écrivons toutes les solutions possibles.

Quatrièmement: choisissons la solution qui semble la meilleure.

Cinquièmement: essayons de découvrir dans notre problème la semence d'une plus grande possibilité de réussite et de bonheur.

Traversez-vous une situation difficile ?

Alors demandez-vous ce qui pourrait vous arriver de pire. Ensuite, acceptez *le pire.* Si vous l'acceptez vraiment, vous deviendrez calmes. Par le fait même, vous serez plus en mesure de trouver une solution adéquate à votre problème. La plupart du temps, le pire ne se produit pas. La loi de la moyenne travaille pour nous.

Lorsque nous avons une difficulté à surmonter, acceptons une transfusion, non pas de sang, mais une « transfusion de bon sens », de confiance, d'optimisme et d'enthousiasme malgré les circonstances. Nous n'avons pas le choix. Si nous voulons être heureux, remplaçons:

— *Chaque pensée négative par une pensée positive.*

— *Chaque pensée de haine et de rancune par des pensées d'amour et de compréhension.*

— *Chaque pensée pessimiste par des pensées optimistes.*

Injectons-nous une forte dose de confiance, d'enthousiasme et de bonne humeur.

Notre septième vitamine du bonheur.

Chaque problème porte en lui la se-
mence d'une plus grande possibilité de
réussite et de bonheur.

Croyez-vous que tout vous est dû ?

Plusieurs s'imaginent que tout leur est dû. Ils s'approprient constamment le moindre objet qui leur est tendu et s'en vont comme si de rien n'était. Croyez-vous que ces gens-là dégagent véritablement un climat de bonheur ? Non. Souvent, ils ne prennent même pas conscience de ce qu'ils reçoivent. Plus tard, lorsqu'un événement se produit au cours duquel ils ne reçoivent rien, ils se sentent frustrés. Ils deviennent malheureux et souvent jaloux. Ils ont oublié *la reconnaissance.*

Soyons reconnaissants !

Tout ne nous est pas dû. Ainsi, lorsque nous recevons, soyons reconnaissants.

La reconnaissance est l'art de recevoir avec gratitude, de manifester qu'on est sensible à toute marque de bonté et de dévouement. Ne manquons pas de témoigner le plaisir que nous ont procuré une aimable hospitalité, des cadeaux ou tout autre service rendu. Nous pouvons toujours parfaire notre manière d'exprimer notre reconnaissance en la rendant aussi personnelle et sincère que possible. Rien ne blesse autant celui qui donne ou rend service que des remerciements exprimés du bout des lèvres.

Merci !

L'ingratitude blesse quiconque en est victime. Il ne suffit pas d'éprouver de la gratitude, encore faut-il l'exprimer. Souvent, un seul mot, merci, du fond du cœur, peut tout changer.

Dans quelle mesure apprécions-nous les innombrables petites manifestations quotidiennes de gentillesse ou de bienveillance qui nous facilitent tant la vie ?

La gratitude se manifeste surtout dans les petits détails. Le facteur, le coiffeur, la fille de table, le laitier, le garçon d'ascenseur, tous nous rendent service à leur façon tout au long de l'année. Remercions-les ! Ainsi, nous rendrons humaines des relations machinales. Les tâches monotones deviendront plus agréables.

Lorsque nous assistons à une représentation théâtrale, nous applaudissons les comédiens lorsqu'ils viennent saluer. C'est là notre façon de les remercier, de leur exprimer notre gratitude. Quand applaudissons-nous le chauffeur d'autobus ? Jamais. Pourtant un simple merci lorsqu'il nous tend notre « billet de correspondance » vaut bien des applaudissements.

La spontanéité

Certains s'abstiennent de manifester leur gratitude, craignant qu'elle ne soit importune. Découvrons plutôt que la meilleure façon de remercier est encore de le faire immédiatement, alors que notre gratitude est vive. Nous ne devons pas attendre que celle-ci s'émousse. Si nous éprouvons un élan de reconnaissance, manifestons-le le plus tôt possible, spontanément.

Rien n'illumine davantage notre vie et celle des autres que la reconnaissance. C'est pourquoi, lorsque nous sommes découragés, pessimistes, aveuglés par nos propres malheurs, procédons comme suit:

Pendant une période d'au moins trois semaines, remercions spontanément quiconque nous rendra service. Pour bien prouver notre sincérité, appuyons ce merci d'un sourire venant du fond du cœur. Rien n'est plus simple et pourtant, c'est une source de bien-être et de bonheur.

Ainsi, nous nous transformerons nous-mêmes. Nous constaterons peu à peu que nul n'est inutile dans le monde. Chacun, par un apport souvent minime, contribue à notre réalisation et à notre bonheur. Nous nous libérerons ainsi de nos griefs. Nous nous convaincrons que les gens deviennent meilleurs et bienveillants. N'oublions pas que la guerre comme la paix, l'amour comme la haine ne résident qu'en nous. C'est notre façon de voir qui fait que les objets, comme les actes, paraissent beaux ou laids. Nous changeant nous-mêmes, nous croirons que notre entourage est changé.

N'avons-nous pas tous plus ou moins besoin qu'un témoignage spontané de reconnaissance réponde à notre bienveillance ? Rien ne contribue plus que l'ingratitude à étouffer l'esprit de bienveillance et de fraternité.

Trop de gratitude ?

Ne craignons jamais de manifester trop de gratitude. C'est sur nos sourires, nos remerciements, nos moindres témoignages de reconnaissance que nos semblables fondent très souvent leur attitude à l'égard de la vie.

Développons notre sens de la gratitude et notre désir de l'exprimer. Nous rendrons les gens plus heureux autour de nous et nous deviendrons plus heureux nous-mêmes. Le mot merci a un pouvoir magique; découvrons-le, il ouvre tant de portes.

Notre huitième vitamine du bonheur:

Elle est aussi efficace pour les autres que pour nous-mêmes.

Soyons reconnaissants et prouvons-le !

Vous aimez-vous ?

Si quelqu'un déclarait, à la télévision ou dans un journal: « Je m'aime », l'auditeur ou le lecteur sursauterait immédiatement. Sa première réaction serait sûrement de trouver ce type d'une suffisance, d'un orgueil, d'un égocentrisme sans pareils. Pourtant, s'aimer soi-même s'avère absolument essentiel à notre bonheur. Comment pensons-nous pouvoir aimer autrui, aimer la vie et être heureux si nous ne nous aimons pas ? Si je me déteste, je ne peux pas aimer les autres... et ma vie devient un enfer.

S'aimer soi-même pour mieux aimer les autres !

Les fréquentes disputes chez les gens mariés ne reflètent pas nécessairement un manque d'amour de part et d'autre, mais plutôt une lacune dans leur amour d'eux-mêmes.

Pour réussir son mariage, l'amour de soi est très important. Le docteur Clark E. Vincent, directeur du Centre Scientifique de Comportement à l'Université de Wake Forest, s'expliquait ainsi lors d'une conférence à l'Université du Michigan: « Quand l'amour de nous-mêmes est fort, nous sommes joyeux et optimistes. Par contre, si nous ne nous aimons pas nous-mêmes, nous sommes malheureux et critiquons tout. Par exemple, poursuit-il, lorsqu'un mari a connu une mauvaise journée à son travail, il revient à la maison malheureux, de mauvaise humeur. Il est alors susceptible de provoquer un malentendu. Il accentue immédiatement la moindre petite faute que sa femme peut faire, faute tellement banale qu'il ne l'aurait jamais vue un jour normal. » Souvent, un désaccord soudain est un signe qui veut dire: « Je ne m'aime pas moi-même. »

Se sentir bien dans sa peau

Pour être véritablement un homme ou une femme dans le vrai sens du mot, ne faut-il pas se sentir bien dans sa peau ? C'est là une condition essentielle à notre propre réalisation: être moi-même et m'aimer moi-même.

En fait, que savons-nous sur nous-mêmes ? Sommes-nous différents des autres ? Notre visage, nos habitudes, nos attitudes intérieures et extérieures,

55

notre manière bien particulière de marcher, de parler, de sourire, de regarder, de nous comporter nous sont propres. Nous sommes exclusifs et originaux. Il n'y a qu'une seule copie; il n'existe qu'un seul modèle comme nous, tant sur le plan physique que psychologique. En sommes-nous vraiment convaincus ?

Vivre pleinement sa vie

Pour s'aimer soi-même, il faut vivre en entier chaque détail de sa vie. Nous devons « sentir » et vibrer de tout notre être. Ne nous contentons pas de penser et de comprendre intellectuellement. Nous sommes beaucoup plus que ça. Nous pouvons vivre beaucoup plus profondément.

La plupart des gens se contentent trop souvent de ne vivre qu'en surface. Ainsi, ils n'arrivent jamais à se connaître pleinement. Pourquoi ne pas vivre en profondeur de façon à ce que chaque cellule de notre corps en vibre ? Vivre ce que nous ressentons au plus profond de notre cœur, même si tous sont contre nous, c'est vivre pleinement. Et vivre pleinement, c'est s'aimer soi-même.

Un des compliments les plus appréciés de nos jours est de dire d'une personne qu'elle est un homme ou une femme de tête. Un être humain équilibré et heureux n'est pas seulement une tête, mais aussi et surtout un cœur. Ce cœur doit tout d'abord s'aimer pour pouvoir aimer les autres. Pour y arriver, apprenons à nous connaître nous-mêmes.

L'épouse qui se détestait

Je me souviens de cette jeune femme, pourtant très intelligente et très jolie, qui ne pouvait absolument pas s'accepter. Elle se cherchait constamment une faiblesse ou une tare. Elle parvenait même à s'affubler des pires défauts de la terre. Rien de ce qu'elle faisait n'était bien. Elle se trouvait laide et grosse. Elle était si bien convaincue de son embonpoint qu'elle mangeait constamment des pâtisseries, des sucreries, etc... «Ah ! pour la différence que ça peut faire», disait-elle. Effectivement, elle engraissait. Elle allait magasiner, revenait à la maison et disait immédiatement à son mari: «J'ai acheté une robe, mais je ne sais pas si je l'aime.» Elle enfilait sa robe et revenait devant son mari en disant: «Je suis laide. Cette robe ne me convient pas. J'hésitais aussi. J'aurais donc dû ne pas l'acheter... mais il n'y a rien de beau dans les magasins, tout est laid. Ah ! si la mode pouvait changer !» Son mari essayait bien de la convaincre que cette robe lui allait à ravir, qu'elle était très belle, mais c'était inutile. Ou elle retournait la robe au magasin, ou elle la laissait dans sa garde-robe sans jamais la porter. Elle était si déprimée qu'elle refusait d'accompagner son mari dans les soirées. Elle critiquait tout constamment. Cela rendait son mari malheureux. Des conflits éclatèrent.

Lorsqu'elle vint me voir, elle se considérait comme une loque humaine. Afin de l'aider à remonter la pente je dus la convaincre de s'aimer elle-même, en changeant l'image qu'elle avait d'elle. Ce fut long, mais dès qu'elle commença à s'aimer, elle délaissa les sucreries et se mit à maigrir. Maintenant, elle s'épanouit et n'a plus peur d'elle-même.

Vous connaissez-vous ?

Pour nous faciliter cette connaissance de nous-mêmes, faisons le bilan des qualités et des défauts que nous nous découvrons du côté: physique, intellectuel, affectif, émotif, moral, spirituel, actif et pratique.

Répondons maintenant par écrit aux questions suivantes:

— Nous acceptons-nous ?

— Sommes-nous heureux dans notre peau ? Pourquoi ?

— Désirons-nous ressembler à autrui ? Imiter quelqu'un d'autre ?

— Nous réalisons-nous pleinement ?

Appliquons-nous à nous connaître et à nous respecter. Acceptons-nous tels que nous sommes. Osons vivre ce que nous sommes. Osons vivre avec ce que nous avons.

Telle une mine, la plupart d'entre nous possèdent de grandes richesses, des trésors inestimables. Nous ne les découvrirons qu'en creusant profondément en nous. Recherchons en nous cet amour profond, unique, illimité.

Acceptons-nous avec plus de facilité. Développons notre confiance en nous-mêmes, en nos talents, en nos capacités. Nous apprendrons ainsi à mieux nous aimer. Notre vie deviendra fascinante et exaltante où que nous soyons et quoi que nous fassions présentement.

Prenons conscience de ce que nous sommes vraiment, car nous rencontrerons toujours quelqu'un de mieux ou de pire que nous, mais jamais exactement semblable à nous. Aimons-nous tels que nous sommes. Soyons bien dans notre peau. C'est le départ essentiel vers le bonheur et la réussite.

Notre neuvième vitamine du bonheur:

Aimons-nous nous-mêmes pour pouvoir aimer autrui, apprécier la vie et être heureux.

Savons-nous pardonner ?

Dans la vie, tout n'est pas facile. Lorsqu'un de nos désirs se réalise à la perfection, nous nous en félicitons, et nous avons raison.

Je ne crois pas à la chance. Je crois plutôt que si nous atteignons un de nos buts, c'est que nous 'avons mis en œuvre toute notre énergie pour le réaliser. Nous avons attiré ce qu'on appelle ordinairement la chance. Nous avons eu confiance. Nous avons cru en notre réussite. Ensuite, chacune de nos actions s'est avérée efficace, justement à cause de notre grande foi. Nous avons donc raison de nous féliciter. Nous sommes responsables de notre réussite.

Qui est le vrai coupable ?

Lorsque tout ne tourne pas rond, nous cherchons le coupable. Nous avons besoin de blâmer quelqu'un ou quelque chose, de rejeter la responsabilité de notre échec.

Certains s'en prennent à Dieu, l'accusant d'injustice et lui reprochant toutes les souffrances qu'Il semble cultiver sur la terre. D'autres condamnent alors la vie en général, décrétant qu'elle n'est qu'une suite de malheurs, que le bonheur est impossible, que l'homme s'en va vers sa perte, etc... D'autres personnes encore cherchent le coupable dans leur entourage. Mettre un nom sur leur malheur et se forger un ennemi, voilà, à leurs yeux, une excellente justification et une consécration du caractère définitif de leurs échecs. Elles disent: « Si mon mariage ne fonctionne pas, c'est à cause de ma femme qui... », « Si j'ai perdu ma place, c'est Untel qui m'a joué un sale tour !, « S'il y a la guerre, c'est à cause de ci, de ça... », etc...

Enfin, un dernier groupe comprend les individus qui s'accusent eux-mêmes de tous leurs maux. D'avance, ils se considèrent comme des ratés et des incapables qui ne feront jamais rien de bon dans la vie.

Si nous sommes ainsi, nous établissons une résistance au libre cours de la vie en nous. Nous fixons des limites dans notre subconscient. Nos accusations provoquent des conditions négatives qui se reflètent dans tous nos actes.

Dans la nature, tout fonctionne harmonieusement. Et si, dans notre vie, nos réalisations semblent condamnées à un échec fatal, nous avons nous-mêmes créé ces conditions par notre façon de penser négative et destructrice. Nous avons entraîné notre subconscient à résister au courant naturel de la vie.

Nos accusations, nos condamnations, nos ressenti-ments, nos colères ne punissent personne d'autre que nous-mêmes. Nous récoltons dans notre vie ce que nous semons dans notre subconscient. Nous ne pouvons vivre heureux et maintenir des activités saines et créatrices si nous entretenons constam-ment des pensées négatives et rancunières.

Que devons-nous faire alors ? Nous devons par-donner.

La nature nous pardonne toujours. Lorsque, par exemple, je me coupe à la main ou me brûle, que se passe-t-il ? La nature, guidée par l'intelligence sub-consciente qui m'habite, se met tout de suite à répa-rer ma blessure. De nouvelles cellules apparaissent pour remplacer les cellules atteintes; ma plaie guérit et, peu à peu, mon corps reprend sa forme naturelle. Ainsi, la nature me pardonne.

A qui devons-nous pardonner ?

Nous devons d'abord et avant tout nous pardon-ner à nous-mêmes.

Une institutrice, possédant pourtant toutes les qualités requises pour bien accomplir son travail, ne pouvait profiter des joies que son action aurait pu lui procurer. « J'aime les enfants et j'aime enseigner, me déclarait-elle. Je sais que je pourrais être heu-reuse dans ma profession et pourtant, chaque année, je ne suis pas satisfaite de ce que j'ai pu accomplir. Je sens que les enfants ne m'aiment pas. Je suis constamment tendue. Je crois que je suis trop sévè-re. »

Nous avons essayé de comprendre pourquoi elle

était si sévère, elle qui, au fond, pouvait être très douce. Peu à peu, nous en avons trouvé la raison.

Sa première année d'enseignement s'était avérée un échec. Ses élèves avaient réussi à lui « monter sur la tête». Elle avait alors eu des reproches de la direction de son école.

Depuis lors, elle craignait qu'une telle situation se reproduise. Elle se montrait d'une sévérité extrême, n'acceptant aucun accroc aux règlements de la part des enfants. En somme, elle ne s'était jamais pardonné son premier échec.

Il lui suffisait de se pardonner pour devenir confiante ! Maintenant, un climat d'amour règne dans sa classe. Elle s'est débarrassée de son sentiment de culpabilité.

Pardonnons pour être heureux

Nous devons aussi pardonner aux autres. Le pardon que nous accordons aux autres est essentiel pour notre bonheur et pour la paix de notre esprit. Souvent, lorsque des gens nous ont blessés, nous nous faisons plus de mal intérieur en ne leur pardonnant pas qu'ils ont pu nous en faire avec la blessure qu'ils nous ont infligée.

La rancune nous rend malheureux. Si nous nous regardons bien quand nous désirons du mal à autrui, nous nous sentons mal à l'aise dans notre peau. Nous ne nous aimons pas. Par contre, en pardonnant réellement, nous ne pouvons entretenir que de bonnes et saines pensées à l'égard de celui qui nous a offensés. Alors, nous nous sentons mieux. Nous nous aimons et nous aimons les autres.

62

Pardonner est un acte d'amour et de bonheur.
Quand nous pardonnons, nous consentons, face à
nous-mêmes, à ne pas entretenir de mauvais sentiments à l'égard d'autrui. Autrement dit, quand nous
pardonnons à quelqu'un, nous lui souhaitons d'être
heureux. N'est-ce pas là le véritable sens de
l'amour ? Nous souhaitons le bonheur pour nous-
mêmes comme nous le souhaitons pour tous les
hommes.

Notre dixième vitamine du bonheur:

*Pardonnons-nous et pardonnons aux
autres. Nous n'en serons que plus heureux.*

Etes-vous pleinement satisfaits de votre vie ?

L'aimant de notre vie

Un aimant a deux pôles: le pâle (+) et le pôle
(−). Le rôle positif attire vers lui le fer et l'acier. Il
exerce une force d'attraction; nous dirons donc, selon notre terminologie, qu'il peut recevoir. Le pôle
négatif repousse les mêmes métaux. Ce phénomène
de répulsion, nous l'appellerons le rejet. Le pôle négatif peut donc rejeter ou donner. Un certain équili-

bre se manifeste à travers l'aimant: celui-ci reçoit et donne.

Notre vie ressemble à cet aimant. Elle possède, elle aussi, deux forces: celle de recevoir et celle de donner. Nous serons satisfaits de nous-mêmes dans la mesure où nous conserverons un équilibre entre ces deux forces.

Certains sont des spécialistes du recevoir. Ils reçoivent tout: argent, connaissances, aides, etc... Ils demandent et redemandent toujours. Ils veulent constamment élargir le champ de leurs possessions. Mais n'allez surtout pas leur demander de vous rendre un service. Ils se trouvent alors toutes les raisons du monde pour se défiler: « Je suis très occupé présentement... dans un mois, peut-être... », « Tiens, demande donc à Pierre, lui, il pourrait t'aider, moi, tu sais... », « Oh ! tu tombes mal, mon vieux, tu tombes vraiment mal... justement, ce soir... »

Ces spécialistes du recevoir s'intoxiquent. Ils ressemblent à des estomacs qui encaisseraient toute la nourriture sans jamais la distribuer. Vous imaginez facilement les conséquences graves qu'une telle anomalie produirait, tant sur l'estomac que sur le corps entier. Croyez-vous que les spécialistes du recevoir soient heureux ?

D'autres sont passés maîtres dans l'art de donner. Ils donnent, ils donnent, ils donnent... constamment, sans regarder, sans jamais penser à eux-mêmes, exactement comme une bouteille qui se renverse toujours. Éventuellement, la bouteille se vide complètement. On la jette et elle se brise. Croyez-vous que les spécialistes du donner intégral soient plus heureux ?

64

L'équilibre entre donner et recevoir

Nous ne pouvons vivre avec l'une de ces deux notions seulement. L'amour véritable tient de l'équilibre entre donner et recevoir.

N'aimeriez-vous pas changer vos peines en joies, vos inquiétudes et vos peurs en confiance et en paix du corps et de l'esprit ?

Découvrez alors la puissance de l'amour. Nous pouvons tous, sans exception, transformer notre vie par cette force, la plus grande de l'univers; cette force qui se veut encore plus grande que la puissance de la pensée. Nos pensées et nos désirs peuvent devenir dangereux s'ils ne sont pas motivés par l'amour, par l'équilibre.

Nous devons admettre que l'amour n'est pas une rue à sens unique. La circulation s'y fait dans les deux sens: donner et recevoir. Si nous recevons trop et ne donnons pas assez, le déséquilibre s'installe dans l'ordre du bonheur. Le contraire aussi est vrai. Si nous donnons constamment plus que nous ne recevons, nous nous vidons. Le véritable amour réside dans l'équilibre entre donner et recevoir.

Les quatre fers en l'air !

Un fermier avait décidé de ne plus nourrir son cheval. Tous les jours, il emmenait sa bête aux champs. Cette dernière travaillait ferme et, de retour à l'écurie, notre fermier l'installait pour la nuit sans lui donner de nourriture. A ce régime, trois jours, quatre jours passèrent. Un bon matin, notre fermier retrouva son cheval les pattes en l'air, mort de faim. « C'est dommage, dit-il. Il meurt juste au moment où il commençait à s'habituer. »

On ne peut s'habituer à toujours donner comme on ne peut s'habituer à toujours recevoir sans en subir les conséquences néfastes. Croyez-vous que le fermier de notre petite histoire aimait son cheval ? Non. Croyez-vous qu'il s'aimait lui-même ? Pas plus.

Le plus urgent !

La plupart d'entre nous estimons tout connaître de l'amour. Si tel était le cas, notre vie serait bien différente de ce qu'elle est. Nous devons être capables de rendre des services désintéressés sans rien attendre en retour et sans pour cela qu'on abuse de nous.

N'est-il pas urgent de faire de l'amour la plus grande règle de notre vie et d'apprendre à agir, à parler, à regarder, à écouter, à penser avec compassion ? Ainsi, nous vivrons avec amour et toute notre attitude intérieure en sera imprégnée. Nous découvrirons le bonheur.

Aimons maintenant. Décidons-nous à rayonner d'amour pour la vie et pour tous.

Les principales étapes de cette voie sont les suivantes:

1 — Ne parlons jamais lorsque nous sommes en colère.

2 — Prenons conscience de l'inutilité de la critique constante.

3 — Essayons de découvrir des occasions d'aider les autres, de façon désintéressée, sans rien attendre en retour.

66

4 — Demeurons optimistes et parlons surtout de sujets positifs.

5 — Donnons une intonation gaie, chaleureuse et confiante à notre voix.

6 — Apprenons à dire plus souvent: « Je vous comprends. » Comprenons sincèrement les autres.

7 — Donnons de franches poignées de main et accrochons un sourire affectueux à nos yeux.

8 — Acceptons tous les gens tels qu'ils sont, sans les juger.

L'amour est à la fois le chemin et le point culminant de notre bonheur. Avons-nous expérimenté ce bonheur ?

======

Notre onzième vitamine du bonheur:

Rendons service de façon désintéressée sans rien attendre en retour, sans pour cela qu'on abuse de nous.

======

Où se trouve la solution à tous nos problèmes ?

Qu'est-ce qu'une invention ?

Pour solutionner un problème, il faut ordinairement faire preuve d'un esprit inventif.

Prenons, par exemple, l'imprimerie. Autrefois, les

livres étaient transcrits par de bons moines. Cette transcription constituait un travail manuel épuisant et très peu efficace. Un moine pouvait prendre toute sa vie pour recopier un seul livre. Bien entendu, à ce rythme, il ne fallait pas compter sur une forte distribution. Il existait donc ici un problème: la transcription des écrits.

Il semble qu'au sixième siècle les Chinois aient trouvé une solution, un moyen d'imprimer. L'Occident attendra quelques siècles de plus avant d'employer un mode d'imprimerie semblable à celui que nous connaissons aujourd'hui. Cette invention a solutionné un problème.

Il en est de même pour toutes les inventions, à partir de la roue jusqu'à la force nucléaire. La solution d'un problème semble être le but de chacune d'entre elles.

« Tous les inventeurs sont des génies ! », pouvons-nous affirmer. Le génie n'est, au fond, qu'un homme normal qui a su développer ses qualités créatrices.

Qu'est-ce donc que le génie ?

Quelles sont les qualités mystérieuses qui élèvent un simple individu à cette hauteur ?

La possibilité de créer et d'inventer est l'apanage du génie. C'est pourquoi certains individus semblent littéralement possédés par le besoin de créer. Leur personnalité même en est affectée et peut les pousser jusqu'à la bizarrerie et à la fantaisie. Nous disons souvent qu'ils sont « *originaux* ».

En somme, ils ont découvert le principe vital suivant: la solution à tous nos problèmes se trouve en nous: elle nous vient de la pensée créatrice soutenue par la puissance merveilleuse de notre subconscient.

Pour être pratiques, essayons, en dix étapes, d'examiner ce qui caractérise le génie:

1 — Une grande puissance de concentration. Les « génies » possèdent cette faculté de s'absorber, de se perdre totalement dans leur travail.

2 — Le génie? *Une once d'inspiration pour une tonne de transpiration.* Autrement dit, le génie est un bourreau de travail.

3 — Comment font ces hommes que l'on dit géniaux, demanderez-vous, pour se concentrer, sans se lasser, durant des années ? Où puisent-ils leur énergie pour consacrer à leur activité leur personnalité tout entière ? Ils mobilisent toutes leurs forces conscientes et inconscientes et les tendent vers un seul but.

4 — La possibilité de distinguer en toute chose l'essentiel, les grandes lignes, la synthèse, l'unité. Ainsi le génie va au fond des choses, au-delà des apparences pour découvrir le réel de façon neuve et satisfaisante.

5 — Ces « surhommes » voient le monde avec un regard émerveillé. Ils sont de grands enfants et conservent un élan d'enthousiasme, le goût du risque et de la nouveauté.

6 — C'est la souplesse mentale. Si une méthode ne réussit pas, ils en trouvent rapidement une autre pour résoudre leurs difficultés. Ils essaient. S'ils se trompent, ils recommencent sans se décourager. Pouvons-nous en dire autant ?

7 — C'est la confiance en soi, la clé de base de toute réussite. Le génie ne se contente pas de suivre les directives d'autrui, il fait preuve d'initiative. Il peut ainsi travailler seul pendant de longues heures à une tâche qu'il s'est imposée lui-même.

8 — Ce qu'il possède au plus haut degré, c'est du caractère et de la volonté pour aller toujours de l'avant vers ce qui l'intéresse.

9 — Les génies oublient leur âge. Pourquoi ? Parce qu'ils savent que l'âge ne nous empêche pas d'apprendre, de nous perfectionner, de nous instruire, même après cinquante, soixante ou soixante-dix ans.

10 — Ils ont appris, consciemment ou inconsciemment, à utiliser la puissance de leur subconscient. Notre subconscient est la source où nous pouvons puiser de l'aide pour résoudre tous nos problèmes, même les plus difficiles. Il peut nous apporter plus de sagesse et d'expérience que notre pensée consciente. C'est en lui que repose notre faculté créatrice.

Il est un moment où il convient de conférer toute notre attention à un problème. Cependant, vient aussi un moment où il faut cesser de nous tracasser. Laissons alors notre subconscient remplir sa part de travail. Rappelons-nous que la détente est une des clés de notre subconscient.

Quatre-vingt-dix pour cent des savants et des génies ont admis avoir fait leurs découvertes grâce à la puissance de leur subconscient. Avons-nous découvert cette puissance ?

Si nous le voulions, nous pourrions tous être des

génies. Examinons nos problèmes et « inventons »-leur des solutions. Nous serons surpris de notre génie.

—————————————

Notre douzième vitamine du bonheur:

La solution à tous nos problèmes se trouve en nous.

—————————————

Le rituel du bonheur

Une formule magique pouvant nous garantir le bonheur !

Imaginons le monde merveilleux dans lequel nous pourrions constamment vivre heureux. « Ce serait trop beau pour être vrai », direz-vous.

Il existe pourtant un *rituel du bonheur* qui ne dure qu'une minute et une seconde par jour. Les résultats sont assurés et il ne vous en coûtera pas un sou pour l'appliquer. Il se compose de trois parties.

Première partie du rituel:

En nous réveillant le matin, notre première pensée, pendant au moins 30 secondes, devrait être de choisir. Choisir quoi ? Choisissons d'être heureux, enthousiastes, pour aujourd'hui seulement. Pas pour demain, pas pour un mois ni pour le reste de notre vie, mais pour aujourd'hui seulement, choisissons le bonheur.

Beaucoup de gens croient que le bonheur nous apparaît à l'improviste, un bon matin, sans raison aucune ! Paf ! ça y est ! Aujourd'hui, je suis heureux ! Boum ! Ah ! que je suis malheureux !

On ne joue pas au bonheur et au malheur. On le choisit. Le bonheur est un choix, une façon de penser, de réagir; une manière de vivre qui devient éventuellement une habitude.

Si nous désirons être heureux, soyons-le immédiatement. Autrement, en attendant le bonheur à cause de ceci, de cela... nous risquons de l'attendre longtemps. Si tout va pour le mieux, ceci vient s'ajouter à notre bonheur, mais n'en est pas la cause.

Ainsi, en nous réveillant le matin, prenons trente secondes de notre temps et choisissons une attitude intérieure, un état d'âme qu'il faudra maintenir toute la journée, quoi qu'il advienne.

Deuxième partie du rituel:

En nous couchant, prenons encore 30 secondes de notre temps et choisissons de nous réveiller heureux et de bonne humeur le lendemain. « Quelle merveilleuse journée ce sera ! »

A notre grande surprise, le lendemain, nous nous réveillerons en pleine forme et heureux. Notre subconscient aura travaillé et développé ce thème toute la nuit.

Troisième partie du rituel:

Durant la journée, n'acceptons aucune idée pessimiste. Remplaçons immédiatement, automatiquement, toute pensée négative par une pensée positive. Nous ne répéterons jamais assez que nous sommes et que nous devenons ce que nous pensons à longueur de journée. Nos pensées habituelles, nos émotions nous rendent heureux ou malheureux.

Voyons-nous vraiment l'importance de n'entretenir que des pensées et des attitudes positives qui créeront le moule de notre bonheur ?

Sommes-nous prêts à pratiquer dès aujourd'hui ce rituel magique du bonheur ?

Quel est votre quotient de maturité ?

Notre quotient de maturité

Nombre de gens sont préoccupés par leur quotient intellectuel. Cela est bien normal. Aujourd'hui, face aux multiples activités qui nous sont offertes, nous devons connaître nos capacités de compréhension et d'exécution. De cette façon, nous pouvons mieux nous orienter.

Par contre, trop peu de gens sont préoccupés par leur *quotient de maturité*. Sommes-nous de ceux-là ?

Souvent, on donne de la maturité des définitions de toutes les couleurs. Par exemple, si un enfant nous semble très sage, s'il demeure enfermé dans sa chambre, s'il ne trouve rien d'amusant dans les jeux, s'il n'a pas de compagnons, nous entendons plusieurs parents dire: « Paul est trop vieux pour son âge... »

Ces personnes croient que Paul a atteint un *niveau de maturité supérieur* à la moyenne des autres enfants. Elles ne se gênent pas pour le donner en exemple au petit gamin qui lance des cailloux dans l'eau, court les papillons, grimpe dans les arbres. « Regarde, disent-elles, Paul est bien plus sage que toi, tu devrais l'imiter. »

Ce qu'elles ne sentent pas, c'est que Paul est peut-être très malade. Souvent, ces gens-là ne possèdent même pas le degré de maturité de leur enfant.

Trop prudent !

Un adulte que nous nommerons F. conserve le même emploi depuis dix ans. Il se prive considéra-

76

blement, s'impose de grands sacrifices pour accumuler le plus d'argent possible. F. n'est pourtant pas avare; il se montre généreux quand il le faut, mais il demeure intransigeant pour lui-même. Son entourage dira: « F. est un homme prudent. Il fait preuve d'assez de maturité pour penser au futur. »

Croyez-vous que ce soit exact? Non. F. a une peur incroyable de ce qui pourrait lui arriver, de l'insécurité. Il possède, au fond, un niveau de maturité inférieur.

Qu'est-ce que la maturité ?

La maturité n'est pas une apparence de sagesse. La maturité n'est pas une prudence maladive. La maturité ne se cache ni derrière la peur, ni dans la bravoure absurde des Don Quichotte. La maturité ? C'est la recherche de l'équilibre et de l'harmonie en tout. Être bien dans notre peau; en d'autres mots, être nous-mêmes.

Au cours des chapitres suivants, nous allons gravir les sept marches de la maturité. Nous tâcherons de voir comment améliorer notre niveau de maturité et comment atteindre *l'équilibre et l'harmonie* en tout.

Sommes-nous patients et persévérants ?

Le siècle de l'instantanéité

Aujourd'hui, à l'époque du café instantané (soluble), des repas instantanés, des records de vitesse, de l'amour et du sexe éclairs, nous exigeons que tout soit rapide, presque subit. Grâce à la télévision, en une heure nous pouvons poser un œil sur chacun des continents sans même nous lever de notre fauteuil. Nous avons même des images de la Lune avec à peine quelques secondes de retard.

Jules Verne parlait du « Tour du monde en 80 jours ». Nous parlons du tour du monde en 80 secondes. En somme, entourés de toutes ces réalisations rapides, nous voulons que nos activités suivent le même rythme. Si nous ne réussissons pas notre travail immédiatement, si un résultat tangible ne nous saute pas aux yeux à la première esquisse, nous sommes prêts à abandonner. Nous voulons, comme le dit l'expression, « tout rôti dans le bec ». Maintenant, nous désirons tout sans en payer le prix.

Suivons le rythme de la nature

La nature ne suit pas ce rythme. Combien d'années faut-il à un arbre pour atteindre sa maturité ? La nature ne fait aucune course. Elle prend le temps qu'il faut. Tout se paie et nous n'obtenons rien pour rien, à moins de croire encore au Père Noël. Nous risquons alors de connaître de sérieuses déceptions.

Quel prix devons-nous payer ?

Il s'appelle C.T.P.P.: Création-Travail-Patience-Persévérance. Souvent nous avons de bonnes idées. Notre cerveau est constamment en ébullition et nous pouvons solutionner une foule de petits problèmes grâce à notre esprit créateur. Il nous faut cependant réaliser ces bonnes idées. Le moyen ? Le travail. Certaines personnes ont une capacité de travail incroyable, mais elles ne réussissent jamais rien. Pourquoi ? Elles manquent de patience et de persévérance.

Les possibilités incroyables de la persévérance

Evangelos Georgakakis, à l'âge de 10 ans, perdit la vue, une main et l'usage presque complet de son autre main.

Il ne se découragea pas. Il apprit le braille avec sa langue. Il fut le premier aveugle à être admis à la faculté de Droit de l'Université de la ville où il demeurait. Des 2 000 candidats qui demandèrent leur admission à cette faculté en septembre 1958, 600 réussirent. Georgakakis se classa cinquième.

A force de travail et de persévérance, il obtint, en octobre 1963, un diplôme de l'Université d'Athènes. Trois ans après, il passa ses examens au barreau de la Cour Suprême de la même ville. Il se classa premier des 333 candidats.

Nous gâchons tant d'efforts à cause de notre manque de patience et de persévérance. Si Evangelos Georgakakis avait décidé de se laisser vivre par la société, vu son infirmité, il ne serait pas avocat, aujourd'hui.

Ne lâchons pas !

Notre patience et notre persévérance peuvent se développer. Si nous sommes persévérants, nous pouvons nous imposer de petits buts, toujours à court terme. Nous devons absolument les réaliser, quoi qu'il nous en coûte.

Ne nous décourageons pas. Soyons comme un enfant qui apprend à marcher. L'enfant tombe, se relève, recommence. Il prend tout le temps qu'il lui faut. Un jour, naturellement, il réussit. Il est debout, il marche. Il nous a fallu beaucoup de patience et de persévérance pour marcher, pour pouvoir courir... et nous avons réussi. Nous pouvons encore tout réussir si nous nous armons de patience et de persévérance.

La patience d'une grand-maman

Mme Miriam Hargrave, une grand-maman anglaise de Wakefield, a échoué 39 fois à ses examens de conduite automobile pour réussir la quarantième fois. Elle avait compris que, tôt ou tard, sa persévérance l'aiderait à atteindre son but.

Malgré les échecs

Revenons sans cesse à la charge, malgré les problèmes accumulés en nous et autour de nous. Rien de valable ne peut être accompli sans patience et persévérance.

La réussite et le bonheur s'obtiennent rarement au premier essai. Il nous faut souvent subir cinq, dix, quinze échecs avant d'y parvenir.

Persévérons.

Quelle est la cause de la majorité de nos découragements ? Ne serait-ce pas, dans la grande majorité des cas, notre impatience ?

80

Le génie

Le génie est fait de travail et de patience. Le talent ne peut remplacer la persistance. Toutes les grandes réalisations humaines dignes d'admiration constituent de merveilleux exemples de la puissance irrésistible de la persévérance. Ces œuvres ont été accomplies par des gens qui ont continué sans relâche leur travail alors qu'il ne semblait plus y avoir d'espoir. Le moindre petit geste répété incessamment surmonte les plus grands obstacles.

Ne laissons rien nous décourager. Continuons, n'abandonnons pas. C'est la devise de tous ceux qui ont réussi. A un moment ou à un autre, le découragement viendra. L'important est de le surmonter. Si nous pouvons faire cela, le bonheur nous appartient.

L'ampoule électrique

Le grand inventeur Edison a échoué près de 10 000 fois avant de réussir à fabriquer l'ampoule électrique à incandescence. N'abandonnons jamais après un ou deux échecs, persévérons.

Pour réussir dans la vie, le talent est souhaitable, les circonstances favorables aussi, mais la persévérance l'est davantage encore. Nous sommes entourés de gens doués et instruits qui ont raté leur vie et qui sont malheureux. Rien au monde ne peut remplacer la persévérance, ni le talent, ni l'instruction.

Le gagnant et le perdant

Quand nous sommes portés au découragement, nous n'avons pas le choix; osons nous répéter: « Je refuse d'abandonner. Je suis de plus en plus persévérant. Je réussirai éventuellement. J'en suis certain. A tout problème, il y a une solution. Je trouverai la solution à mon problème. »

Soyons déterminés à persévérer sans nous laisser abattre par les problèmes, les critiques et les circonstances. Rappelons-nous la fable du lièvre et de la tortue.

Nous pouvons réussir et être heureux, quoi que nous ayons fait ou omis de faire dans le passé, pourvu que nous décidions de persister vers notre but. Cette persévérance nous permet de survivre à toutes les épreuves.

Quoi que les gens disent de nous, quoi qu'ils pensent ou fassent, ne lâchons pas, continuons. Le bonheur appartient à ceux qui persistent, à ceux qui continuent alors que tous les autres ont abandonné. La persévérance est cette qualité essentielle qui différencie le gagnant du perdant.

Ainsi, voilà la première marche à gravir pour atteindre notre maturité: la patience et la persévérance. Devenons plus patients sans nous emporter à la moindre contrariété. Persévérons et nous mènerons toutes nos tâches à leur fin.

Première marche:

Patience et persévérance.

Avez-vous du tact ?

Le tact vs l'hypocrisie

Pour plusieurs, avoir du tact c'est faire preuve d'hypocrisie. Quand, devant eux, on parle de tact, leur esprit dessine aussitôt l'image du vendeur qui, avec de belles paroles, des sourires « à tout casser » et des boniments, réussit à nous vendre un produit de mauvaise qualité en nous le vantant tellement que nous croyons acheter la Lune.

Voilà l'erreur ! Le vendeur qui met tout en œuvre pour « rouler » son client n'agit pas avec tact. Il fait preuve de malhonnêteté. Il se sert de ce que nous appelons de la fausse représentation. Le tact est bien différent puisqu'il est l'art des relations humaines.

Lui marchons-nous sur les pieds ?

Beaucoup de gens se disent qu'il faut être franc, sincère; en somme, qu'il faut être loyal dans les relations avec autrui. Ils ont raison. Mais ils croient que, pour être loyal, il faut constamment exprimer une opinion telle qu'elle se présente, sans restrictions. Ils parlent avec toute l'émotion qu'ils ressentent face à un problème donné. Ils brisent bien des plats. Ils disent agressivement leur façon de penser, obligeant leur interlocuteur à se camper dans une position défensive, et immédiatement le dialogue devient négatif. Chacun fonce avec « son » idée en tête, chacun tente de détruire l'opinion de l'autre. Il en résulte deux monologues qui s'affrontent. Pourtant, avec un peu de tact, la discussion prendrait un tout autre aspect.

Pour convaincre quelqu'un de notre sincérité ou de nos idées, est-il nécessaire de lui marcher sur les pieds ? Non ! On attire plus de mouches avec du miel qu'avec du vinaigre. Ainsi, le tact est simplement une question de respect des autres.

Qui réussit sa vie agit avec tact. Il sait amener les autres à coopérer avec lui dans un esprit amical, ce qui lui permet de réaliser plus facilement ses buts. Celui qui rate sa vie, au contraire, aime critiquer et montrer constamment du doigt les erreurs des autres.

Celui qui réussit réfléchit avant de parler. Il pèse ses mots avec soin. Il admire ouvertement ce qu'il apprécie chez les autres et se montre plus discret face à ce qu'il désapprouve. Cela signifie qu'il préfère penser positivement plutôt que de se laisser gagner par la pensée négative. Il n'oublie pas que le fait de penser du bien des autres l'amène automatiquement à penser du bien de lui-même.

Le côté positif des événements s'avère toujours plus enrichissant que leur côté négatif. Par exemple, si, à chaque fois que nous voyons un film, une pièce de théâtre ou une émission de télévision; si, à chaque fois que nous lisons un article de journal, nous faisions un bilan de l'aspect positif, nous trouverions toujours quelque chose. Cela, même si nous désapprouvions l'événement en général. Après avoir dégagé l'esprit positif, nous pourrions plus facilement, plus objectivement, voir ce qui nous semble moins agréable.

Celui qui échoue parle avant de réfléchir. Il blesse tout le monde par ses propos inopportuns et se crée ainsi constamment des ennemis.

L'être équilibré et le raté

L'être équilibré ne donne son opinion qu'après s'être bien renseigné. Le raté expose constamment ses vues même s'il ne connaît pas le sujet dont il parle.

Celui qui réussit s'intéresse aux gens, surtout à ceux qui ont beaucoup en commun avec lui. Celui qui échoue n'essaie de cultiver l'amitié que de ceux dont il veut obtenir des faveurs. Ainsi, ses démarches aboutissent souvent à une impasse.

L'être équilibré est ouvert à tout et à tous. Autrement dit, il vit comme il l'entend et laisse les autres vivre à leur façon. Il sait qu'avant de changer ou de réformer ceux qui l'entourent, il doit se changer, se réformer lui-même.

Sommes-nous prêts à payer le prix de la réussite et du bonheur ? Si oui, changeons notre attitude mentale envers nous-mêmes, envers les autres et envers la vie. Étudions l'art des relations humaines.

N'entretenons aucun préjugé

Souvent, nous avons la mauvaise habitude de classer les gens avant même de les connaître. Nous entendons parler de quelqu'un et nous nous disons immédiatement que nous ne pourrions jamais nous entendre avec lui. Sans même que nous en soyons conscients, cette attitude s'imprime dans notre subconscient. Un jour, rencontrant la personne en question, nous constatons qu'il nous est impossible de nous entendre avec elle. C'est souvent à cause de notre préjugé. Si nous avions pensé le contraire, il en aurait été autrement. Nous sommes responsables de l'état de nos relations.

Nous ne devons jamais condamner quelqu'un dans notre cœur. Il est certain que tous les gens ne sont pas d'un caractère facile. Parfois, même si nous employons toute notre bonne volonté, même si nous faisons preuve de beaucoup de tact, nos relations avec certaines personnes peuvent s'avérer bien difficiles. Il y a des gens qui sont malades psychiquement. A cause de leur éducation, de leur enfance, d'expériences malheureuses, ils n'acceptent personne. Si, à ce moment, nous nous élevons contre eux, il est certain que nous ne pourrons jamais espérer établir une relation sincère avec eux. Il faut les comprendre, de la même façon que nous comprenons un infirme. Certaines personnes souffrent d'infirmités psychologiques. Si nous n'acceptons pas ce handicap au départ, nous ne réussirons jamais à les approcher.

Soyons donc équilibrés. Permettons aux autres de ne pas être d'accord avec nous comme nous nous permettons de ne pas partager leurs pensées. Nous pouvons ne pas être d'accord sans pour cela devenir désagréables. Apprenons à nous contrôler.

Un dicton nous suggère de nous « tourner sept fois la langue dans la bouche avant de parler ». Si nous appliquions ce principe, que d'erreurs nous pourrions éviter. Le respect de l'autre, la compréhension et l'amour, voilà les clés des bonnes relations humaines.

Deuxième marche:

Ayons du tact !

Peut-on plaire à tout le monde ?

Sommes-nous des caméléons ?

Certains ne peuvent jamais dire non. Ils se montrent toujours prêts à rendre service, à changer ceci ou cela dans leur façon d'agir, selon leur entourage. Lorsqu'ils parlent avec autrui, ils acceptent ses idées comme si elles leur étaient acquises. Et souvent ces gens ne sont pas heureux.

Nous ne doutons pas qu'une personne qui rend constamment service sera « bien vue ». Tout être prêt à se plier aux désirs des autres, à effectuer les changements nécessaires pour toujours s'adapter pourra nous apparaître comme le collaborateur idéal. Alors nous nous trompons. Les gens qui disent toujours oui ne sont pas heureux. Ils n'ont pas de maturité. Pourquoi ? Parce qu'ils ne sont pas bien dans leur peau, pour la simple raison qu'ils n'en connaissent pas la couleur. Ils ressemblent aux caméléons. Avez-vous déjà pensé au cauchemar d'un caméléon posé sur un tissu rayé ?

Tout cela peut vous sembler impossible, caricatural, mais il existe effectivement des situations dans lesquelles nos « caméléons » se sentent véritablement mal à l'aise. Une expression nous dit: « Ils ne savent plus sur quel pied danser ! » C'est vrai. Imaginez les acrobaties et le ridicule d'un danseur qui voudrait suivre trois musiques à la fois.

Le meunier, son fils et l'âne

Lafontaine, dans une fable intitulée « Le meunier, son fils et l'âne », nous a merveilleusement dépeint

87

les situations malencontreuses vécues par un pauvre meunier qui, accompagné de son jeune fils, allait vendre son âne à la foire. Tout le long du parcours, quoi qu'il fit, les gens considéraient qu'il n'agissait pas comme il aurait dû le faire. Et, comme notre homme se fiait au « qu'en-dira-t-on », il en vint à ne plus savoir comment se comporter.

Sommes-nous esclaves de l'opinion des autres ?

Pour chacune de nos opinions, quelles qu'elles soient, il se présentera toujours des gens qui ne partageront pas nos idées. Alors que devons-nous faire ? Agir comme nous l'entendons.

Cela ne signifie nullement que nous devons nous enfermer dans notre coquille et marcher droit devant nous. Non, nous pouvons demander l'opinion des autres si nous ne sommes pas certains de la nôtre, mais, une fois que nous avons choisi une direction, si nous croyons sincèrement qu'elle est la meilleure, nous devons la suivre jusqu'au bout. Ne craignons pas la sincérité et sachons dire non quand il le faut. Cest là un facteur essentiel de notre maturité.

Faut-il que les autres nous approuvent constamment ?

Sommes-nous effrayés d'être totalement nous-mêmes ? Il n'y a pas deux personnes semblables. Celui qui accepte cette différence développe véritablement sa maturité. Il est immunisé contre les sarcasmes, les critiques destructives et les opinions variées que ses actions et ses paroles peuvent provoquer chez les autres. Il est impossible de plaire à tout le monde.

Nous reconnaissons-nous le droit de différer d'opinion d'avec la majorité ? Ce que la plupart des gens croient et font n'est pas nécessairement « correct ».

Osons développer notre individualité. Trop de gens parmi nous sont des « copies ». Osons devenir des originaux. Agissons selon nos convictions sincères.

Ne nous excusons pas constamment d'être différents. Ne nous préoccupons pas continuellement de plaire à tout le monde. Cessons d'avoir peur d'exprimer notre véritable opinion. Il n'y a rien de plus frustrant que de telles attitudes.

Troisième marche:

Ayons le courage de nos convictions !

Êtes-vous de bonne humeur ?

N'est-il pas merveilleux de pouvoir faire naître, par notre sourire, la joie dans les cœurs ? Soyons toujours de bonne humeur, où que nous allions et quoi que nous fassions.

« Créateurs de joie » demandés !

Nous avons un urgent besoin de « créateurs de joie », de gens qui refusent de voir constamment l'aspect négatif et pessimiste des gens et de la vie. Répandre le soleil autour de soi revêt une valeur incalculable. Gardons notre cœur ensoleillé. Tout est moins pénible à supporter quand nous sommes bien disposés intérieurement envers ce qui nous entoure. En maintenant notre humeur enjouée, nous recevons immédiatement notre récompense.

Notre expression triste et figée contribue-t-elle à répandre un froid dans notre entourage ?

Le sourire et la gaieté, au contraire, communiquent la joie de vivre. Nous avons besoin d'hommes et de femmes gais et souriants qui remplissent leur esprit de beau, de bon pour que le pessimisme ne puisse y trouver place.

Pensons positif, chassons le négatif.

Avez-vous découvert cette baguette magique qui transformera votre vie: le sourire sincère ?

Comment retrouver cette joie de vivre que nous avons perdue ?

Maintenons constamment une attitude joyeuse dans notre vie. Parlons et agissons comme si la joie nous était déjà revenue.

Semons partout nos sourires et notre bonne humeur, comme des fleurs. Substituons-les aux critiques et aux rancunes. Recherchons toujours ce qui nous unit plutôt que ce qui nous divise.

Le sourire et la bonne humeur sont les plus beaux cadeaux à offrir et à recevoir. Ils enrichissent tout le monde, tant celui qui donne que celui qui reçoit.

C'est une fontaine merveilleuse: plus on en donne, plus on en a. « Que ça fait du bien de regarder votre visage rayonnant de bonheur », diront les gens.

Le sourire transfigure tout. Il possède une éloquence que ne peuvent exprimer les mots. Oui, tout sourire parle.

Comment maintenir notre bonne humeur ?

Fuyons l'oisiveté comme la peste. Ayons toujours quelque chose à faire, à aimer ou à espérer. Réjouissons-nous de la réussite des autres. Voyons toujours ce qu'il y a de meilleur en chacun. Prononçons constamment des paroles encourageantes et non dénigrantes.

Avançons encore plus loin sur la route du bonheur et de la maturité. Admettons sans aucune restriction qu'il n'est pas nécessairement facile de trouver le bonheur en nous-mêmes, mais qu'il est impossible de le trouver ailleurs.

Comment cultiver le sourire en nous ?

Premièrement, dressons l'inventaire de toutes nos joies quotidiennes, de tout ce que nous prenons pour acquis, de tous les bienfaits de notre vie y compris les plus petits. Révisons cette liste tous les jours.

Deuxièmement, rendons service à quelqu'un avec bonne humeur.

Troisièmement, prenons l'habitude de chanter gaiement, surtout si nous sommes enclins au découragement ou à la dépression. Notre entourage n'appréciera pas nécessairement notre talent, avec raison peut-être, mais cette méthode nous servira cependant de véritable tonique de bonne humeur.

Si nous gardons dans tout ce que nous entreprenons un sourire sincère, toutes nos activités seront colorées de joie et de bonheur. Comment nous y prendre ?

1— Soyons aimables. Sans nous laisser marcher sur les pieds, ne blessons personne.

2— Intéressons-nous à tous ceux que nous rencontrons.

3— Réveillons-nous. Soyons plus dynamiques et plus enthousiastes.

4— Apprécions ce qu'il y a de bien au lieu de critiquer ce qui nous semble mal.

Notre plus riche contribution à la vie pourra être notre bonne humeur. C'est un des meilleurs remèdes pour notre corps, notre cœur et notre esprit.

Comme le poète l'a si bien dit: « Le monde est un miroir qui nous renvoie notre propre image. Sourions, il nous sourit. »

Quatrième marche:

Cultivons le sourire et la bonne humeur.

Donnons-nous toujours le meilleur de nous-mêmes ?

Nous croyons souvent que certains travaux ne sont pas importants. Nous ne fournissons alors aucun effort pour les réaliser. Que remarquons-nous quand ils nous semblent terminés ? Nous n'éprouvons aucune satisfaction. Non seulement sommes-nous insatisfaits du travail exécuté, mais en plus nous sommes mécontents de nous-mêmes. Bref, nous ne sommes pas heureux.

Le bonheur appartient à ceux qui donnent leur plein rendement en tout. Ils vont jusqu'au bout de leurs possibilités en se donnant totalement à tout ce qu'ils entreprennent. Le bonheur leur vient par surcroît.

Il faut du courage pour se donner à fond. D'ailleurs on n'a jamais rien accompli de grand sans prendre les choses passionnément à cœur. Oui, donnons-nous à fond.

Si nous enlevons à la vie cet élément unique, rien n'a plus guère de sens. Cependant, plus le mouvement qui nous pousse à prendre les choses à cœur est désintéressé, plus il est fécond et plus il nous rendra heureux.

Le champion

Le champion n'est pas nécessairement celui qui possède le plus. Mais c'est toujours celui qui donne le plus. Le champion risque tout. Que de fois n'avons-nous pas vu, au cours de compétitions sportives, celui que les experts ont négligé remporter la victoire. Comment a-t-il fait ? Il y a mis tout son cœur... alors que souvent le champion respecté, adulé, se repose sur ses lauriers. Celui qui met tout son cœur dans ce qu'il fait peut véritablement espérer une réussite.

Le bonheur, c'est la récompense accordée à celui qui se donne corps et âme à sa tâche, quelle qu'elle soit. Cela exige un effort supplémentaire. Une fois qu'on a goûté à ce mélange de fierté, d'enthousiasme et de soulagement qui en résulte, notre vie se trouve irrémédiablement transformée. On peut se répéter: « Voilà du bon travail ! Je m'y suis mis en entier ! » Toutes les besognes qui nous paraissent actuellement monotones et ennuyeuses deviendront alors intéressantes. Nous en tirerons des étincelles qui nous enflammeront.

N'essayons-nous qu'à moitié ?

C'est souvent la crainte de l'échec qui nous empêche de foncer et de réussir. Pourtant, nous perdre dans la besogne entreprise constitue le seul moyen de nous découvrir nous-mêmes à travers elle. Plus nous nous donnons, plus nous avons à donner et plus nous créons notre bonheur.

Certains ne jugent pas leur travail assez important pour y consacrer le meilleur d'eux-mêmes. Ils se ménagent toujours pour la grande occasion. . . qui ne vient jamais. Ce que nous oublions trop fréquemment, c'est que toute grande œuvre est composée de nombreux petits travaux qui paraissent sans importance mais qui doivent être bien faits.

Un homme d'affaires inutile

Un homme d'affaires me racontait récemment la difficulté qu'il éprouvait à participer à des travaux d'équipes. « Lorsque je travaille seul, me déclarait-il, je perçois le résultat. Je me donne facilement. Mais lorsque nous travaillons en équipes, je ne vois pas de résultats tangibles. Il me semble toujours que ma part de travail est mal faite et inutile. Je ne suis pas satisfait de moi-même. »

Je lui ai demandé s'il croyait pouvoir effectuer seul toute sa tâche. Il m'a répondu que c'était impossible, qu'il avait absolument besoin des autres. Je lui ai alors fait comprendre que les autres aussi avaient absolument besoin de lui. Sa part de travail était aussi importante pour la réussite finale du projet que celle des autres.

Dernièrement, il m'avoua comment toute son attitude vis-à-vis des travaux d'équipes avait changé. Il peut maintenant se donner à fond et fournir tous les efforts dont il est capable pour le moindre travail.

Les moindres choses ont leur importance

Il en est ainsi pour chacun de nous. Rien n'est inutile. Tous les travaux, si petits soient-ils, méritent d'être bien faits parce qu'ils font partie d'un grand tout.

L'important, dans toute vie heureuse, n'est pas de réussir de grandes choses de façon plutôt ordinaire ou moche, mais d'accomplir, de se donner entièrement, de mettre tout son cœur dans les choses les plus ordinaires. En nous y mettant sérieusement nous pouvons tout accomplir de façon extraordinaire. Ainsi, tout nous procurera une immense satisfaction et un authentique épanouissement.

La dispersion mentale

Souvent, des gens me disent qu'ils ne peuvent donner le meilleur d'eux-mêmes, non parce qu'ils n'aiment pas ce qu'ils font, mais parce qu'on les dérange, parce qu'on les distrait constamment. Ils aiment trop de choses, voudraient tout accomplir à la fois. Ils n'obtiennent alors pas la réussite à laquelle semblaient les prédestiner leurs talents et leurs connaissances. Quelle en est la cause ? La plupart du temps: la dispersion mentale.

Pouvez-vous vous concentrer facilement ?

Plusieurs me répondront: « Mais comment pouvons-nous nous concentrer quand le bruit, le téléphone, la télévision, les problèmes, les amis viennent constamment nous distraire et nous interrompre ? »

Tous, sans exception, nous pouvons acquérir l'habitude de la concentration.

Rappelons-nous la facilité de concentration d'un enfant: il s'absorbe tout entier dans ce qu'il entreprend. Souvent, nous le regardons, nous lui parlons et il ne fait pas attention à nous. En fait, il possède véritablement un pouvoir de concentration.

Conservons ou retrouvons cette merveilleuse capacité de concentration que nous possédions lorsque nous étions enfants. Elle nous permettra de nous absorber totalement dans tout ce que nous faisons.

Que devons-nous faire pour réapprendre à nous concentrer ? Apprenons tout d'abord à nous plonger résolument dans notre besogne présente.

Le cinéaste

Le cinéaste qui prépare un film obéit à un but précis. Il désire attirer l'attention du spectateur. Il veut que ce dernier se concentre sur l'image qu'il lui expose. Ainsi, il agira de façon à ce que chaque image, chaque plan soit une étape. En somme, il exécute une chose à la fois. Nous devons suivre son exem-

96

ple: faire une chose à la fois. Sans cette disposition d'esprit, notre travail aussi bien que nos loisirs seront gâchés.

La concentration s'acquiert par l'entraînement

Cette pratique exige une grande patience et un effort assidu. Obstinons-nous à ramener sans cesse notre esprit à un sujet déterminé. A la fin, nos pensées indisciplinées finiront par céder le pas à la concentration. A notre grande joie, nous découvrirons que nous pouvons à volonté diriger notre attention sur n'importe laquelle de nos activités.

Rien ne porte plus préjudice à notre réussite que le vagabondage de notre imagination.

Trois exercices pratiques de concentration

1— Plaçons devant nous une photo en couleurs d'un magnifique paysage tropical. Observons celui-ci très attentivement. Ensuite, fermons les yeux et reconstituons la scène. Rappelons-nous en imagination ce paysage plaisant. Mettons-y le plus de détails possibles. Répétons régulièrement cette expérience de concentration tous les jours.

2— Lisons attentivement une page d'un volume ou d'un article intéressant. Sans nous référer au texte, résumons en quelques mots ce que nous avons lu. Graduellement, lisons 2, 3, 4 pages. Transcrivons ensuite de mémoire les principales idées de l'auteur.

3— Rappelons-nous que la méthode la plus rapide pour développer notre concentration est de nous exercer à bien faire tout ce que nous avons à faire avec attention.

Cinquième marche:

Donnons constamment le meilleur de nous-mêmes.

Avez-vous l'esprit de décision ?

L'indécision est une des causes majeures de la misère et des problèmes de bien des gens. Elle est la source de nombreux désappointements et de beaucoup d'échecs.

Toute personne très lente à prendre une décision et rapide à la changer atteint rarement la réussite et le bonheur qu'elle désire.

Admettons que celui qui prend souvent des décisions commet certainement plus d'erreurs que celui qui n'en prend jamais. Malgré tout, il accomplit beaucoup plus que tout autre dans son domaine.

Qui n'a entendu ce proverbe populaire: « La fortune sourit aux audacieux » ? Napoléon disait: « Si j'ai eu tant de supériorité sur mes contemporains, c'est que j'ai toujours su me décider sans hésiter. »

La vie nous demande chaque jour de prendre des décisions. Les prenons-nous ? Les gens qui réussissent leur vie possèdent l'esprit de décision. Ils se décident rapidement, ce qui nous permet de les prendre au sérieux. Ils donnent aussi une impression de sécurité à ceux qui les entourent.

Hésitons-nous en pesant toujours le pour et le contre sans jamais nous décider ? Acquérons l'esprit de décision et nous économiserons ainsi notre temps et notre énergie. Par le fait même, nous accroîtrons notre bonheur.

On lui vole ses inventions !

Sommes-nous capables d'accepter la possibilité de nous tromper ? Certains hésitent indéfiniment et le regrettent amèrement par la suite.

Ainsi, un de mes amis d'enfance, dont le passe-temps était d'inventer mille et une choses, n'osa jamais développer au maximum ses inventions les plus géniales. Le temps passait et il ajournait sa décision de peur de se tromper.

D'autres s'inspirèrent de ses trouvailles et prirent, eux, la décision de les développer et de les exploiter brillamment.

Jamais de promotion !

Un autre homme, pourtant bon travailleur, s'aperçut un jour qu'il demeurait toujours à la même position dans sa compagnie. Les jeunes acquéraient des postes plus élevés. Il était vraiment chagriné car il mettait véritablement tous ses efforts à bien effectuer son travail. Il en vint à croire qu'il n'aurait jamais d'avancement.

Il confia son problème au chef du personnel et lui demanda les raisons de cet état. Le directeur lui répondit qu'il faisait toujours bien son travail mais qu'il lui manquait l'esprit de décision. Il ne prenait jamais d'initiatives. Il fallait toujours qu'il attende la permission avant d'exécuter un ouvrage.

Il vint me rencontrer. « Je travaille fort, me dit-il,

mais quand je fais quelque chose par moi-même, j'ai peur de me tromper et je préfère attendre qu'on me donne un ordre. » En somme, il craignait de prendre une mauvaise décision.

Je lui dis que les seuls qui ne se trompent jamais sont ceux qui ne prennent aucune décision et qui ne font rien. Je lui exposai une méthode pour prendre une bonne décision. Il la mit en pratique et, quelques mois plus tard, le chef du personnel remarqua des changements dans son attitude. Il obtint l'avancement désiré.

Mes conseils sont simples: ils comprennent six points:

1 — Compilons le plus de faits susceptibles d'affecter notre décision. Réfléchissons-y. Cependant, employons notre bon sens. Que le temps de notre réflexion soit proportionné à l'importance de notre décision. Décidons-nous rapidement quand il s'agit de bagatelles comme l'achat de bas ou de souliers, mais réfléchissons plus longuement s'il est question de changer d'emploi ou de résidence.

2 — Écrivons le pour et le contre de ces faits.

3 — Distinguons entre les faits importants et ceux qui ne le sont pas.

4 — Choisissons au meilleur de notre connaissance, en admettant que nous puissions nous tromper, ce que nous croyons être la meilleure solution applicable. Il reste toujours un fossé à sauter pour réussir. Il s'agit à la fin de décider si nous le sauterons ou non.

5 — Oui, admettons au départ qu'il est humain de se tromper. La plupart du temps, toute réussite est

précédée de nombreux échecs.

6 — Passons rapidement à l'action. Si nous attendons constamment le moment propice pour démarrer, nous ne commencerons jamais. Passons à l'action avec ce que nous avons, où nous sommes, et faisons de notre mieux, sans craindre de nous tromper. Nous serons émerveillés des résultats.

Il vaut mieux se décider sincèrement, passer à l'action et se tromper que de ne rien faire et de critiquer continuellement.

Prenons immédiatement la décision de... développer notre esprit de décision. Décidons-nous, que diable !

Sixième marche:

Ayons l'esprit de décision.

Avons-nous le sens des responsabilités ?

Que faisons-nous quand il n'y a personne autour de nous pour nous surveiller ?

Aujourd'hui, nous entendons souvent dire qu'on ne peut se fier à personne. Un de mes patients me disait: « Je ne peux même pas me fier à moi, comment voulez-vous que je me fie aux autres ? »

Sommes-nous toujours honnêtes ? Les gens peuvent-ils compter sur nous ? Peuvent-ils nous faire confiance ?

Nombreux sont ceux qui se plaignent de ce que leur patron ne leur fait pas confiance. Hélas ! souvent ils ne font rien pour attirer la confiance d'autrui. Je pense aux vieux clichés relatifs à la lenteur de ceux qui sont payés à l'heure ou au travail d'une qualité douteuse de ceux qui sont payés à la pièce. Il est certain que nous ne travaillons pas pour « la gloire et les prunes ». Nous devons gagner notre vie. Mais l'argent doit-il annihiler notre sens des responsabilités ? Doit-on ne plus garder le respect du travail bien fait sous prétexte que le temps est de l'argent ?

Trop zélé !

Un jeune homme qui avait beaucoup d'ambition me racontait les difficultés qu'il éprouvait à bien effectuer son travail. Pourquoi ? Ses confrères n'approuvaient pas le zèle exagéré dont il faisait preuve devant ses patrons. « Lorsque je m'aperçois que, pour une raison ou pour une autre, je me suis embourbé, me disait-il, je redouble d'énergie, surtout quand le patron est là, quitte à travailler parfois pendant quelques heures supplémentaires. Mais voilà, cela ne plaît pas aux autres employés. Ils me traitent de « zélé », disent que je suis un « vendu », un hypocrite, etc... Cela me met véritablement mal à l'aise. »

Peu à peu, en mettant en pratique mes conseils, il développa son caractère. Il améliora la qualité et l'efficacité du travail qu'il exécutait sans surveillance; et, ayant le courage de ses convictions, il répondit avec humour et gentillesse aux remarques désobligeantes de ses compagnons. Aujourd'hui, il est respecté non seulement de ses patrons, mais aussi de ses confrères.

Qu'est-ce qu'avoir du caractère ?

Avoir du caractère, c'est être intègre, quoi que les autres en pensent ou fassent. Bien exécuter ce que nous avons à faire de façon à être pleinement satisfaits de nous-mêmes, toujours et en tout, est un signe de maturité. La maturité et le sens des responsabilités et du devoir sont synonymes.

Beaucoup de personnes se laissent emprisonner dans le carcan de la moyenne, de la normalité. Elles se disent: « Un homme normal abat telle somme de travail en une heure; je ferai exactement cela, ni plus ni moins. » Au lieu de se demander ce qu'elles-mêmes peuvent véritablement donner, elles préfèrent se retrancher derrière des statistiques. Croyez-vous que ces gens finiront par se connaître ? Non. Ils n'avancent pas, ils piétinent. Ils ne fonctionnent qu'à moitié.

Qu'arrive-t-il à un moteur puissant qui ne tourne qu'à petite vitesse ? Il s'encrasse. Il vient un moment où on ne peut lui demander son plein rendement. Si un coureur veut devenir champion, il doit s'entraîner à fond, vraiment « se vider » pour connaître sa pleine capacité, son potentiel. S'il ne s'entraîne qu'à courir lentement, il ne pourra, au moment de la compétition, fournir l'effort nécessaire pour aller au bout de lui-même.

C'est la même chose dans tous nos travaux. Pourquoi ne donner que notre demi-mesure lorsque nous pouvons fournir davantage ? Ce n'est là qu'une question de responsabilité, face à soi-même d'abord, et face aux autres ensuite. C'est une question de maturité.

Notre bonheur dépend en réalité du degré de maturité auquel nous sommes parvenus. L'âge où nous devenons physiquement adultes n'a pas grand-chose à y voir. A chaque âge correspond une authentique maturité.

Assouplissons-nous !

La plupart des jeunes possèdent certaines qualités que nous, adultes, devons retrouver si nous voulons atteindre notre pleine maturité. Ils ont souvent l'esprit plus ouvert et plus souple. Les jeunes sont prêts à expérimenter tout ce qui est nouveau. Ne sont-ils pas à l'affût d'une cause à embrasser, d'une nouvelle amitié, d'une aventure à courir ?

Ne rejetons pas tout de la jeunesse; conservons ce qui est sain chez elle. Découvrons cette bonne grâce à entrer dans le jeu, cette perméabilité qu'elle « affiche » devant des faits nouveaux. Les jeunes désirent constamment aller au bout d'eux-mêmes. Ils veulent se connaître. C'est là notre première responsabilité.

Soyons nous-mêmes !

Qu'est-ce donc que la maturité ? C'est la conscience de n'être ni aussi admirables, ni aussi méprisables que nous le croyions. C'est s'accepter et être bien dans sa peau.

Notre bonheur réside dans la faculté d'être nous-mêmes, de découvrir que les choses les plus simples et les plus modestes de la vie sont souvent celles qui comptent le plus. Nous devons nous y donner entièrement.

Ainsi, apprenons à demeurer constamment en contact avec la partie la plus profonde de nous-mêmes; celle-là même où résident la stabilité et le bonheur, notre subconscient. Nous acquerrons alors la maturité et, par le fait même, une secrète maîtrise intérieure qui nous assurera le bonheur.

Notre première responsabilité, si nous voulons réellement faire preuve de maturité, est de nous découvrir nous-mêmes, en tout; de toujours donner le maximum de ce que nous possédons comme talent, courage, respect des autres et de nous-mêmes.

Le véritable sens des responsabilités réside dans la satisfaction personnelle que nous pouvons éprouver dans tout ce que nous faisons.

Développons notre caractère !

Mais comment atteindre cette satisfaction personnelle ? Comment donner véritablement le meilleur de nous-mêmes ? En développant notre caractère.

Nous faisons toujours ce que nous aimons faire, ce que nous voulons faire, ce que nous sommes forcés de faire.

Ainsi, il nous faut du caractère et de la volonté pour réaliser ce que nous voulons faire.

Passons à l'action !

Avons-nous de la facilité à passer à l'action ? Cela dépend en partie de l'intensité de notre désir. Plus notre désir est intense, plus le rôle de notre volonté est faible. Que nous le voulions ou non, le désir intense se traduit par l'action. Rappelons-nous que le désir précède toujours l'acte de volonté.

De plus, quel est l'essentiel pour nous ? C'est de réaliser les actes que nous avons décidé d'accomplir après avoir compris leur utilité par la réflexion.

Qu'est-ce qui nous permet de faire l'effort nécessaire pour vaincre et surmonter chaque difficulté ? L'esprit de combativité, élément essentiel de notre volonté et de notre caractère. Cette combativité qui nous permet d'oser et de foncer vers ce que nous considérons comme le plus important est à la base de toute réussite. Il faut « prendre le taureau par les cornes ».

Vingt-cinq mille dollars pour 20 minutes !

Un trait essentiel de notre caractère, que nous devons appliquer à tout ce que nous faisons, est d'accomplir le plus urgent en premier et maintenant.

Ivy Lee a déjà reçu des industriels américains $25 000 pour une période de 20 minutes de son temps. Son secret: il disait aux patrons et aux employés de toujours faire le plus urgent en premier.

Notre bonne vieille nature humaine nous dicte souvent le contraire. Nous commençons, devant une somme de travail, par exécuter les petites choses. Nous effectuons toutes les bagatelles d'abord pour passer au plus difficile ensuite.

Si une bagatelle s'avère plus urgente que le reste nous devons nous en occuper en premier. Par contre, si le travail le plus urgent est en même temps le plus difficile, nous devons ne pas hésiter et nous y attaquer immédiatement.

106

Les pompiers

Pourquoi attendre ? Les pompiers n'hésitent pas un seul instant lorsqu'un incendie est annoncé. Ils accourent. Nous devons, nous aussi, toujours prendre le travail « qui brûle » en premier. Une fois celui-ci terminé, nous n'en serons que plus satisfaits et les bagatelles nous paraîtront encore plus petites que nous le croyions.

Septième marche:

Développons notre sens des responsabilités !

Le prix du bonheur

Le poison no 1: la peur !

Un remède à la peur

L'angoisse: voilà une des caractéristiques de notre vie moderne. C'est une chose de se faire dire de ne pas être anxieux et une autre d'apprendre à ne pas l'être.

Il y a quelques mois, je participais à une émission radiophonique au cours de laquelle on invitait les auditeurs à me téléphoner. Une dame découragée, sans travail et malade m'entretint de ses problèmes. Elle envisageait le suicide comme unique solution à son angoisse et à ses peurs. Plus elle devenait anxieuse devant ses problèmes, plus il lui était difficile de les résoudre. Pourquoi ?

Nous ne pouvons vraiment surmonter les obstacles qui s'entassent sur notre route que lorsque nous voyons clairement la situation. Nous ne pouvons vaincre que ce que nous ne craignons pas d'affronter. Ainsi, nous pouvons nous tirer de toutes les difficultés en réagissant positivement à la vie, aussi difficile soit-elle.

Certains ne peuvent supporter l'annonce d'une nouvelle tragique lorsque celle-ci les concerne. Ils abandonnent alors tout désir de vivre, de s'aider ou d'être aidés et meurent de peur.

D'autres, au contraire, se servent de leurs épreuves pour se motiver et acquérir coûte que coûte, puisqu'ils n'ont plus rien à perdre, un bonheur au-delà de la moyenne. Ils apprennent alors à mettre en pratique, comme ils ne l'ont jamais fait auparavant les lois naturelles d'une vie heureuse. Les épreuves qu'ils savent affronter avec courage leur servent de tremplin vers une vie meilleure.

Nos peurs peuvent se comparer à un ciel nuageux. Nous savons que le soleil est là, caché bien sûr; mais nous savons qu'il reviendra. Affirmer que le soleil ne brillera plus et en être convaincu peu s'avérer extrêmement angoissant, même si, en fait, le soleil brillera sûrement un jour.

Mourir de peur !

Le docteur Robert Duguay de la faculté de Médecine de l'Université de Montréal rapportait cette anecdote:

Enfermé par erreur dans un wagon frigorifique, un homme connut soudain une peur si intense qu'il se persuada qu'il allait mourir. Il commença donc à décrire, sur un calepin, sa mort par réfrigération. Quelques jours plus tard, on retrouva son cadavre. L'homme était véritablement mort de peur. Pourtant, le système de réfrigération ne fonctionnait pas. Il régnait d'ailleurs, à l'intérieur du wagon, une température très confortable. La puissance de sa peur et de son angoisse avait tué le malheureux.

Il en est ainsi de nos problèmes. Nous pouvons être éventuellement criblés de dettes et abandonnés par ceux que nous aimons. . . Ce n'est pas parce qu'actuellement nous traversons de pareilles difficultés que nous ne nous en sortirons jamais. Il ne faut pas avoir peur. L'anxiété ne résout aucun de nos problèmes. Au contraire, elle les multiplie, les complique et les aggrave.

111

Il montre le bout de son nez

Prenons une attitude positive et courageuse devant toutes les difficultés de la vie. Nous serons émerveillés de constater les résultats. Quand le soleil montre tranquillement le bout de son nez entre les nuages, il métamorphose toute la journée.

La peur et l'angoisse ne servent à rien. Nous n'avons pas à devenir des victimes de la vie. La seule solution est de nous en sortir. Mais alors où trouver la solution à nos difficultés ?

En nous. En changeant notre attitude intérieure.

Le remède à l'anxiété et à la peur est d'acquérir cette foi qui nous permet d'attaquer nos difficultés, de trouver des solutions heureuses, de passer à l'action et de persévérer jusqu'au triomphe de la victoire.

Ainsi, la situation la plus impossible commencera à changer quand nous entreprendrons de modifier notre attitude intérieure en substituant à la peur une confiance de plus en plus inébranlable.

Êtes-vous hypnotisés
sans le savoir ?

Toutes nos habitudes, bonnes ou mauvaises, demeurent jusqu'à un certain point une forme d'auto-hypnose quotidienne. Par exemple: prendre nos repas toujours à la même heure, cirer nos chaussures, nous brosser les dents.

Celui qui réussit s'hypnotise avec l'idée positive de la réussite. À certains moments, cependant, il

112

peut se décourager et tout abandonner. Alors, il doit détruire le charme hypnotique de cette croyance négative s'il veut réussir.

Toute attitude négative maintenue constamment agit exactement de la même façon que toute pensée négative implantée dans l'esprit d'une personne hypnotisée par un hypnotiseur professionnel.

En chacun de nous existe la possibilité d'être heureux et de réussir. Nous possédons tous le pouvoir de nous défaire d'un sentiment d'infériorité en rompant le flux hypnotique de nos croyances négatives et pessimistes.

La foi et la confiance sont des formes positives de l'hypnotisme: la peur et le pessimisme en sont des formes négatives.

Nous commençons à renverser la vapeur quand nous cessons d'imiter les autres ou d'agir de telle ou de telle façon parce que la plupart des gens agissent ainsi. Osons plutôt être nous-mêmes en faisant ce que nous aimerions faire ou être.

L'hypnotisé tout-puissant

Nous sommes tous hypnotisés. Hypnotisés par qui ? par quoi ? Par ces idées des autres que nous nous répétons et que nous acceptons comme vraies.

Avez-vous déjà assisté à une séance d'hypnotisme ? L'hypnotiseur dit au champion haltérophile (qui pèse 200 livres et qui est doué d'une force herculéenne): « Tu ne pourras pas lever cette chaise ! » Notre champion essaie... et, en effet, ses efforts demeurent vains.

En fait, l'hypnotisme n'affaiblit pas notre athlète.

113

Pendant quelque temps, celui-ci ne réalise pas sa force. Il en a perdu conscience, quels que soient les efforts qu'il déploie.

Certains croiront que l'hypnotiseur possède une force magique ou occulte. Il est scientifiquement prouvé que le pouvoir se trouve plutôt chez l'hypnotisé; celui-ci s'est laissé convaincre qu'il ne pouvait pas lever la chaise. En d'autres mots, l'hypnotisé s'est hypnotisé lui-même en croyant à son incapacité, même si sa force existe encore de façon latente.

Croyez-vous en votre puissance ?

Nous sommes tous plus ou moins dans la même situation. Notre réussite ou notre échec, notre bonheur ou notre malheur dépendent de ce que nous admettons comme vrai au plus profond de nous-mêmes. En nous, présentement, nous pouvons découvrir cette puissance latente pouvant nous permettre d'accomplir tous nos rêves les plus chers. Cette puissance ne sera mise à notre disposition que si nous croyons en elle. Aussitôt que nous changerons nos pensées de « Je ne peux pas » en « Je peux ». Oui, si nous croyons en cette puissance de notre subconscient, nous pouvons réussir n'importe quoi et être heureux.

Notre sommeil est-il du temps perdu ?

« Quand je dors, je ne fais rien ! » Que de fois n'entendons-nous pas cette phrase ! Chez des milliers de gens, le sommeil correspond à un moment d'arrêt où rien ne se produit. Pour eux, c'est un instant figé, un point mort.

Notre subconscient dort-il ?

Pourtant, le sommeil ne ressemble pas du tout à la mort. Au contraire, il est une période de vie intense. Si nous savons profiter de ses pouvoirs, il peut devenir un élément important de notre bonheur, non seulement par son rôle réparateur, mais aussi par son rôle créateur.

Nous dormons pendant le tiers de notre vie. C'est une loi naturelle qui s'applique à tout être vivant. Si notre conscient s'endort, notre subconscient, lui, ne dort jamais. Il continue son œuvre même pendant notre sommeil.

Lorsque nous dormons, notre cœur bat-il, nos poumons respirent-ils, notre estomac continue-t-il d'assimiler les aliments ? Oui, n'est-ce pas ? Notre subconscient contrôle nos fonctions vitales de la même façon que lorsque nous sommes en période de veille.

Le sommeil n'est donc pas une période de temps où tout s'arrête. C'est un moment nécessaire, un temps de repos au cours duquel notre corps se recharge. D'une autre façon, il est aussi une continuation de notre tâche. Comment ? Par le travail de notre subconscient.

Lorsque nous dormons, notre subconscient n'est plus soumis au stress de notre conscient. Il peut ainsi nous aider avec plus d'efficacité. Le sommeil s'avère donc un moment propice à la résolution de nos problèmes.

Rêvez-vous ?

Oui, vous rêvez. Tout sommeil normal est parsemé de rêves. Nous rêvons tous. Cependant, la majeure partie des gens ne se souviennent pas de leurs rêves. Ils n'en rêvent pas moins.

Nous rêvons toutes les nuits à des intervalles d'environ 90 minutes. Chez les adultes, les rêves occupent ainsi entre 20 et 25% de la durée totale de leur sommeil. Comme nous dormons pendant au moins le tiers de notre vie, nos rêves constituent donc le douzième de celle-ci. Et, sachant que l'homme moyen vit durant à peu près 70 ans, nous rêvons donc pendant près de six années.

Contrairement à ce que nous pouvons souvent imaginer, nos rêves ne durent pas que quelques secondes. Ils ont plutôt tendance à durer de plus en plus longtemps, au fur et à mesure que la nuit avance. Ainsi, le premier rêve peut ne durer que dix minutes alors que le dernier peut atteindre la durée d'une heure.

Nos rêves prédisent nos maladies

Par nos rêves, nous pouvons prévoir nos maladies prochaines. Le Dr Vasily Kasatkin, un psychiatre de Leningrad, en arrive à cette conclusion après 28 ans d'études approfondies sur plus de 8,000 rêves.

Selon lui, nos rêves peuvent faire ressortir les symptômes d'une maladie comme la tuberculose, et ceci, deux mois avant que les véritables symptômes de la maladie n'apparaissent. De la même façon, la dysenterie peut être prévue avec deux jours d'avance, et les bronchites, rhumes ou maux d'estomac nous sont indiqués 24 heures plus tôt.

Deux médecins montréalais, les docteurs Hector Warnes et A. Finkelstein racontèrent certains cas similaires lors d'une convention de l'Association des Psychiatres canadiens, à Winnipeg..

Un homme de 29 ans, entre autres, avait rêvé que son estomac s'ouvrait parce qu'il avait mangé une pizza. Le lendemain, un examen médical a révélé qu'il souffrait d'un ulcère crevé à l'estomac.

Nos rêves: puissance créatrice !

Nos rêves possèdent également un rôle créateur important. De nombreux artistes, savants, hommes d'affaires confient leurs projets à leur subconscient en s'endormant. Ce dernier poursuit son travail durant leur sommeil. Le lendemain, ils sentent clairement comment ils peuvent réaliser leurs œuvres.

On a également constaté qu'une personne qui est réveillée chaque fois qu'elle commence à rêver devient irritable, et peut en venir à souffrir de troubles de mémoire et à éprouver des malaises étranges ainsi que des problèmes de personnalité.

Le rêve est l'activité par laquelle notre cerveau emmagasine toute l'information qu'il a reçue pendant la journée. Il place le tout dans un certain ordre. Le phénomène est semblable à celui qui se produit quand on veut programmer à nouveau un ordinateur.

Dormez-vous suffisamment ?

L'adulte moyen a besoin d'environ 7 heures et 35 minutes de sommeil par jour. Cependant, le tout varie selon les individus. Les petites siestes sont excellentes pour notre bonheur et notre santé. Pendant ce temps, nous rêvons un peu et nous nous libérons ainsi d'une partie de notre tension. Des personnages illustres avaient pris l'habitude de ces petites siestes. Citons entre autres: Napoléon, Harry Truman, Churchill et John F. Kennedy.

D'autres recherches nous apprennent qu'un homme dort plus longtemps qu'une femme (selon les lois de la moyenne, bien sûr !), que les personnes grasses dorment plus longtemps que les personnes maigres et que les extravertis ont davantage besoin de sommeil que les introvertis.

Pendant notre sommeil, nous ne sommes jamais immobiles. Nous exécutons entre 35 et 40 mouvements par nuit. De plus, en une seule nuit, nous pouvons rattraper le sommeil perdu au cours des nuits précédentes.

La longévité et le sommeil

Notre sommeil est-il du temps perdu ? Non. Il peut même prolonger notre vie. Des spécialistes affirment que la longévité est fort probablement liée, entre autres choses, à la qualité de notre sommeil.

Ne craignons donc pas le sommeil. Il est un des moments les plus importants de notre vie, de notre bonheur.

Nos pensées et nos émotions influencent notre santé[1] !

Plusieurs s'imaginent que la santé ou la maladie ne relèvent que d'une question de microbes. de virus,

---

1— L'auteur a aussi démontré l'influence des facteurs physiques sur notre santé mentale dans son livre précédent: « L'Alimentation et votre santé psychique », Éditions La Presse, Montréal 1972.

de chance ou de malchance. Ce qu'ils oublient c'est que nos pensées et nos émotions jouent un rôle primordial pour notre santé. Notre santé, qu'elle soit physique, mentale ou spirituelle, est contrôlée entre autres par l'état de nos pensées, par notre façon de réagir devant les événements de la vie et par nos croyances et notre imagination.

Nous possédons véritablement le pouvoir d'être en santé ou d'être malades. Tous les jours, des expériences scientifiques prouvent que nos pensées et nos émotions influencent toute notre vie. Le pessimisme, un état d'esprit négatif, une critique constante de tout, le malheur peuvent engendrer des maladies. Par contre les gens heureux ou qui tendent constamment vers le bonheur, ceux qui font preuve d'optimisme, d'un état d'esprit positif, ou qui contrôlent leurs pensées et leurs émotions, ceux-là se donnent eux-mêmes une meilleure santé.

Voici quelques exemples basés sur la recherche scientifique, prouvant que la santé dépend véritablement de soi.

Le rhume et la dépression

À l'Université de l'État de New York, des recherches nous ont démontré qu'un état d'esprit dépressif atténuait la résistance physique et rendait ainsi le corps plus suceptible d'attraper le rhume. On a constaté, dans la majorité des cas, qu'un sentiment de dépression chez le sujet précédait invariablement les symptômes du rhume.

Votre nervosité peut carier vos dents

L'ennui et l'anxiété peuvent causer la perte de

nos dents. Cette révélation a été faite lors d'une convention qui réunissait plus de 12,000 dentistes et 800 techniciens dentaires, par le docteur Marvin Smiring, professeur au Collège des Dentistes de l'Université de New York. « Comme nous sommes à l'âge de l'anxiété, déclara-t-il, les gens expriment leur nervosité et leurs frustrations par des serrements et des grincements de dents. Cela abîme les gencives, ébranle les dents et aide l'extension des infections à toutes les régions de la mâchoire. De plus, poursuit-il, la tension émotive contracte les vaisseaux sanguins autour de la racine des dents, réduisant la circulation sanguine dans la gencive. Ainsi, un manque de sang prive les dents de l'oxygène dont elles ont besoin et provoque leur maladie. »

Le stress occasionne des maux de dos

Plusieurs spécialistes considèrent que les maux de dos résultent, entre autres, d'une tension nerveuse trop forte. « Quand le bagage du stress et de la tension nerveuse est trop élevé, les muscles tendent à se contracter involontairement », nous confie le Dr Charles Wahl, psychiatre et psychanaliste de Los Angeles. «La plupart des gens qui ont des problèmes de rigidité dorsale ont aussi un caractère très rigide », ajoute-t-il.

Dans le même sens, le Dr Jack Goldfarb, directeur du Département des Services Psychologiques à l'Hôpital Orthopédique de Los Angeles, déclare que les maux de dos ne proviennent pas, dans la plupart des cas, de carences physiques. Selon lui, plusieurs maux de dos sont des symptômes de problèmes psychiques. « Ces patients vivent ordinairement sous une forte tension, dit-il, et plusieurs ne reçoivent pas l'affection qu'ils désirent. Souvent, ils demandent plus de respect et veulent recevoir plus d'approbation dans ce qu'ils font. Plusieurs ne peuvent accepter de responsabilités. Ce stress cause leur mal de dos. Ainsi, ils reçoivent d'autrui l'attention qu'ils ont toujours espérée. »

Cette tension, ce stress cause aussi de nombreuses autres maladies.

La principale cause des accidents d'automobiles

De récentes recherches aux Universités de Californie, du Missouri et du Michigan ont révélé que 80% des accidents de la route étaient causés par des problèmes émotionnels. Une auto conduite par un chauffeur émotivement ébranlé devient un instrument encore plus dangereux que celle dont le conducteur a bu. Les docteurs Norman D. Tabachnick et Robert E. Litman, de Los Angeles, qui ont mené cette enquête, ont basé leurs dires sur une étude des émotions de centaines de chauffeurs accidentés.

Le Dr John F. Edland, de l'École de Médecine du Missouri, explique: « Les candidats au suicide se servent de leur véhicule pour exprimer leur hostilité et leur agression envers la société. »

Est-ce fréquent ?

Une enquête faite par le Service de la Santé publique des États-Unis a prouvé que 14 accidents fatals sur 124 étaient de toute évidence des suicides ou des tentatives de suicide.

Plusieurs autres enquêtes effectuées un peu partout aux États-Unis et en Amérique du Nord démontrent que 5% des accidents mortels arrivent à des gens qui veulent se suicider ou à leurs victimes.

Le bonheur améliore notre santé

Nombre de gens développent des maux de tête, des problèmes digestifs et d'autres maladies par le seul fait d'être obligés de se rendre à un endroit où ils ne désirent absolument pas aller.

Comme nous l'avons vu précédemment, des scientistes, dans des universités et des instituts de recherches, ont tenté de connaître les causes premières de certaines maladies. Qu'ont-ils trouvé ? Ils peuvent maintenant prouver que les personnes qui prennent facilement une mauvaise grippe ou un virus arborent une attitude générale différente de celles qui ne sont jamais malades.

Le psychologue Horace Stewart, du Collège Augusta aux États-Unis, a effectué une expérience concluante. Il a étudié l'état de santé de centaines d'étudiants de son département. Il a divisé ses sujets en deux groupes: ceux qui étaient souvent malades et ceux qui ne l'étaient presque jamais.

Sa conclusion ? Ceux qui sont rarement malades ont une plus grande confiance en eux-mêmes. Ils semblent être en paix avec ce qu'ils font. Ils se sentent davantage concernés par le bien commun. En somme, ils sont plus heureux.

Les chercheurs du Centre Médical Cornell ont tenté une expérience similaire avec un certain nombre de sujets qui avaient vécu dans des milieux identiques. Ils les ont, eux aussi, divisés en deux groupes selon leur état de santé. Les interviews des psychiatres ont démontré que ceux qui étaient le plus souvent atteints par la maladie considéraient leur vie comme très difficile, monotone et non satisfaisante. Les autres, par contre, trouvaient leur vie intéressante, variée et relativement satisfaisante.

La conclusion des chercheurs est celle-ci: Ce n'est pas l'ampleur du problème, du désappointement ou de la frustration qui détermine le bien-être physique du sujet. La différence se trouve plutôt dans la façon d'affronter et de régler telle ou telle situation malencontreuse. Ce n'est pas ce qui nous arrive qui nous affecte, mais plutôt la façon dont nous réagissons.

Conservons toujours un regard optimiste sur les événements, quels qu'ils soient. L'optimisme et la paix intérieure sont les facteurs premiers d'une bonne santé.

Guérison du cancer

En 1931, Christian Winkler, de Lakewood, Ohio, « était condamné » par ses médecins. Il souffrait d'un cancer à la gorge et aux cordes vocales. Il était alors âgé de 56 ans. Devant l'impuissance de ses médecins, Monsieur Winkler employa son propre remède. Aujourd'hui, ses médecins sont morts, il a enterré quatre de ses six enfants et il vit toujours, presque centenaire. Quel est son remède secret ? Vous pouvez vous-mêmes vous le procurer. Où ? En vous-mêmes ! « Mon secret, déclarait-il de la voix qu'il a su s'« inventer » grâce à l'action des muscles de son estomac, est un amour immense de la vie. »

Les docteurs Arthur H. Schmale, Howard P. Iker et William A. Greene, du Centre Médical de l'Université de Rochester, affirment qu'à la suite de leurs nombreuses recherches ils peuvent conclure que notre état émotionnel peut nous rendre plus sujets au cancer ou atténuer les progrès de cette maladie. [1]

Équivalences psychiques des maladies

La cause première de la plupart de nos maladies relève souvent du domaine psychique. Certains sentiments négatifs longuement entretenus, le pessimisme et un état d'esprit maladif engendrent une foule de maladies physiques.

Voici un tableau qui vous présentera les causes psychiques probables et les solutions possibles à un certain nombre de maladies et symptômes. Ce tableau ne doit cependant pas être pris à la lettre. Si quelqu'un est convaincu que sa santé ne dépend véritablement que de lui et s'il prend tous les moyens intérieurs nécessaires pour guérir, il a déjà franchi une étape importante vers son bien-être.

Je le répète, vous ne devez pas prendre ce tableau à la lettre. Néanmoins, mon expérience clinique m'a prouvé que, dans bien des cas, les causes psychiques que je vais énumérer correspondent effectivement aux maladies et symptômes mentionnés. Vous pourrez vérifier vous-mêmes la justesse de ces données, en analysant votre cas personnel et celui de vos proches.

1— Pour de plus amples renseignements sur le cancer, consultez le livre du même auteur: « Les Maladies Psychosomatiques », Éditions de l'Homme 1971.

TABLEAU
DES ÉQUIVALENCES PSYCHIQUES
DES MALADIES

MALADIES, SYMPTÔMES OU PARTIES AFFECTÉES	ÉQUIVALENCES PSYCHIQUES PROBABLES	SOLUTIONS POSSIBLES
Alcoolisme	Sentiment d'infériorité, manque d'assurance et d'amour, non-acceptation de soi.	Confiance en soi, amour, discipline, acceptation de soi, réalisation de soi.
Anémie	Manque d'intérêt dans la vie, découragement.	Intérêt, enthousiasme, joie de vivre, optimisme.
Appétit (Perte de l')	Non-acceptation des autres, sentiment de rejet.	Acceptation de soi, adaptation, confiance en soi.
Arthrite	Ressentiment, amertume, rancune.	Compréhension, pardon, liberté et tolérance.
Asthme	Susceptibilité, hypersensibilité, peur d'être blessé.	Confiance en soi, force d'expression.
Cancer	Désappointement intensif, blessure émotionnelle profonde, dépression.	Pardon, oubli, self-control, réalisation de soi.
Coeur	Stress, tension, blessures émotionnelles, frustrations, colère, haine.	Relaxation, sécurité, pardon, encouragement, amour.

MALADIES, SYMPTÔMES OU PARTIES AFFECTÉES	ÉQUIVALENCES PSYCHIQUES PROBABLES	SOLUTIONS POSSIBLES
Constipation chronique	Rejet du présent, sentiment de limitation, cupidité.	Détente, participation active à la vie présente, liberté, générosité.
Diabète	Nombreux complexes, manque d'amour.	Confiance en soi, sécurité intérieure, amour.
Dos	Sentiment d'insécurité financière, peur de ses responsabilités, stress.	Confiance en soi, optimisme, détente.
Épilepsie	Rébellion, tendance à la violence, rejet de son milieu.	Sécurité, amour, pardon, oubli, paix intérieure.
Fatigue chronique	Haine de ses propres actions et de son travail, stress, manque d'intérêt dans la vie.	Intérêts, relaxations, esprit de coopération.
Fièvre	Instabilité, irritabilité, peur.	Sérénité, foi, confiance, optimisme.
Foie	Refoulement, découragement, dépression.	Accomplissement, paix, adaptation.
Glandes	Manque d'ordre, mauvaise organisation.	Ordre et méthode, (chaque chose en son temps, chaque chose à sa place.)

MALADIES, SYMPTÔMES OU PARTIES AFFECTÉES	ÉQUIVALENCES PSYCHIQUES PROBABLES	SOLUTIONS POSSIBLES
Gorge	Blessures émotionnelles, tristesse, manque d'expression.	Pardon, joie, gaieté, liberté d'expression.
Hémorroïdes	Tension, peur profonde, sentiment d'écrasement, de surcharge face aux événements.	Foi, confiance, détente.
Indigestions constantes	Anxiété, insécurité, peur.	Confiance, paix, compréhension, intégration.
Menstruations douloureuses	Peur, croyances périmées, frustration.	Relaxation, confiance, compréhension, équilibre sexuel.
Migraines chroniques	Confusion, refoulement sexuel, tension.	Relaxation, paix, ordre, méthode, équilibre sexuel.
Obésité	Manque de contrôle, frustrations générales et sexuelles, non-acceptation de soi.	Self-control, acceptation et réalisation de soi.
Paralysie	Peur des responsabilités, violent choc émotionnel.	Confiance en soi, relaxation physique et mentale, sens des responsabilités.

MALADIES, SYMPTÔMES OU PARTIES AFFECTÉES	ÉQUIVALENCES PSYCHIQUES PROBABLES	SOLUTIONS POSSIBLES
Peau	Manque d'amour, irascibilité, hypersensibilité.	Amour, sécurité, acceptation de soi, paix intérieure.
Pieds	Instabilité, incertitude constante, sentiment d'incompréhension de la part d'autrui, insécurité.	Confiance, stabilité, sécurité, adaptation.
Poumons	Découragement, manque d'intérêt, sectarisme, sentiment de limitation.	Confiance, intérêt et joie de vivre, réveil spirituel, tolérance.
Prostate	Découragement, défaitisme, négligence.	Nouvel intérêt, persévérance, application.
Reins	Confusion, frustrations, mauvaises intentions.	Relaxation, paix, bonnes intentions.
Rhumatismes	Vengeance, amertume, irritabilité.	Pardon, compassion, don de soi, tolérance.
Rhumes	Confusion, refoulement.	Ordre, méthode, organisation, défoulement.
Surdité	Entêtement, misanthropie.	Coopération, intérêt pour autrui, esprit d'équipe, confiance.

MALADIES, SYMPTÔMES OU PARTIES AFFECTÉES		SOLUTIONS POSSIBLES
Tension artérielle (basse)	Chagrin, dépression, découragement.	Enthousiasme, intérêt, joie de vivre, sens de l'humour.
Tension artérielle (haute)	Peurs, craintes.	Confiance, foi, paix intérieure, relaxation.
Toux chronique	Ennui, nervosité, intolérance.	Intérêt, enthousiasme, relaxation, compréhension.
Ulcères	Stress, anxiété, peur, irritabilité.	Relaxation, paix, foi, optimisme.
Varices	Désappointements, découragement, sentiment de limitation.	Enthousiasme, joie de vivre, sentiment de liberté.
Vésicule	Sentiments d'infériorité, anxiété.	Confiance, foi, relaxation, paix.

Notre santé résulte de notre façon de vivre. Tout ce que nous pensons, ressentons, disons, mangeons et faisons influence notre santé. Soyons donc sereins, tempérants, actifs, détendus, joyeux et équilibrés.

Les lois physiques de la santé

Nous ne sommes pas soumis qu'à des lois psychiques. Cette machine que constitue notre corps doit obéir aussi à des lois physiques naturelles.

Dans leur recherche du bonheur, trop de gens oublient d'étudier et de mettre en pratique les principales lois physiques de la santé.

Quels sont ces principaux facteurs physiques de santé tant oubliés ?

Tels que mentionnés et expliqués en détail dans mon livre: « Les Maladies Psychosomatiques, comment les éviter, les surmonter, en triompher » [1], ces principaux facteurs sont:

1   l'hérédité
2   l'air
3   l'équilibre psychique
4   l'eau
5   l'alimentation naturelle
6   l'exercice
7   le repos
8   le soleil
9   la propreté.

1— Éditions de L'Homme, Montréal 1971.

La santé dépend de lois tant physiques que psychiques; à nous d'en maintenir l'équilibre. Ainsi, nous rayonnerons de santé et, partant, serons plus heureux.

Recette infaillible pour réussir n'importe quoi !

Existe-t-il une recette merveilleuse qui, tout en étant simple, nous permettrait de réussir infailliblement quoi que ce soit ?

Oui. Elle comprend dix étapes et résume différents points que nous avons déjà approfondis dans les « Douze Vitamines du Bonheur » et le « Quotient de Maturité ». Désirez-vous réussir tout ce que vous entreprenez ? Voulez-vous savourer une réussite à votre goût ? Alors suivez bien cette recette et appliquez-la à tout ce que vous entreprenez. Le succès viendra... peut-être tardera-t-il un peu, peut-être la cuisson s'avérera-t-elle plus longue que prévue, mais il viendra.

Première étape: *Déterminons précisément le but que nous voulons atteindre.* C'est à nous seuls de choisir exactement le ou les buts qui nous satisferont pleinement.

Deuxième étape: *Fixons-nous une date limite pour atteindre notre but.* Une limite nous pousse davantage à tout mettre en action pour réussir. Sans limites, nous pourrions tellement étirer notre but qu'il se détendrait sans jamais retrouver sa forme originale.

131

Troisième étape: *Écrivons notre but.* En l'écrivant, nous l'extériorisons. Déjà, nous passons à l'action.

Quatrième étape: *Planifions, programmons et organisons* nos journées en fonction de notre but. Ne perdons pas notre temps; fixons-nous un programme nous permettant d'employer notre temps libre pour avancer vers notre but, une étape à la fois, un pas à la fois.

Cinquième étape: *Soyons prêts à payer le prix pour réussir.* Complétons une liste de tout ce que nous sommes prêts à sacrifier pour appliquer efficacement notre plan et atteindre notre but.

Sixième étape: *Passons à l'action véritable,* sans attendre le moment idéal qui ne viendra probablement jamais. Que puis-je faire aujourd'hui pour m'approcher de mon but ? Commençons immédiatement à travailler en vue de la réalisation de notre but.

Septième étape: *Maintenons à leur paroxysme notre intérêt, notre motivation et notre enthousiasme pour notre but, jusqu'à ce que celui-ci soit atteint.* Sans intérêt, sans motivation soutenue, que pouvons-nous accomplir ? Inscrivons sur une feuille de papier tous les avantages que nous retirerons en atteignant notre but. Relisons cette liste deux fois par jour, matin et soir. Ainsi, notre motivation se maintiendra constamment à son plus haut degré.

Huitième étape: *Conservons une confiance inébranlable en notre réussite,* malgré nos problèmes, nos erreurs et les critiques.

132

Neuvième étape: *Soyons déterminés à persévérer et à patienter,* malgré tout, jusqu'à ce que nous atteignions notre but. La persévérance est toujours cette qualité essentielle qui différencie le gagnant du perdant. Avec de la patience, tous nos rêves peuvent devenir réalité.

Dixième étape: *Mettons notre cœur dans tout ce que nous faisons.* Donnons-nous à fond. Le bonheur et la réussite viendront quand nous oserons nous donner corps et âme à notre tâche, à notre but, quels qu'ils soient.

Etes-vous prospères ?

Prospérité vs pauvreté

Quelle est la différence entre la prospérité et la pauvreté ? La chance, le hasard, la classe sociale dans laquelle nous sommes nés, l'instruction ? Nous pourrions mentionner un tas de facteurs qui nous sembleraient tous aussi bons les uns que les autres.

Pourtant, ni la chance ni le hasard ne créent la prospérité. Toute croyance maintenue intensément dans notre subconscient se matérialise automatiquement dans notre vie. Les situations prospères ou désavantageuses se dessinent tout d'abord dans le subconscient de chacun avant de prendre véritablement place dans la réalité.

L'individu né de parents riches peut nous sembler plus « enclin » à la prospérité. Pourtant, plusieurs personnes nées et ayant toujours vécu dans le luxe et la richesse ont connu la ruine. D'autres, par contre, partant de milieux pauvres et défavorisés, ont atteint les plus hautes sphères de la richesse. Henry Ford n'était qu'un simple vendeur de journaux... peut-être cet exemple est-il devenu classique, mais il n'en est pas moins réel.

L'instruction ne correspond pas nécessairement à la prospérité. J'ai connu, entre autres, un président d'industrie qui n'a jamais pu apprendre à lire. Il n'en devint pas moins prospère... alors que des avocats, des médecins et des professionnels ne peuvent joindre les deux bouts.

La clé de la prospérité

Si la prospérité ne dépend pas de tous ces facteurs, alors de quoi dépend-elle ? Elle ne dépend que de nous. Nous devons absolument nous convaincre que la prospérité est un état d'âme.

Pour devenir prospères, nous devons *décider* de l'être. Notre meilleur moyen d'action est alors de *demander* l'aide infaillible de notre subconscient.

La prospérité est un état d'âme, une conviction intérieure. Nous devons imprimer l'idée de la prospérité dans tout ce que nous faisons. C'est dans notre mentalité même que la prospérité germera.

La plupart des gens causent leurs propres malheurs en ne se servant pas des moyens invisibles mis à leur disposition pour réussir. Une image vaut mille mots ! Voyons-nous prospères pendant environ cinq minutes tous les soirs avant de nous endormir. Notre subconscient produira alors la prospérité dans notre vie. N'oublions jamais: le sentiment continu de la prospérité produit la prospérité.

Il faut alors que notre conscient et notre subconscient s'harmonisent. Notre subconscient n'accepte que ce que nous ressentons profondément comme étant la vérité. Il ne développe que l'idée chargée de confiance, qu'elle soit négative ou positive. Nous devons alors entretenir l'idée profonde de la prospérité et non celle de la pauvreté.

La vraie prospérité

Un jour, un patient me dit: « C'est bien beau tout ça, mais il y a l'argent. La prospérité ne correspond-elle pas à l'argent ? Il me semble, moi, que l'argent n'est pas important. »

Il avait bien raison. L'accumulation de l'argent ne doit pas devenir un « leitmotiv ». Certains ne pensent qu'à accumuler les billets de banque sans jamais s'en servir. Le moindre geste qu'ils font pourrait porter comme sous-titre: « Combien ça rapporte ? ». Les gens qui n'auront vécu que pour l'argent, mourront souvent riches. Auront-ils vraiment atteint la prospérité ?

Nous ne voulons sûrement pas toujours vivre avec le strict minimum. Nous désirons posséder l'argent nécessaire à la réalisation de ce que nous voulons. Ainsi, l'argent prend valeur de symbole. Il n'est qu'un outil. Il ne faut pas le condamner. L'argent peut prendre différentes formes: un voyage, un spectacle, une maison, une auto, la réalisation d'un désir.

La vraie prospérité ne correspond pas à notre compte en banque. Elle se situe dans notre esprit. Nous ne vivrons heureux que dans la mesure où nous mènerons une vie équilibrée.

Certains s'imaginent que la pauvreté est vertueuse. Elle résulte plutôt d'un conflit intérieur. Elle est une maladie. Personne ne doit accepter fatalement la pauvreté comme un état normal.

Surmontons ce conflit en nous répétant constamment: « Tous les jours, je deviens de plus en plus prospère. Je passe immédiatement à l'action. »

Quelle est votre attitude ?

Un autre obstacle fréquent sur le chemin de notre prospérité est notre tendance à toujours nous comparer aux autres. Notre prospérité n'a de vrai sens que par rapport à nous-mêmes. Cessons de nous imaginer que ceux qui réussissent n'atteignent leur prospérité qu'en volant. L'envie et la jalousie nous barrent la route du bonheur. Réjouissons-nous plutôt de la prospérité des autres. Ainsi, les portes de l'écluse de notre abondance s'ouvriront.

Plusieurs travaillent d'arrache-pied. Toute œuvre qu'ils entreprennent est pénible. Au fond, si la prospérité ne leur sourit pas, ce n'est pas à cause d'un manque de travail, mais d'une mauvaise orientation de leur esprit. Ainsi, ils gaspillent leurs efforts.

Pour devenir prospères, il nous faut surtout maintenir la certitude que notre prospérité ne dépend, avant tout, que de nous, que de notre état d'âme.

Comment devenir prospères ?

Je connais un millionnaire né dans un milieu défavorisé et pauvre. Nous l'appellerons Paul. À l'âge de sept ans, il fut placé dans un orphelinat. À treize ans, on l'envoya travailler sur une ferme où il fut exploité pendant quatre ans. À la fin, il s'enfuit en ville avec l'intention de travailler comme livreur à bicyclette.

Ne pouvant trouver d'emploi, il osa approcher tous les épiciers qu'il pouvait, leur offrant gratuitement ses services pour une période de trois jours afin qu'ils puissent juger de son efficacité. Plusieurs rirent de lui, d'autres déclinèrent son offre. Cependant, un des plus gros détaillants de la région, émerveillé par l'audace de ce petit jeune homme, l'engagea comme aide-camionneur.

Paul décida de devenir le meilleur aide-camionneur que son patron ait jamais employé. En très peu de temps, ce dernier remarqua la qualité et la quantité du travail accompli par sa recrue.

Il s'empressa de donner une promotion à Paul, lui offrant le poste de commis dans un de ses magasins à chaîne. Rapidement, Paul devint chef de rayon. Après quelques années, on le nomma gérant de magasin.

Tout ce qu'il entreprenait, il essayait de l'accomplir comme personne d'autre ne l'avait fait avant lui. Il mit en pratique les différentes étapes de notre chapitre « Comment réussir n'importe quoi ! »

Aujourd'hui, en tant que directeur général il est devenu non seulement le bras droit de son patron, mais aussi le principal actionnaire après ce dernier. Il va sans dire qu'il est maintenant prospère.

Comment a-t-il acquis sa prospérité ? Par son attitude intérieure.

Quelle est votre attitude intérieure ?

Équilibre = harmonie = bonheur !

Découvrir cette source de bonheur

« Qu'il est donc chanceux d'être heureux ! », entendons-nous souvent. Oublie-t-on que l'homme réellement heureux obéit aux lois naturelles du bonheur; qu'il se soumet à la grande loi de l'équilibre universel: donner et recevoir ? Il ne s'agit pas ici de chance, mais plutôt d'un choix.

L'homme sera heureux dans la mesure où il comprendra et vivra ce principe unique de notre univers. L'équilibre et l'harmonie sont les clés de notre bonheur et de tout ce que nous pouvons désirer.

Le boomerang d'Australie

Une fois lancé, le boomerang des aborigènes australiens peut sembler se perdre au loin pendant quelques instants. Tôt ou tard, cependant, il revient à son point de départ. De même, dans la vie, tout ce que nous donnons nous est redonné. Tout ce que nous prenons nous est repris à moins d'en payer le juste prix. C'est la loi de l'univers, du bonheur. Nous ne pouvons pas l'éviter.

L'homme doit tous ses malheurs à son ignorance de cette loi de base de l'équilibre: donner et recevoir dans tous les domaines de sa vie. Trop de gens se contentent de prendre au maximum et de ne donner qu'au minimum. Ils deviennent ainsi les principaux artisans de leur perte.

L'unique leçon de la vie

La seule leçon de la vie est d'apprendre à équilibrer harmonieusement toutes nos activités.

Depuis des millénaires, l'homme « emprunte » à l'océan, à la terre, à l'air, aux plus faibles, à son propre corps et, en essayant de donner le moins possible en retour, il crée le déséquilibre et le malheur autour de lui et en lui.

Tant et aussi longtemps que les époux, les employeurs et les employés, les dirigeants et les dirigés, etc... n'auront pas compris et assimilé cette loi naturelle infaillible, ils ne vivront pas en harmonie et ne pourront être heureux totalement.

L'homme heureux nourrit son subconscient de pensées et d'émotions harmonieuses. En retour, son subconscient lui procure le bonheur.

Si nous n'offrons à notre subconscient que des pensées négatives, il ne pourra faire mieux que de nous apporter le malheur et la dépression.

Notre première et notre dernière étape sur la voie du bonheur, c'est de découvrir et d'expérimenter cette source illimitée de bonheur en nous. Dépassons l'acceptation intellectuelle de ce principe. Réalisons-le en l'assimilant de plus en plus à chaque instant, aujourd'hui même.

Quel est le but de ce livre ?

Le but de ce livre n'est pas nécessairement de vous montrer quelque chose de nouveau à propos de la vie, de l'amour et des gens, mais plutôt de vous faire vivre et expérimenter plus profondément le bonheur, l'harmonie, comme vous ne l'avez jamais fait auparavant.

Pour toute joie ou tout bonheur, il y a un prix à payer. Êtes-vous prêts à le payer ?

ROGER FOISY, N.D., Ph.D., auteur de plusieurs volumes, conférencier, naturopathe consultant, est l'un des pionniers de la naturopathie et de l'approche «holistique» ou globale au Québec.

Il travaille depuis plus de 25 ans à promouvoir l'équilibre, l'harmonie et l'épanouissement de l'être humain sur tous les plans (physique, mental, émotionnel, spirituel et social).

Il est directeur du Centre de Synthèse et n'emploie que des méthodes naturelles éprouvées: naturopathie, psychosynthèse, programmation neuro-linguistique, thérapie transpersonnelle, reiki, etc.

Roger Foisy offre des consultations privées et des ateliers uniques régulièrement. Tous ceux qui aimeraient y assister ou le consulter en privé peuvent se renseigner au (514) 388-1402.

• Cap-Saint-Ignace
• Sainte-Marie (Beauce)
Québec, Canada
1995

« L'IMPRIMEUR »

COMPLETE

ERIC KENNEWAY

COMPLETE ORIGAMI

ERIC KENNEWAY

EBURY PRESS
LONDON

Published by Ebury Press
Division of the National Magazine
Company Ltd
Colquhoun House
27-37 Broadwick Street
London W1V 1FR

First impression 1987
Text copyright © 1987 The Estate of
Eric Kenneway

Illustrations copyright © 1987 The
National Magazine Company Ltd

Illustration of Japanese Wrestlers (page
51) reproduced by permission of The
Mary Evans Picture Library

ISBN 0 85223 622 0 hardback
ISBN 0 85223 617 4 paperback

Senior Editor: Fiona MacIntyre
Editor: Sandy Shepherd
Designer: Jerry Goldie, Grub Street
Design
Photographer: Jon Bouchier

Computerset by Stratatype Ltd, London
Printed and bound in Yugoslavia by
Mladinska Knjiga, Ljubljana

CONTENTS

*I*NTRODUCTION

*O*rigami, or-i-gäm′ē, n. the Japanese art of folding
paper. (Jap. *oru*, to fold, *kami*, paper.)

'Why do people become paperfolders? The reasons are about as many as the folders. I suspect that most non-creative folders learn origami in order to be able to teach it – as an entertainment for children, as therapy for patients with physical or mental handicaps, as a means of cultivating dexterity, or as a demonstration of the principles of geometry. Others fold paper because they want to use the models they make – as decorations for holidays and parties or to make individual greeting cards...'

So American paperfolder Alice Gray once wrote in answer to a Japanese correspondent who was curious to know why Westerners were interested in this traditional Japanese children's pastime.

It has always been a children's pastime – in Japan as well as in the West. In Japan the play origami of children, at least until the modern era, was regarded as a preparation for the functional origami they would need to know as adults. But there it has also had a religious and ceremonial function too.

Now, in the West, origami is a form of play that grown-ups can join in too, and since the early 1960s increasing numbers of adults have discovered the many pleasures that paperfolding can bring. Even if you are among them and already have some experience of origami, you should find aspects of the subject in this book which you have not considered before (if only because origami is interpreted widely here to include not only paperfolding but such related subjects as handkerchief and headscarf folding). If you hope to become a creative folder, you should be able to find suggestions throughout this book which will help you to get started and remain inspired.

Beginners would do well to study the section which deals with vocabulary and procedures before attempting any of the projects which follow. The projects may be tackled in any order you prefer but, as a guide, they are starred according to degree of difficulty. One star ★ denotes a straightforward project. Two stars ★★ indicate that there is one step in the project which prevents it from being completely straightforward. Three stars ★★★ indicate that the project contains two or more origami procedures. Four stars ★★★★ are reserved for projects which contain complex procedures or many, time-consuming steps.

Among the entries in this book you will find many suggestions for further reading, should you want to learn more about some particular aspect of origami. Books published in Japanese are also included because origami diagrams are really a form of international language. Once you are familiar with the standard instructions, you will be able to profit from origami books published in any language and feel yourself part of the international origami community.

Eric Kenneway

7

SYMBOLS

Make sure that you understand the following symbols because they are used throughout this book. The first of each pair of diagrams indicates an instruction and the second demonstrates what the paper should look like once the instruction has been carried out.

A line of dashes indicates a 'valley' fold – a concave crease. A solid arrow is generally used to indicate the direction of a fold.

A line of dots and dashes indicates a 'mountain' fold – a convex crease. A hollow-headed arrow is used when paper is folded to the rear of a model.

An arrow which returns on itself means 'Fold, crease firmly and return the paper to its previous position'. A faint, solid line represents an existing crease line – one which is the result of a previous step.

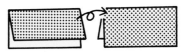

A looped arrow means 'Turn the folded paper over'.

A multi-curved arrow means 'Fold the paper over and over again'. Each curve represents one fold.

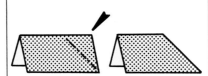

A hollow arrow refers to a fold made in a previous step and means 'Pull out'.

A black arrow-head refers to a crease made in a previous step and means 'Press' or 'Push in'.

A swollen arrow indicates that the diagram that follows is drawn to a larger scale.

VOCABULARY AND PROCEDURES

Certain words and phrases are frequently used in origami. They are, for the most part, names of combinations of folds known as 'procedures'. By using these procedures, as well as simple valley and mountain folding, paperfolders are able to modify the shapes of their papers in various ways to achieve the final shape.

In the diagrams below, the first of each set shows the instruction and the second or final diagram illustrates the procedure as it appears when completed.

Pleat

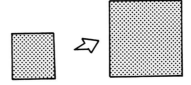

Make parallel folds by folding a section of paper in one direction and then bringing the fold over in the opposite direction to make a second fold.

Swivel

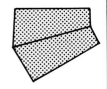

This is similar to a pleat, but instead of making a parallel fold, the second fold meets the first at the edge of the paper and then goes off at an angle.

Inside reverse fold

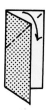

This takes place only when the paper has already been folded into two or more layers. Pull part of the folded edge – the spine – between the layers and fold it into a trough.

Outside reverse fold

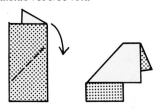

This is also done when the paper has already been folded into two or more layers. Take two corners, one from either side of the spine, and fold them back over the spine to form a cap.

Squash fold

Take a folded sheet of a paper and fold it in half, spine to spine, and return. Then push the spine between the two layers to meet the edge of the second fold.

This fold is also done when the paper has already been folded. Separate the layers and flatten the spine so that the residual crease meets the edge of the second fold.

Crimp

Take a folded sheet of paper and fold it in half, spine to spine, and return. Then make a swivel fold so that the second fold meets the first at the spine, and return. Turn the paper over and make a swivel fold along the same line. Open and then push the lower half of paper between the layers of the upper half so that the swivel folds lie flat on either side of it.

This fold is also done when the paper has already been folded into two layers; it consists of a pair of swivel folds, one at either side of the spine. Make a swivel fold on one layer; then turn the paper over and repeat on the other side so that all the creases meet at the spine.

Rabbit-ear fold

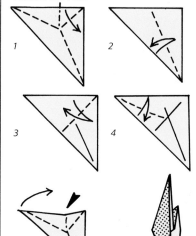

A method of raising a point from a triangular shape. The first diagram (1) shows the instructions when this fold is used in the creation of

a particular model. Proceed as follows: (2) Fold two edges together and return. (3) Fold another two edges together and return. (4) Fold the remaining pair of edges together and return. (5) Finally bring all three edges together by folding two adjacent edges together and making a tuck along one of the short creases. (6) The final diagram shows the completed rabbit-ear fold.

Sink

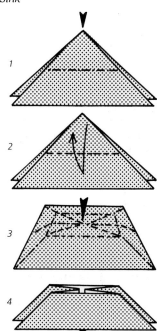

A method of pushing in a point or edge between four layers of paper. The first diagram (1) shows the instruction, when this fold is used in the creation of a particular model. This starting point is a waterbomb base, see page 22. (2) First mark the fold line by a simple valley fold and return. (3) Open up the paper and flatten the point. Make the square of crease lines into mountain folds and, squeezing adjacent mountain folds together, push the centre point down. The final diagram (4) shows the completed sink.

Petal fold

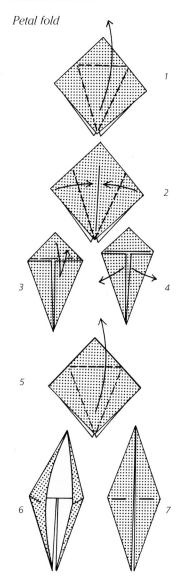

Repeat on three other sides/flaps

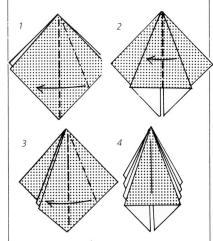

This phrase is used when there are four flaps clustered around a central axis. See preliminary base (page 20). (1) The first diagram indicates the procedure (in this case a squash fold). (2) Then turn the paper over and repeat the procedure on the reverse side. Turn the paper back again. To complete the procedure on the remaining two flaps, take the top flap to the left. (3) Then squash the right flap. Turn over and repeat behind. (4) The finished construction.

X-Ray view

A dotted line is sometimes used to indicate a concealed edge.

Ratios

For projects in which rectangular paper is used, the shape of paper is, in some instances, expressed as a ratio between the width and length. For example, 1:2 indicates that the paper should be twice as long as it is wide.

Raw edges

The outer edges of the original sheet of paper are called raw edges to distinguish them from folded edges.

Another method of raising a point. The first diagram (1) shows the instructions. To reach this point, see preliminary bases (page 20). (2) Fold the raw edges to the vertical centre line. (3) Fold the top point down over the horizontal edges and return; now return the side points (4). Raise the bottom point allowing the side points to come together (5). The penultimate diagram (6) shows this move in progress. The final diagram (7) shows the completed petal fold.

BASIC ADVICE ON FOLDING

*T*eachers of origami are divided between those who advise working with the paper on a flat surface, such as a table top, and those who recommend holding the paper in one's hands and folding it in the air. The former method will probably suit most beginners.

Whichever method you choose, always try to fold neatly and accurately. If, at the outset, your folds are too casually made this may create difficulties later on. Some people are naturally neat folders. Those who consider themselves clumsy at folding may find the following guidelines helpful.

How to sweep the paper

To ensure that your initial crease is accurately placed, sweep the paper with your fingers before committing yourself. The first pair of illustrations (1) demonstrates the sweeping motion that is made when two edges of a sheet of paper are brought together while working on a flat surface.

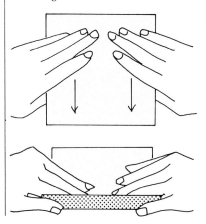

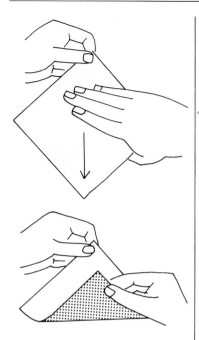

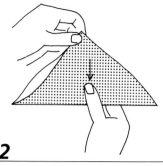

The second pair (2) shows how the sweep is made with one hand while bringing together two corners of a square of paper which is being held in the air. Both of these moves can be easily adapted to suit other initial folding procedures.

How to fold on a flat surface

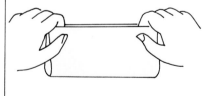

1

Lay the paper flat and bring two edges together.

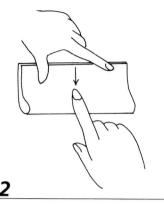

2

Use one hand to keep the edges together and run the finger of your other hand vertically down the middle to fix the centre of the crease.

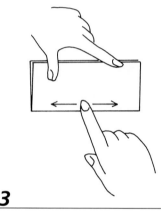

3

Run your finger first to one side and then to the other to complete the crease.

How to fold in the air

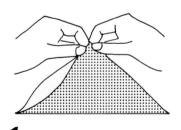

1

Bring the two corners together while holding the paper in the air.

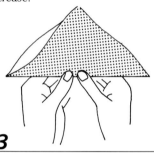

2

Use one hand to hold the corners together and run the finger and thumb of your other hand down the middle to fix the centre of the crease.

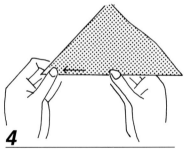

3

With both hands, hold the paper at the centre of the crease.

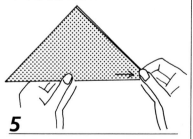

4

Then run the finger and thumb of one hand to the side. Return this hand to the centre.

5

Run the finger and thumb of the other hand to the side to complete the crease.

ACTION MODELS

Certain origami models are particularly popular. These are the 'action models' – models which can be pressed, or pulled, or manipulated in other ways so that they move, or parts of them do, in ways which can be quite startling to the unprepared observer. Some action models also have a second surprise effect, such as the creation of sound.

People do not always realize how much elasticity paper possesses. It is this elasticity and the energy generated through it that make movement possible in most action models. See for yourself how much energy can be stored in a piece of paper by making the following experiment.

How to make a
coiled spring ★★

Prepare a strip of paper about 2×25cm (¾×10in) (e.g. by cutting along the edge of a sheet of writing paper).

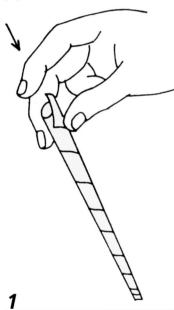

1

Curl the paper slightly by running it between the thumb and forefinger of one hand, and then wind it tightly into a spiral. Let the edges of the strip overlap by just a few millimetres (not more than ⅛ of an inch) all the way along its length. Stand the completed spiral on a flat surface, holding it between thumb and finger with the narrow end down.

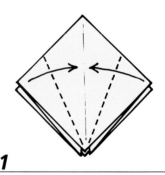

2

Press it down into a coil (you should be able to feel the tension this creates). Let the coil go.

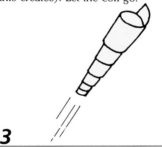

3

The paper should spring into the air reaching a height two or three times greater than its own length.

This coiled spring exemplifies the simplest type of action model – one in which the natural elastic force of the paper is directly exploited, i.e. by pinching or pressing it to create a counter-movement. Models such as jumping frogs (page 69) operate on this principle, although they are more complex in construction.

There is a second type of action model in which the natural elastic force of the paper is indirectly exploited. In this version, one movement causes another. The best-known model to have this kind of action is the traditional Japanese flapping bird: a stylized representation of a bird which lowers its wings when its tail is pulled. By continuing to pull and release the tail, the bird's wings flap. (For a history of the flapping bird, see WESTERN TRADITION, page 186.)

How to make a
flapping bird ★★★

Use a square of paper. Fold the preliminary base (page 20).

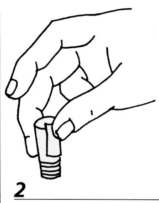

1

Fold the left and right raw (unfolded) edges to the centre crease. Turn the paper over and repeat behind.

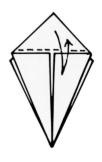

2

Fold the top point down over the horizontal edges. Crease the fold firmly and return.

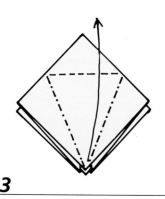

3

Unfold to step 1. Then make a petal fold. Turn the paper over and repeat behind.

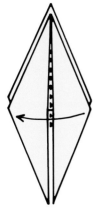

4

Fold the right flap across the left. Turn the paper over and fold the right flap to the left.

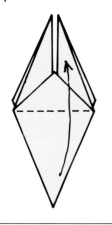

5

Fold the bottom point up to meet the top points. Turn over and repeat behind.

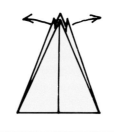

6

Take hold of the two inner flaps. Pull first one and then the other, down to the left and right.

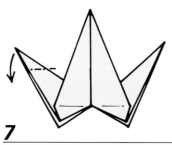

7

Crease firmly at the bottom (where the paper will have spread). Inside reverse fold the left point.

8

The bird is now completed. Curl the wings slightly by running them between your thumb and forefinger.

9

Hold the base of the neck and pull the tail – the wings will flap.

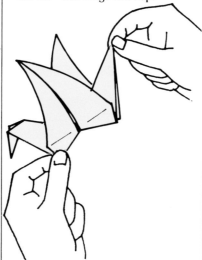

A third type of action model works through forces caused by shifting balance. There are comparatively few of this type, but the following is an outstanding example.

How to make a

magic tipper ★★
(Seiryo Takekawa)

Use a square of paper. Note that the model thickens with accumulated layers of paper during construction, and that this thickness can cause the paper to tear in step 6. Start by making a diagonal crease.

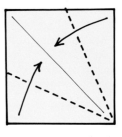

1

Fold two adjacent edges to lie on either side of the centre crease.

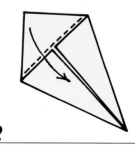

2

Fold the top point down over the horizontal edges.

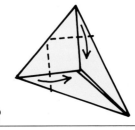

3

Fold the two top corners down to lie either side of the centre crease. ▶

magic tipper continued

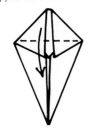

4

Fold the top point down once more, to form a horizontal edge.

5

Again, fold the two top corners down on either side of the centre crease.

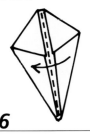

6

Fold in half, taking care that at this stage the paper does not tear.

7

The model is completed. Place it on a flat surface in the position as shown.

8

It should gradually lift its tail and then tip over suddenly. The model works by the two little triangular flaps inside pushing against each other. If the model tips over too quickly, or fails to tip at all, these may need adjusting.

AEROPLANES

*I*t has been said that Leonardo da Vinci was the first person to design a paper aeroplane, although there is no conclusive evidence of this. It seems certain, however, that folding paper aeroplanes first became popular among children during World War I.

Considerable interest in the techniques of making paper aeroplanes was created by the First International Paper Airplane Contest – an event organized in San Francisco, in 1967, by a local newspaper. The interest taken in this project by the world's press was quite remarkable. A full account of the contest and instructions for making the winning designs (including James Sakoda's SST Airplane, winner of the origami section) appeared in Jerry Mander *et al*'s *Great International Paper Airplane Book*, published by Simon and Schuster, New York, in 1967.

Other paper aeroplane contests followed in various parts of the world. In England, a National Paper Glider Championship was held for the first time in the Strand Palace Hotel, London, in 1974, since which there have been similar events.

A thorough grounding in the principles of flight for the paper aeroplane maker is provided by Ralph S. Barnaby's *How to Make and Fly Paper Airplanes*, first published in the USA by Four Winds Press, New York, 1968, and published in the UK by John Murray and Armada Books. Seymour Simon's *The Paper Aeroplane Book*, Puffin Books, 1974, covers similar ground but is less technical, being intended for younger readers. For a purer origami approach to flying models, see Stephen Weiss's *Wings and Things: Origami that Flies*, St Martin's Press, New York, 1984. This book contains many curiosities, including a Flying Nun, and has an extensive annotated bibliography.

See also KLINE-FOGLEMAN AEROFOIL (page 91).

How to make an aeroplane ★

Use a rectangular sheet of paper. Crease the vertical centre line.

1

Fold two upper corners to lie one on either side of the centre line.

2

Fold the top point down on a line some way below the raw horizontal edges.

3

Again, fold the top corners down to lie against the centre line.

4

Fold up the protruding bottom point so that it lies over the horizontal edges.

5

Mountain fold the paper in half along the centre crease.

6

Fold the left flap to the right. Mountain fold the remaining left flap behind to the right.

7

Raise the wing flaps so that they are at right-angles to the body of the model.

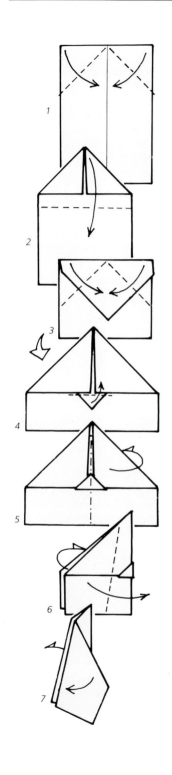

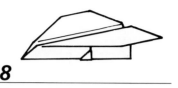

8

The completed aeroplane. The reason why it flies well is discussed under KLINE-FOGLEMAN AEROFOIL.

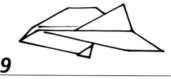

9

Origami aeroplane expert Eiji Nakamura prefers to pull up the centre fold to give the plane a vertical stabilizer, like this.

How to make a

dart ★

Use a sheet of notepaper. Crease the vertical centre line.

1

Fold the two top corners inwards to lie on the centre line.

2

Fold down the folded edges once more, against the centre line.

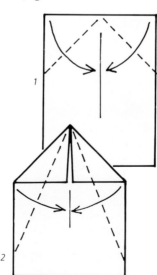

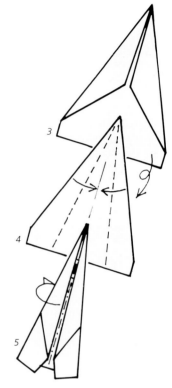

3

Turn the paper over.

4

Fold the folded edges in so that they lie against the centre line.

5

Mountain fold the paper in half, along the centre crease.

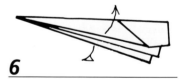

6

Raise the wing flaps so that they are at right-angles to the body of the dart.

7

The completed dart.

15

ANE-SAMA NINGYO

*A*ne-sama ningyo, literally 'elder sister dolls', are stylized, small-scale figures, dressed in the fashion of the Japanese Edo period (eighteenth and nineteenth centuries), and made from paper.

Strong white WASHI paper is rolled and tied to make the elaborate hairstyles, while traditionally patterned chiyogami paper is used to make the kimono. Making ane-sama ningyo became a pastime for Japanese girls in the early nineteenth century and is still a popular activity. Instructions for making them are included in some of the more traditional Japanese origami books.

Japanese doll made entirely from washi *paper (page 186)*

APPLIQUE

Making models from small, folded squares of dress fabric and using them to decorate dresses – by sewing them in a frieze around the hem of a skirt, for example, or in a line down a side seam – is an idea some readers may like to adopt from the Japanese to give a new look to an old dress.

A pioneer in fabric folding is Japanese designer Chieko Usuike, who believes that countries should develop their own characteristic fashions, now that France no longer dominates the fashion industry. Some of the models she uses on her clothes are traditional symbols of good fortune, such as the cranes that decorate the skirts of her wedding dresses. Others are modern, such as the pandas and sailing boats that provide cheerful and summery motifs for her children's clothes.

Two pages of photographs of Miss Usuike's designs appear in the Nippon Origami Association's journal *Origami*, October 1976.

ARCHITECTURE

The possibility of using paper to manufacture cheap, portable houses was first considered seriously during World War II. It was thought that they would provide shelter quickly for large numbers of people who might suddenly become homeless as a result of enemy action. Paper houses were later developed during the 1960s, by exponents of the survival culture, a culture based on self-sufficiency and closeness to nature.

Origami has had no direct influence on these developments, but it is interesting that one of the architectural designs considered most successful is, in essence, origami. This is the plydom, designed in 1966 by the Canadian architect Herbert Yates, to house migrant agricultural workers in California. Its appearance is not unlike a giant concertina.

The material used in constructing these houses actually comprises two layers of paper with a layer of polyurethane foam between them. The exterior is coated with polyethylene. The combination is considered to be warm and waterproof.

The article 'Influence of origami, the Japanese art of paperfolding, on the possible development of paper architecture', by B.M. Muhlestein in the trilingual Swiss journal *Werk*, May 1970, indicates that origami is not unknown to architects. For more about paper houses see *Architectural Design*, October 1970.

ART

*I*n the sense of 'skilled activity' origami is unquestionably an art, but is it art in the sense of 'Art-with-a-capital-A'? From time to time this possibility is considered, generally by paperfolders who hope to sell their models for large sums of money.

The argument can be approached in the following way. All art produces works which consist of two elements: matter and form. In music, notes (matter) are arranged together and in sequence (given form) to create a work of art. In painting, colours (matter) are mixed and arranged (given form) to create an art work. In these and other instances it is by perceiving the formal arrangement of matter that the listener, or viewer, has his or her aesthetic experience.

But does an origami model have these two essential elements? Yes. It has matter (a square of paper); it also has form (folding). But can the formal arrangement of the matter be perceived in an origami model? People seeing a model which attracts their interest will probably ask: 'Is it folded from a square? ... Is it folded from one piece?' They are asking what constitutes the matter of the work, although they may not think of it in those terms. Next they may ask: 'Is it cut?' They are now questioning the nature of the form. Quite properly they may feel uneasy until they know the answers to these questions. They may feel unable to evaluate the work without them. The mere fact that the questions are posed demonstrates that the formal arrangement of the work is not being perceived. I propose that an object in which neither the matter nor the form can be perceived cannot be described as an art work.

Of course, a model can look charming, as can many objects which are not art works, but it is the rhythm of fold lines and balance of shapes *apparent on the surface* which are admired in such a case.

If there is art in origami it exists within the sequence of folds which transform a sheet of paper into a model. The point is worth making because some people are inclined to compare origami models unfavourably with apparently similar decorative arts such as paper sculpture. In fact, like is not being compared with like. A proper perception of origami can only be achieved by doing it.

BANGERS

*H*ere are two action models which should make a loud crack or bang when operated. The first, simple banger has a single pocket which pops out to create the sound; the second has two pockets and is called a double-barrelled banger. Try making both types and consider whether there is any difference in the bangs; it may be that the double-barrelled banger produces greater resonance.

The type of paper you choose is quite important. Generally a sheet of newspaper or brown wrapping paper gives a good result. Sculptor Paul Jackson demonstrated 'The Largest Origami Banger Ever Made' as a piece of performance art at University College, London, in 1980. The banger in question measured 165×270cm (64×106in) and the material used was photographic print paper – this is the material Jackson recommends for getting the biggest bangs.

How to make a
simple banger ★

Use a large rectangle of paper. Crease the horizontal and vertical centre lines.

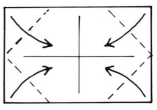

1

Fold the four corners so that the raw edges lie on the horizontal centre line.

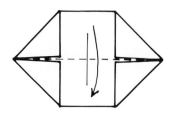

2

Fold the paper in half, in a valley fold.

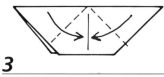

3

Bring the top points down so that the two folded edges lie on the centre line.

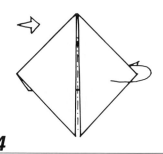

4

Mountain fold the paper in half along the centre line.

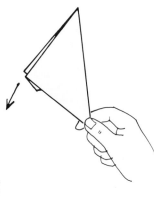

5

The banger is completed. Take hold of the bottom point between your thumb and forefinger. Raise your arm and bring it down smartly.

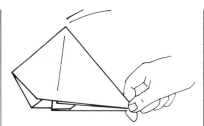

6

The inside pocket should pop out with a loud bang.

How to make a double-barrelled banger★★

Use a large rectangle of paper. Crease the vertical centre line.

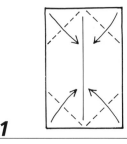

1

Fold the four corners so that the raw edges lie along the centre crease.

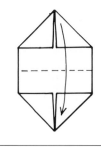

2

Fold the paper in half from top to bottom, point to point.

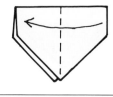

3

Fold the paper in half from right to left, in a valley fold.

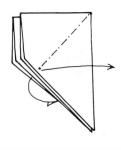

4

Make a squash fold, as shown, and open the fold right out. Turn the paper over and repeat the squash fold.

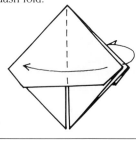

5

Take the right flap across to the left. Mountain fold the remaining right flap behind.

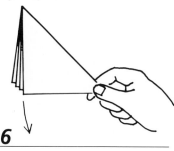

6

The completed banger. Hold the bottom point between your thumb and forefinger (make sure that the inside pockets are not trapped by your fingers). Raise your arm and bring it down smartly.

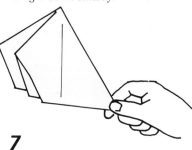

7

This should make a sharp bang.

*B*ASES

'*B*ase' is a term used to describe any folded construction which is common to the creation of more than one model. It also describes any construction which is generally recognized as a potentially fruitful point of departure for creative folding.

One of the simplest and most fruitful bases is the 'preliminary base' – a cluster of four right-angled triangular flaps, around a central axis. By manipulating these flaps in various ways it is possible to construct other bases and an infinite number of models.

How to make a preliminary base

Method 1 ★

Use a square of paper, plain side up. Fold it along the vertical centre, and return.

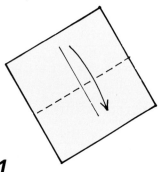

1

Fold the top edge down to the bottom edge in a valley fold.

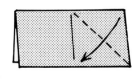

2

Fold the top right corner to centre bottom, so that the folded edge lies along the centre crease.

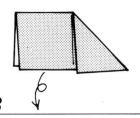

3

Turn the paper over.

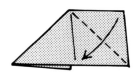

4

Fold the top right corner to centre bottom so that it lies on the centre crease.

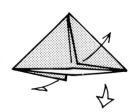

5

Put your thumbs into the model and separate the front from the back, allowing the side points to come together and form a square.

6

The completed preliminary base.

Method 2 ★★

Use a square of paper. First fold it diagonally in half.

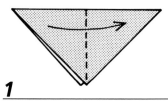

1

Fold the paper in half, from left to right in a valley fold.

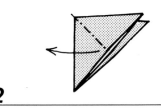

2

Squash fold the upper flap and open it right out.

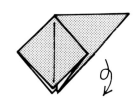

3

Turn the paper over.

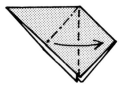

4

Squash fold the remaining flap, and open it right out.

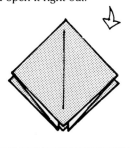

5

The completed preliminary base. ▶

Clockwise from the top: Carp (page 94); Crane (page 156); Japanese jumping frog (page 69); Frog base (page 25); Bird base (page 25); Fish base (page 24)

How to make a waterbomb base

A waterbomb base can be made in one of three ways. In the latter two methods, it is unnecessary to fold a preliminary base first – the waterbomb base can be folded directly.

Method 1 ★

Make a preliminary base and turn it upside down. Take hold of two opposite corners and pull them apart. Apply pressure to the centre point (with your thumb, for example) and it will instantly turn inside out into a new form. This form is known as the 'waterbomb base' because it is the base from which the traditional waterbomb (see page 184) beloved by generations of school children, is constructed.

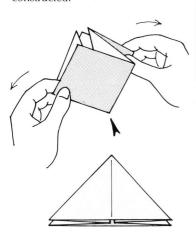

Method 2 ★

Use a square of paper. First fold it diagonally in half.

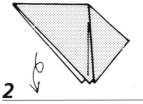

1

Fold the top right corner to the bottom point so that the folded edge lies in the centre.

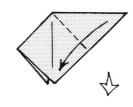

2

Turn the paper over.

3

Fold the top right corner to the bottom point, in a valley fold.

4

Put your thumbs inside and separate the front from the back, allowing the two side corners to come together.

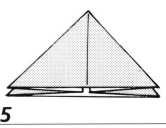

5

The completed waterbomb base.

Method 3 ★★

Use a square of paper, plain side up.

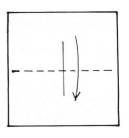

1

Fold the top edge to the bottom edge in a valley fold.

ORIGAGS BY R. MORASSI

FLIP!!

FLOP!!

SOME GYMNASTICS EVERY MORNING...

...KEEPS YOUR BODY SLIM AND HEALTHY!

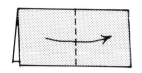

2

Fold the paper in half from left to right.

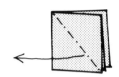

3

Squash fold the upper flap and open it right out.

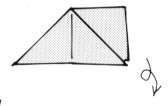

4

Turn the paper over.

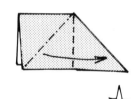

5

Squash fold the left flap, and open it out.

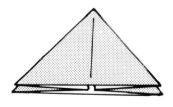

6

The completed waterbomb base.

THE CLASSIC BASES

Some teachers of origami, and authors of origami books, have organized bases into groups so that it is possible to see the relationship between them, making them easier to memorize.

The best-known bases are sometimes given the collective name of 'classic bases'. They were first established in Japan in the 1960s by the distinguished Japanese origami teacher Akira Yoshizawa, and in the English-language books of the Japanese author Isao Honda. These bases were adopted in the 1960s by Samuel Randlett and others in America, and by Robert Harbin, in England. Consequently, most English-language origami books published during the past twenty years refer to these bases.

The classic bases are the fish base, the bird base and the frog base. They derive their names from the most popular of the models to be developed from them, but they are not restricted to these models – far from it. These three bases form a valuable tool for the creative paperfolder.

The relationship between the classic bases can best be understood if you first look at a very simple construction: a square of paper in which two adjacent edges have been folded into a diagonal crease line. This is sometimes known as an 'ice-cream cone fold' and, when turned over, the kite base.

If you compare the pattern of creases produced by opening up a kite base with the crease pattern of an opened-up fish base, you will see that the fish base could be considered as a double kite base. The crease pattern of a bird base shows that it may be considered as a quadruple kite base. Similarly, the frog base is eight kite bases or a quadruple fish base.

There is nothing mysterious about this relationship. It indicates only that all the classic bases are formed similarly, by folding edges to diagonal creases in order to create narrow points from right-angled corners. These narrow points can be more easily manipulated to make legs for animals, petals for flowers, wings for birds and so on.

Creative paperfolders will often consider the number of points possessed by the various bases and select the base with the number most suitable for their projects. They will note that the fish base has two long and two short points; that the bird base has four long points in addition to the point formed by the centre of the paper; and that the frog base has four long points and four short ones as well as the central point.

It is possible to combine these bases. For example, you can fold a quadruple bird base and a quadruple frog base, both of which have very many points and have been found useful for folding such subjects as flowers and insects. The Japanese teacher Kosho Uchiyama has used a base which is a combination of sixteen frog bases. From this he constructs a thirty-two-petalled chrysanthemum, the Japanese imperial emblem.

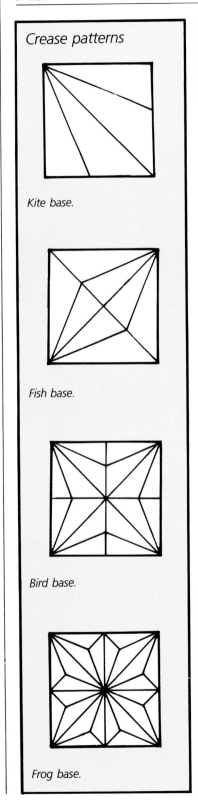

Crease patterns

Kite base.

Fish base.

Bird base.

Frog base.

How to make a
kite base ★

Use a square of paper. First make the diagonal crease.

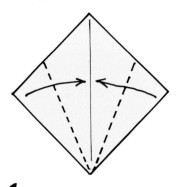

1

Fold two adjacent edges to the centre crease so that the edges lie along the crease.

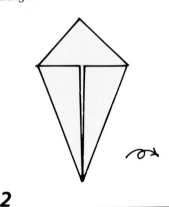

2

Now, turn the paper over.

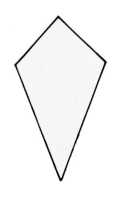

3

The completed kite base.

How to make a
fish base ★

Use a square of paper, plain side up. First make the diagonal crease.

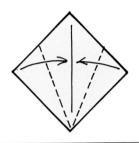

1

Fold two adjacent edges in so that they lie along the centre crease.

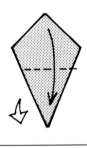

2

Turn the paper over.

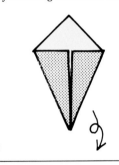

3

Fold the top point down to the bottom point in a valley fold.

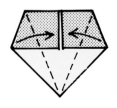

4

Fold the raw edges in to the centre crease.

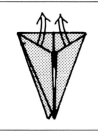

5

Pull out the concealed points and flatten them.

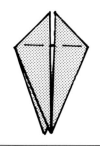

6

The completed fish base.

How to make a
bird base ★★

Start by completing the preliminary base (page 20).

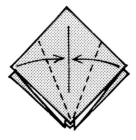

1

Fold the raw edges in so that they lie along the centre crease. Turn the paper over and repeat.

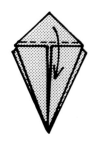

2

Fold the top point down over the horizontal edges.

3

Pull the left and right flaps out from under the top flap and return them to their previous positions. Repeat behind.

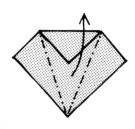

4

Petal fold the bottom point upwards. Turn the paper over and repeat.

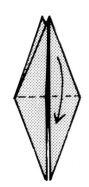

5

Bring the top flap down. Turn the paper over and repeat.

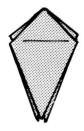

6

The completed bird base.

How to make a
frog base ★★★

Start by completing the preliminary base (page 20).

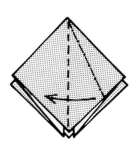

1

Squash fold the right flap and open it out.

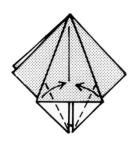

2

Fold in the raw edges of the front flaps so that they lie along the centre crease.

3

Repeat the first two steps on the remaining three flaps. ▶

frog base continued

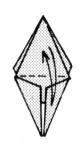

4

Fold the top point to the bottom point and return.

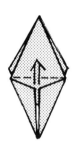

5

Pull out the concealed edge and form it into a point. Repeat steps 4 and 5 on the three other sides.

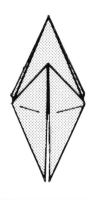

6

The completed frog base.

THE UCHIYAMA BASES

Kosho Uchiyama, who represents the third generation of a family of paperfolders, prefers to use the system of bases first organized by his father. This system includes not only the classic bases but also, for example, a square of paper folded in half or simply pleated.

In the Uchiyama system, bases that have crease patterns in which diagonal or radiating lines predominate are called 'A' bases, and those in which lines parallel to the edges of the paper predominate are called 'B' bases. Thus a square of paper folded diagonally in half is base A1, and a square of paper folded horizontally in half is base B1. The higher the number the more complex the base.

Study the accompanying charts which show the crease patterns of the Uchiyama bases and see if you can recognize the bases that have already been introduced in this book under other names. Base A2 in the Uchiyama system is what has been described as the kite base. Base A8 is the fish base, A9 the preliminary base, or its reverse, the waterbomb base. A10 is the bird base and A13 is the frog base.

See if you can fold other bases after studying the crease patterns. (Remember that the crease lines in this chart may represent either valley folds or mountain folds.) When you have succeeded in folding the bases, consider how they can be developed into creative models of your own.

A Bases

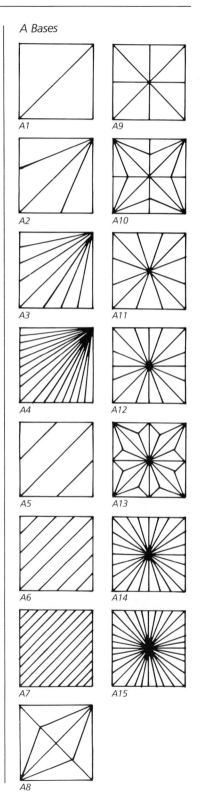

B Bases

B1

B2

B3

B4

B5

B6

B7

B8

B9

B10

B11

B12

B13

B14

B15

*B*LINTZ

*I*t is curious that a Yiddish word of Ukrainian origin should have become so established in the vocabulary of origami that even Spanish paperfolders nowadays refer to '*el plegado blintz*', the blintz base.

A blintz is, literally, a thin pancake folded to contain a cheese or other filling. Because of the way it is folded, its name was taken by Gershon Legman and other New York paperfolders in the 1950s to describe a square of paper after all four corners had been folded to the centre. It can be considered as a base – you will find more than one model in this book which begins by being 'blintzed' – but it is fundamentally a method of transforming an ordinary square of paper into a square with an extra layer. If you fold a base, or any construction, on a square which has been blintzed, its appearance will be as normal, but it will have extra paper inside which can be released and used to make extensions. Multiple bases are generally constructed by folding one or other of the classic bases into a blintz, and then releasing and folding the surplus paper.

For descriptions of some of these multiple 'blintz bases' and for examples of the kinds of complex models that can be developed from them, see Samuel Randlett's *The Best of Origami*, Faber & Faber, 1964, and John Montroll's *Origami for the Enthusiast*, Dover Publications, New York, 1979.

How to make a blintz base ★

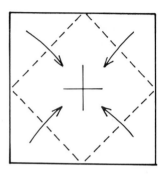

1

Fold the four corner points in to the centre.

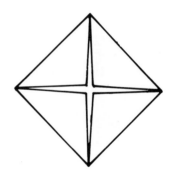

2

The completed blintz base.

BOATS

*T*he two boats shown below are suitable for floating in a bath or stream. The methods of construction are similar: the key difference is that the second boat is folded from a square of paper which has first been formed into a BLINTZ (page 27); it is included here to demonstrate one way in which surplus paper provided by the blintz can be used to develop the form of a model.

How to make a boat

Method 1 ★★
Use a fairly thin but strong square of paper. First make the centre crease.

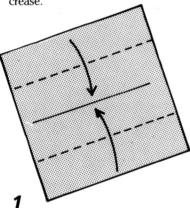

1

Fold top and bottom edges to centre.

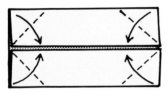

2

Fold the side edges diagonally to the horizontal centre line.

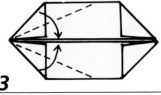

3

Fold on the left again, bringing the diagonal folded edges to the centre line.

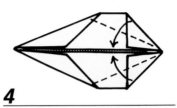

4

Now fold on the right, bringing the diagonal folded edges to the centre line.

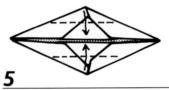

5

Fold the top and bottom points to the centre.

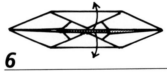

6

Put your fingers in the centre pocket and separate the raw edges, raising the form of the boat.

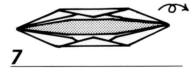

7

Turn the paper over.

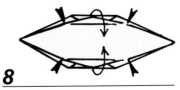

8

Carefully bring the raw edges to the front, putting pressure on the points indicated, so that the boat turns inside out.

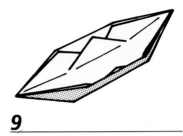

9

The completed boat.

Method 2 ★★
First complete a blintz (page 27).

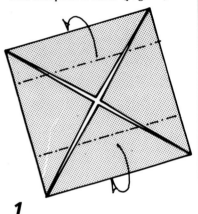

1

Mountain fold the top and bottom edges behind to the centre of the paper.

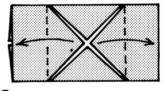

2

Fold the left triangular flap to the left, and the right one to the right.

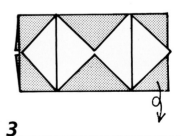

3

Turn the paper over.

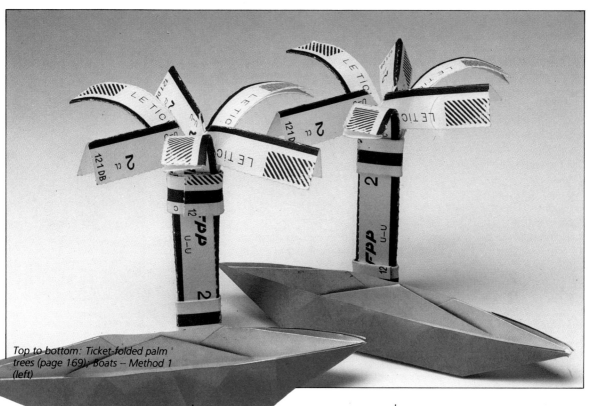

Top to bottom: Ticket-folded palm trees (page 169); Boats – Method 1 (left)

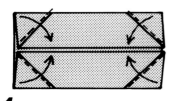

4

Fold the four corners of the rectangle across the diagonal edges.

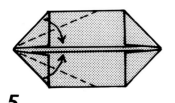

5

Fold in the diagonal edges on the left so that they lie along the centre line.

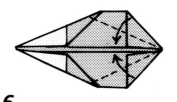

6

Repeat the previous step on the right, folding the diagonal edges to the centre line.

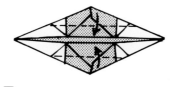

7

Fold the top and bottom points in to the centre.

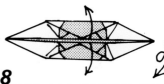

8

Put your fingers into the centre pocket and start raising the form of the boat. Turn it over.

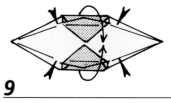

9

Bring the horizontal edges to the front, putting pressure on the points indicated.

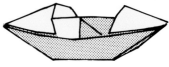

10

The completed boat.

BOOKLET

*T*he four-page booklet (below), together with front and back covers, can be constructed from a single sheet of paper in which only one incision has been made.

There is a museum in Tokyo, which uses this method for making copies of its monthly bulletin in which forthcoming exhibitions and lectures are announced – one page for each week's events. Each booklet can be reproduced (when unfolded) by making a single photocopy, so it is a method which may appeal to anyone who wants a simple, but attractive, programme for a sports event, school concert, or something of the sort. Constructed from a smaller sheet of paper, it will make a notebook for a child or a miniature greeting card to attach to a gift.

Peter McHugh, a resident of Rome, has discovered that it is possible to adapt the method to make booklets with many more pages. If the length of the paper is divided into sixths instead of quarters (and the central incision made between the outermost vertical creases), the result will be a booklet of eight pages plus covers. If it is divided into eighths, the result will be a twelve-page booklet and so on. He says that he uses this method to write many-paged letters to friends who complain that his letters are too short.

How to make a

booklet ★

Use a rectangle of paper. First divide the length into quarters; then fold the longer edges together. Open the sheet out.

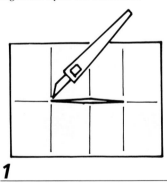

1

Make an incision along the horizontal centre line between the outermost vertical creases.

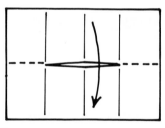

2

Fold the paper in half, bringing the top edge down to the bottom edge.

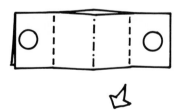

3

Hold the paper at its left and right edges. Allow the two layers at the centre to separate.

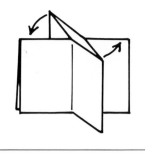

4

Flatten each 'page'.

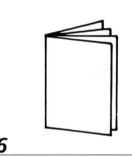

5

Fold the rectangle of pages in half.

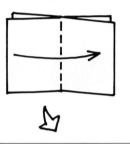

6

The completed booklet.

BOX PLEATING

*I*f you divide a sheet of paper into small squares by making a series of creases parallel to the edges, first one way and then the other, and if you then turn the paper over and make creases diagonally both ways across all the squares, the result is a crease pattern which resembles row upon row of little preliminary bases.

In theory it is possible to collapse the paper into a multiple preliminary base. But in practice it is easier to treat the crease pattern as the base and to 'mould' the paper into the forms you want.

By using paper prepared in this way, you will find that you can create structures much more complex than those traditionally made from the classic bases. By reinforcing some creases and disregarding others it is possible to raise box-like forms within the margins of the paper as well as pleated parallel-edged flaps.

This technique of creative origami, known as box pleating, was pioneered in the early 1960s by the American folders Fred Rohm and Neal Elias. Much of their work is too complex to be published in step-by-step form (Elias's ambition, as yet not fully realized, is to fold a 'Last Supper', with the figure of Christ and twelve apostles, from a single uncut sheet of paper). Yet their influence is strong on paperfolders who favour the 'engineering' approach – those who enjoy the challenge of selecting and analyzing a difficult subject and reproducing it in origami.

It was their choice of a Jack-in-the-box as a subject in 1963 that led to the development of box pleating. They each succeeded in producing working origami models. Since then there have been others, most notably the following version by the English paperfolder Max Hulme.

How to make a Jack-in-the-box ★★★★
(Max Hulme)

Use a 1:2 rectangle of thin but resilient paper, plain side up. A 15×30cm (6×12in) rectangle of paper will fold into a box with sides measuring 2.4cm (about an inch). This is a convenient size for most people to handle.

Start by making firm creases as shown to establish, first, the horizontal and vertical centre lines, then the quarter line at the left and, finally, the division of the right half into sixths.

1

Fold in the top and bottom edges to the centre in valley folds.

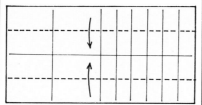

2

Make valley and mountain folds in the centre-left square area and collapse the paper into a waterbomb-type construction by mountain folding the paper back, and then inside reverse folding the top and bottom corners.

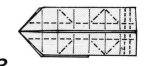

3

Carefully make these mountain and valley folds. Then open up the paper completely.

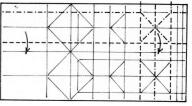

4

At the top, raise a 'wall' broken towards the right by a form which resembles a waterbomb base standing on its side. At the same time, form a standing pleat at right-angles to the main wall which is straddled by the waterbomb base form.

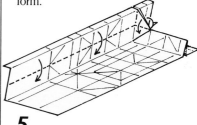

5

Fold down the top half of the wall on either side of the standing pleat, turning the two top corners of the waterbomb base form inside out so that they fit snugly into the corners in front of and behind the standing pleat on the left.

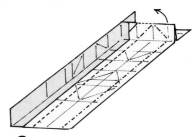

6

Raise the edge of the lower half in a way similar to step 4. ▶

jack-in-the-box continued

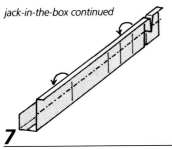

7

Fold down the upper edges in a way similar to step 5.

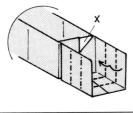

8

(Detail seen from behind) Hide the white triangle, marked X, by tucking it beneath the pleated flap on which it lies. Then fold the near edge over and over to form the sides of the box lid.

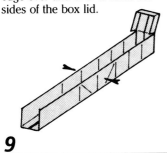

9

At this point, test the hinge action of the box lid to ensure that it is working satisfactorily. If it doesn't work well, unfold and check creases are properly made. Then pinch the sides together.

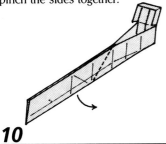

10

Bring the end down by outside reverse folding on the existing crease line.

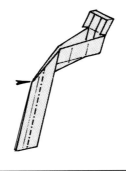

11

Halve the width of the vertical strip by pushing in the folded edge.

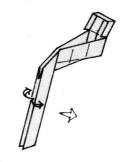

12

Pull out the concealed raw edges and fold them across on either side of the vertical strip.

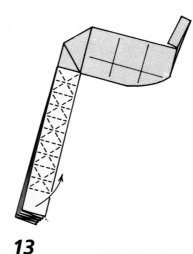

13

In preparation for later, when you will form the spring, note the square areas of the strip and crease their diagonals and horizontal centre lines. Start to form the Jack by lifting the upper three layers at the bottom.

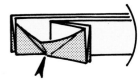

14

(Detail) Flatten the spine of the centre pleat in a squash fold.

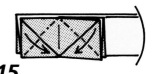

15

Make two inside reverse folds, taking the corners from the top to the centre bottom.

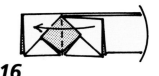

16

Bring the right flap over to cover the pleats.

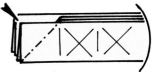

17

Inside reverse fold the pleat. Turn the paper over and repeat.

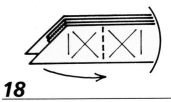

18

Start to lift the left point.

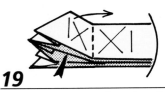

19

At the same time, push against the spine of the second pleat so that the flap will stretch.

Jack-in-the-box (page 31)

jack-in-the-box continued

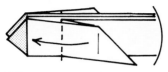

20

Valley fold the flap down. Turn the paper over and repeat steps 18–20.

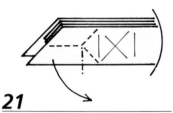

21

Rabbit-ear fold the pleat to form an arm. Turn the construction over and repeat.

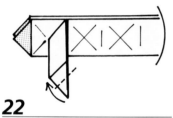

22

Outside reverse fold the point of the arm to form a hand. Repeat behind.

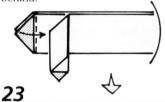

23

Lift the front left flap.

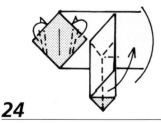

24

Rabbit-ear fold the arm again. Turn the paper over and repeat. Form the square flap on the left into the Jack's head by swivel folding two opposite corners into ears.

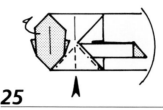

25

Turn the head to face the left. Push in the chest between the chin and arm. Repeat behind.

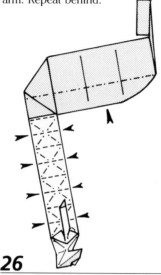

26

Convert the strip into a chain of waterbomb bases at front and behind; this forms the spring. At the top, flatten the base of the box structure.

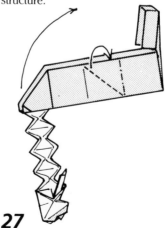

27

Form the mountain and valley folds. This will collapse the two walls, overlapping them and raising them to form the front of the box.

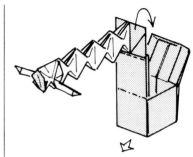

28

Make a mountain and valley fold to make the Jack stand in his box.

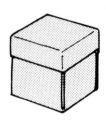

29

Push the Jack down by his head, holding his face against the inside front of the box while closing the lid. To keep him inside, hold the box between your thumb and middle finger with the forefinger pressing down on top.

30

The Jack pops up when you release the lid. When not in use, leave the lid open otherwise the model will cease to work effectively.

BUTTERFLIES

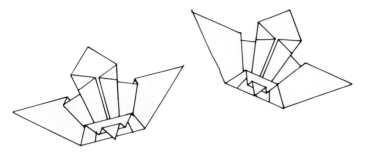

*T*he butterfly is a symbol of womanhood in Japan, and paper butterflies are attached to the wine cups that are exchanged by bride and groom during the Japanese wedding ceremony (see JAPANESE TRADITION). These stylized forms are believed to be among the oldest known traditional origami designs, and their use is strictly ceremonial. The fluttering butterfly, below, is another traditional design but it is used specifically for play. Japanese teacher Dokuohtei Nakano has written a booklet devoted entirely to the techniques of folding butterflies: *Challenge Origami: Butterfly (1),* published by Kodomoni Yumeo Jigyodan, Tokyo, in 1986. He uses the model for a decorative butterfly as an exercise in practising miscellaneous origami procedures.

How to make a
fluttering butterfly ★

Use a small square of brightly coloured paper. First make the vertical diagonal crease, and open.

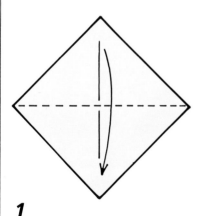

1

Fold the top point to the bottom point in a valley fold.

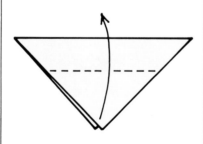

2

Fold up the bottom point so that it overlaps the top edge.

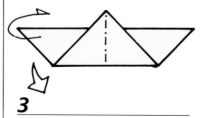

3

Mountain fold the paper in half by taking the left half behind the paper.

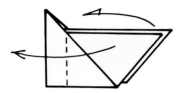

4

Fold the long flaps, the upper one to the left, and the lower flap behind.

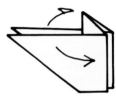

5

Raise the wings so that they are at right-angles to the body of the model.

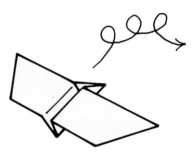

6

The completed butterfly. Throw it in the direction shown and the butterfly will spin rapidly as it falls, so that it appears to flutter to the ground. ▶

How to make a decorative butterfly ★★★

(Dokuohtei Nakano)

Use a 1:2 rectangle of paper. Start by making the vertical centre crease.

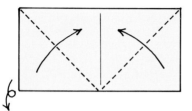

1

Fold the bottom corners to top centre so that the bottom edges lie along the crease. Turn the paper over.

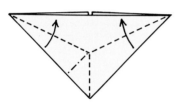

2

Rabbit-ear fold the folded edges, letting the corners kick out from behind.

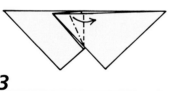

3

Squash fold the centre flap, opening it out.

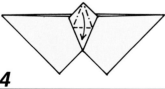

4

Petal fold the flap by folding the two upper corners back, as indicated, and then folding the top point down.

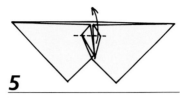

5

Raise the petal point.

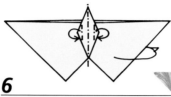

6

Mountain fold the left and right corners of the centre flap. Then mountain fold the model in half.

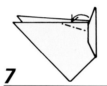

7

Reverse fold at top to shape the front flap into a wing. Repeat on the rear flap.

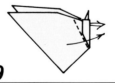

8

(Detail) Double reverse fold to form a head.

9

Raise the wings so that they are at right-angles to the body.

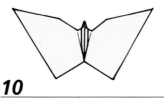

10

The completed butterfly.

Decorative butterflies (left)

CATALOGUE FOLDING

Mail-order catalogues were an important feature of American domestic life in the late nineteenth and early twentieth centuries when the country was largely rural and distances between communities were great. It must have been during this time that somebody first discovered that one of these bulky volumes could be transformed into an attractive Christmas decoration simply by folding each page in a similar way, then taking the front and back pages behind and folding them together as one.

Bob Allen of Northfield Falls, Vermont, USA, believes that catalogue folding can be described as a minor Amercian folk-art. He has collected several traditional folding methods, the simplest of which results in a Christmas tree; he himself has devised a method of folding a catalogue into a bell (see right).

Of course, not only mail-order catalogues but other disposable publications will provide you with the necessary material. Magazines colour-printed on glossy art paper are particularly suitable. Try using a periodical with comparatively few pages, such as a Sunday colour supplement or magazine, for your first attempt. The front and back pages may be left unjoined so that the decoration appears in relief and not in the round; this can be used as a wall decoration. Stiff covers, if there are any, should be removed before you start.

5

Finally, bring the front and back pages together and fold them as one to raise the form of the Christmas tree.

It is better not to place the Christmas tree directly on a flat surface because this can cause the folded pages to buckle. Let them stand free by placing the tree on an upturned saucer or a similarly convex surface.

How to make a
bell ★★★★
(Bob Allen)

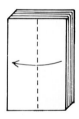

1

Arrange the catalogue so that the spine is on the left. Fold the top page so that the outer edge meets the spine.

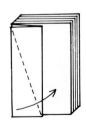

2

Fold the bottom left corner of the folded page across on a diagonal crease line.

How to make a
christmas tree ★★★★
(Traditional)

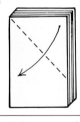

1

Place the catalogue, or other suitable volume, so that the spine is on the left. Fold the top edge of the first page down to the spine.

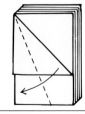

2

Fold the page again so that the folded edge lies along the spine.

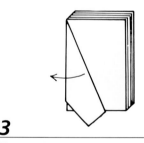

3

Turn the folded page over to the left.

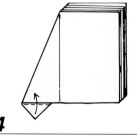

4

Fold up the bottom point, tucking it beneath the horizontal edge. Repeat these steps on each of the remaining pages.

3

At the top of the fold, fold the doubled edge to meet the raw edge of the flap. At the bottom, fold up the point on a line between the two corners.

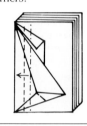

4

Pleat the page to the left, first with a mountain fold and then with a valley fold.

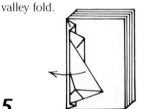

5

Turn the folded and pleated page to the left.

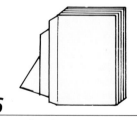

6

Repeat the above steps on the remaining pages of the catalogue.

7

Bring the front and back pages together and fold them as one to complete the bell.

CHAPEAUGRAPHY

Chapeaugraphy has many similarities with the TROUBLEWIT (page 174): they are both music hall acts which flourished in Victorian and Edwardian times; and both entail manipulating material into a variety of shapes. In the latter respect they are both related to origami too.

The word chapeaugraphy, literally 'hat-writing', was coined in eighteenth-century France to describe an act in which a hat brim, or a felt ring resembling a hat brim, was folded and twisted to take on the appearance of various types of headgear. The performer would amuse his audience by holding each 'hat' to his head in turn while adopting a matching facial expression.

The well-known French entertainer Felicien Trewey added chapeaugraphy to his magic act in the 1870s. Through his travels in Europe and America, chapeaugraphy became very popular at the turn of the century and it was adopted by many amateur performers as a drawing-room entertainment.

How to make a chapeau ring

You will need strong paper (for the pattern), black felt, scissors, a sewing machine and binding tape.

Take the paper and cut a circle about 40cm (15½in) in diameter. In the exact centre of this, cut out a circle about 15cm (6in) in diameter. This completes the pattern. Place it on your head to test the size. Trim it, if necessary, so that the hole is big enough for you to pull the paper down over your head.

Use this pattern to cut three similar-sized rings from the felt. Lay them on top of each other and machine sew them together thoroughly so that the surface becomes criss-crossed with stitches and the ring feels fairly stiff. Complete by binding the raw edges with binding tape.

Manipulation
It is better to discover for yourself, by folding, twisting and curling the ring, and holding it at various angles to your head, what hat-like shapes can be created. For example, fold it in half and hold it over your head broadside on to represent Napoleon. Pull the outer rim of the ring through the centre hole, either from the front or from behind to make other shapes.

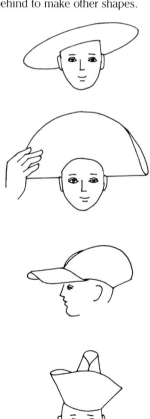

CHINESE TRADITION

*T*here is a line in a poem by the eighth-century Chinese poet Tu Fu which runs like this: 'Old wife draws on paper, squares for a game of chess'. What does this mean?

For centuries the Chinese have used not a board for what we call board games, but a square of paper folded and unfolded into a chequered pattern of creases. An inked brush is run lightly along each folded edge to achieve a series of fine black lines drawn with greater accuracy than can be done with a ruler. If the line from Tu Fu refers to this practice, as seems likely, then it is the first recorded reference to paperfolding anywhere in the world.

Paper originated in China. Its invention is attributed to Tsai Lun, in the year 105 A.D. The main use for paper then, as now, was as a writing material, but someone must have soon discovered that paper could be bent and flattened to create a straight folded edge.

The main tradition of Chinese paperfolding is to be found within the tradition of Chinese funerary art, in which replicas or representations of money or household goods were made to be placed in the tombs of the dead, or burnt on funeral pyres. This custom grew out of the very ancient practice of burying all a mañ's possessions with him to take on his journey to the next world. This was a constant temptation to grave robbers and paper replicas were substituted for the real thing. To this day, the burning of paper offerings is a feature of funerals in Chinese communities where there is a strong Buddhist or Taoist tradition.

There are specialist shops which sell, along with ready-made paper artefacts, prepared sheets of paper which the purchaser is expected to fold into funerary or celebratory items at home. These 'joss papers' are in the form of rectangular sheets, of various proportions, often in bundles of one hundred. On each sheet there may be an area covered in gold or silver foil (for funerary offerings) or, for example, printed symbols of Taoist deities representing Happiness, Prosperity and Longevity (used in celebrating the Chinese New Year). A family will burn a vast number of these folded sheets – several hundred at least and sometimes thousands on each occasion.

It is possible that no description of how these items should be folded has ever appeared in print until now. Francis Ow of Singapore explains that folding traditions are passed down within families and there may be many slight differences between them. 'The grandchild folding such nuggets for his deceased grandparent will one day have his grandchildren folding for him. Such is the Chinese tradition,' he says. But now Ow has revealed two traditional methods of Chinese ceremonial paperfolding which are described below. Both are called nuggets, although the second does resemble a boat and there is clearly a

Left to right: Chinese junks (page 42); Joss paper (left)

relationship between this fold and the Chinese Junk (page 42), a traditional model sometimes described in nineteenth-century English publications and now well known throughout the world. It has been suggested that the Chinese Junk may not be Chinese at all but Spanish in origin. It seems clear, however, that its similarity to a Chinese ceremonial fold places it firmly in the Chinese tradition.

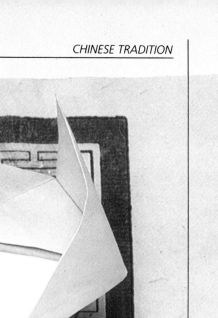

How to make a traditional Chinese funerary offering ★★

Use any rectangle of paper to represent funerary paper.

1

Without creasing the paper, take the top edge behind and down to the bottom edge.

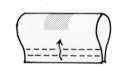

2

Fold both layers of the bottom edge over and over in two valley folds to form a cylinder.

3

Mountain fold the cylinder along the folded edge to create a flattened area. This will form the base of the structure later.

4

(New position.) Tuck the paper into the structure at either end of the base so that it becomes stable. Allow points to form on the layer behind.

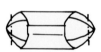

5

Mountain fold the points so that they stick up when the structure is turned over.

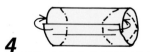

6

(New position) The completed offering, which represents a gold nugget. ▶

How to make a
traditional Chinese
celebratory offering ★★

Use any rectangle of paper to represent joss paper. Fold both pairs of opposite edges together in turn to mark the vertical and horizontal centre creases.

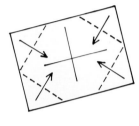

1

Fold in all four corners so that they lie along the horizontal crease.

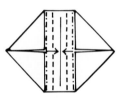

2

Pleat the vertical area between the flaps to the centre, and bring the flaps together.

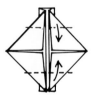

3

Fold in the top and bottom corners so that they meet at the centre.

4

Fold by bringing the bottom half to the top, in a valley fold.

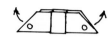

5

Take hold of the left and right points, and pull them.

6

The completed offering.

How to make a
Chinese junk ★★★

Use a square of paper. Start by blintzing (page 27).

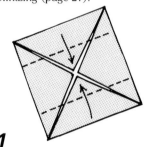

1

Fold the top and bottom edges in to the centre, in a valley fold.

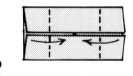

2

Fold the left and right edges in to the centre, again in valley folds.

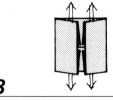

3

Pull out the four corners concealed under each folded edge and form them into points.

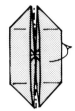

4

Mountain fold the construction in half, taking the right half behind.

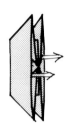

5

Pull out the triangular flap inside the upper folded edge. Turn the paper over and repeat.

6

Fold the three corners of the front flap to the centre. Turn the paper over and repeat.

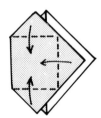

7

Fold the front flap in half, across to the left. Turn the structure over and repeat, folding the flap across to the right.

8

Bring the back two flaps forward.

9

Mountain fold the left and right edges behind to the centre.

10

Now open the central edges, taking them to the left and right. Allow the centre points to flatten and form two new edges at the top and bottom.

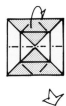

11

Mountain fold the figure in half, taking the top half back behind the figure.

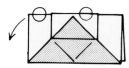

12

Take hold of the top folded edge between the fingers and thumbs of both hands. Pull at the left edge.

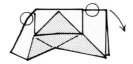

13

The form will start to rise. Hold it at the left edge and pull on the right edge.

14

This action completes the raising of the form. Now turn the paper over.

15

The completed vessel. The concealed edges may be pulled out.

16

One or other of these flaps can be opened further to represent a sail.

CIRCULAR ORIGAMI

At some time or other, most paperfolders consider the creative possibilities of working with circles of paper instead of the customary squares and rectangles. But, as the veteran American paperfolder Fred Rohm has pointed out, as soon as a fold is placed in the material the paperfolder is confronted with a straight edge as usual – and the circularity of the paper becomes either an inconvenience or irrelevant. If you remain unconvinced and want to experiment, packets of circular paper can sometimes be found in shops which supply craft materials to makers of artificial flowers.

COMPUTER ORIGAMI

The first known attempt at designing origami by computer took place in the United States in 1971. Arthur Appel, under the direction of the IBM World Trade Corporation's art director Bob Salpeter, programmed an IBM System 360 Model 91 computer to print out simple geometric configurations at the rate of more than one hundred a minute. Ninety percent were considered unsuccessful, but the remainder were folded on a large scale by Yokio Kono and displayed in the windows of the company's headquarters at United Nations Plaza, New York.

CONSEQUENCES

There is a form of paper-folding play, sometimes called Consequences after the parlour game, in which a sheet of paper is passed around a group of people who each add a fold in turn until a recognizable shape emerges. Several competitive variations, with systems of winning points, were tried out by British paperfolders in the early 1970s. Those who take part in Consequences are compelled, by the nature of the game, to study the folded shape from every angle at each stage of its development and to exercise their imagination by trying to 'read' what the shape might reasonably represent. Its purpose is to stimulate creativity.

COOKERY

'Food baked in paper parcels has a special appeal which is something to do with the anticipation which always goes with opening a package,' is the way that Shona Crawford Poole once introduced an item on cooking *en papillote* in her cookery column in the London *Times*.

The conventional method of preparation is to place the food towards one side of a buttered circle of greaseproof paper, to fold the paper in half over the food and then to seal the edges of the two layers by turning them over together. The result does not look at all decorative; paperfolders may like to explore new ways of folding a papillote by using origami techniques.

Children who enjoy folding paper may also enjoy making – and eating – pastry folded into the form of a favourite model. It probably will not matter to them if the model loses some of its shape in the cooking. Paper-thin sheets of filo pastry are available in packets, but they quickly become so dry and brittle that they are almost impossible to fold. It is better to roll out puff pastry as thin as you can and to then trim into the required square or rectangle. Choose a simple model for your first attempt – perhaps one which will accommodate a fruit or other filling, such as the paper hat on page 76.

See also FOIL and NAPKIN FOLDING.

Salmon cooked en papillote *(left)*

CORNER FASTENERS

Most people, when they find it necessary to keep several sheets of paper together, fasten them in one corner with a pin, paper-clip or staple, but origami enthusiasts do not require these accessories.

Here are two original methods of fastening documents devised by paperfolders. The first is most effective when not more than two or three sheets are being fastened. The second method will fasten a greater number of sheets. You can use different coloured corners as a means of identifying different sets of documents.

How to make a corner fastener

Method 1 ★★
(Martin Wall)

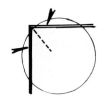

1

Place the collated sheets together and pinch one corner in a valley fold.

2

First raise the corner by swivelling it to the left, then flatten it.

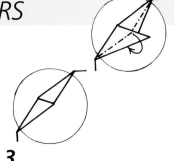

3

Tuck the point and the raw edges under to complete the fastening.

Method 2 ★
(John Cunliffe)

Use a sheet of paper about 10cm (4in) square. Fold a waterbomb base (page 22).

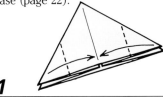

1

Arrange the base as shown. Fold the two opposite corners of the top flap to the centre of the diagonal edge.

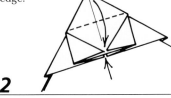

2

First tuck one corner of the collated sheets into the rear pocket, as far as possible, then fold the top left corner to the centre of the diagonal edge.

3

Tuck the two small triangular flaps up into the adjacent pockets.

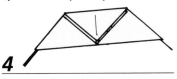

4

The completed fastener.

CROSS PLEATING

Most traditional origami of any complexity is constructed by using, as a point of departure, any of the bases described on pages 20–26: the simple form of these bases can be developed and extended because of their surplus paper, in the form of flaps and points which can be freely manipulated. A somewhat different technique is employed by the contemporary Japanese origami teacher Yoshihide Momotani. The basic forms he uses have their surplus paper not in the form of flaps but as pleats that lie one across another. By stretching, or spreading, these pleats, he transforms a flat shape into a three-dimensional form.

The dish which follows illustrates the fundamental technique of cross pleating. More advanced examples appear in Yoshihide Momotani's book *Shumi no Origami* (Origami of Taste), published by Natsume, Tokyo, in 1981.

See also TAPE FOLDING.

How to make a
dish ★★★
(Yoshihide Momotani)

Use a square of coloured paper, plain side up.

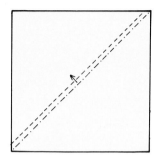

1

Make a diagonal pleat across the square. Note that the mountain fold crease line is the true diagonal and that the pleat is formed by a second, valley fold crease.

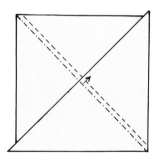

2

Make a similar pleat at right-angles to the first, with both a mountain and a valley fold.

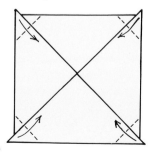

3

Fold in all four corners of the square equally.

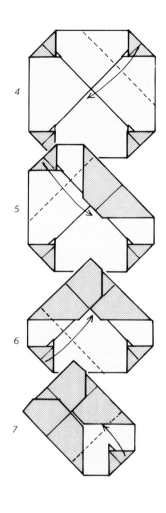

4

Fold the top right diagonal edge to the edge of the *concealed* pleat (you should be able to feel the edge through the paper).

5

Fold the top left edge in the same way.

6

Fold the bottom left edge similarly.

7

Fold the bottom right edge to meet the other three, but form an inside reverse fold at right so that the four flaps become interlocked.

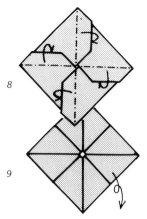

8

Make mountain folds on the diagonals of the square, tucking the four little flaps into the structure.

9

Turn the paper over.

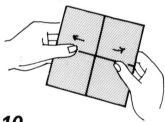

10

Take hold of the model and start to form the dish by spreading the crossed pleats in the centre.

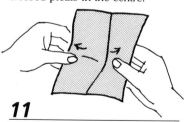

11

Turn the paper around and continue to spread the pleats.

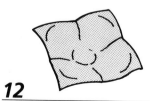

12

The completed dish.

CRUMPLING PAPER

Paper is sometimes crumpled for a purpose – for packing china or providing insulation, perhaps. Here are a few unusual ways which show how crumpled paper can be used.

A character in Dashiell Hammett's crime novel *The Maltese Falcon* surrounded his bed with crumpled sheets of newspaper before retiring so that no-one could approach him silently during the night.

Gypsy Rose Lee recalled, in her autobiography, that a fellow strip-tease artiste appeared on stage dressed in newspapers – her act was to tear off strips and crumple them into paper balls which she threw at favoured members of the audience.

A practical joke from Martin Gardner: place crumpled cellophane in a glass of *tepid* water and it will look like a cold and refreshing *iced* drink. Offer it to an unsuspecting friend.

CUP

This cup has the distinction of once being included in a 'restricted' manual issued to flight crews of the United States Air Force. It was recommended that they learn how to fold it because, should they ever find themselves stranded in hostile territory, they would then be able to tear a page from the manual and provide themselves with the instant means of collecting water for drinking.

How to make a

cup ★

Use a square of paper. Fold it diagonally in half.

1

Fold the bottom edge to the right diagonal edge. Pinch the left corner and return.

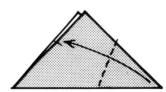

2

Fold the bottom right corner up to the point marked in the previous step.

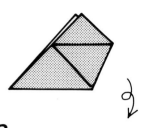

3

Turn the paper over.

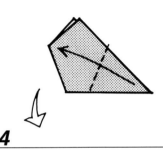

4

Fold the bottom right corner over to the upper corner on the left.

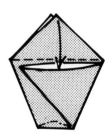

5

Tuck the front flap of the top point into the front pocket. Repeat behind. Put a little pressure on the bottom and raise the form of the cup.

6

The completed cup.

*Top to bottom: Cross-pleated dish
(page 47); Cup (left)*

DIAGRAMMING

*W*hen you have suc-ceeded in creating an origami model, particularly if this is the result of a happy accident, you will probably want to unfold it so that you can see how you did it, per-haps so that you can fold cop-ies for your friends. Unfor-tunately, if you try to retrace your steps by unfolding the model too quickly, you may find that you have forgotten how to refold it – and another origami masterpiece will be lost.

Methods of folding origami models are generally re-corded in the form of dia-grams. Even if you do not know how a model was folded, it is possible to use diagrams to discover a way of folding it. One simple method is to place the completed model on a sheet of paper and draw around its edges to record its outline. Then unfold one step, replace the model on the paper and draw the new outline. By con-tinuing to unfold the paper and recording each step in outline, you will eventually have a full set of diagrams from the completed model to the original square or rect-angle of paper – that is to say, a set of diagrams in reverse. This should be sufficient to enable you to re-create your design.

DIPLOMA

*'D*iploma' is derived from a Latin word meaning 'a letter folded in two'. Nowadays diplomas are more likely to be presented either rolled or unfolded, but it is clear that in former times great significance was at-tached to the fact that the document was folded.

In Japan, a second mean-ing of the word 'origami' (lit-erally 'fold-paper') is a 'cer-tificate', in the sense of a guarantee or provenance, at-tached to a work of art. These documents are also folded in two. Is it not curious that in two very different cultures the mere fact of folding a docu-ment in two should endow it with such authority?

DISASTER SITUATIONS

*O*rigami has been used to create calm and avert panic in situations where this could have arisen.

For example, professional entertainer Milton Halpert has described how, when caught in a suburban train on the night of the New York power failure of 1965 and when fel-low passengers became rest-less and uneasy, he handed out stage money which he was carrying and taught sev-eral origami novelties. 'Mr Halpert and origami con-verted what might have been a nightmare into a pleasant memory,' a friend recalled.

Emily Rosenthal has writ-ten of her experience making toy animals with a group of children during a wartime air raid. She was so successful that when the 'All Clear' sounded, one of the children said, 'Could we go on with the air raid, please?'

*E*LECTRONIC ORIGAMI

J apanese paperfolder Toyo-aki Kawaii constructed full-scale models of birds and animals in the 1960s, which he activated with electronic mechanisms. Richard Brokop has seen film of an origami show by Kawaii in which 'the elephants lift their trunks and shoot water, the pandas climb trees, the peacocks fan their tails, etc'.

Kawaii organized a similar display at one of the commercial pavilions at Expo 70, the international trade exhibition held in Osaka, Japan, in 1970.

*E*NVELOPE FOLDING

L etters have not always been put into envelopes before being posted. Originally, the pages of a letter were simply folded, and then often held together with a drop of sealing wax.

In 1844, Sir James Graham, the British Home Secretary of that time, was involved in what was to become the first mail-opening controversy. Interference with the mail by the authorities became known as 'grahaming', a practice which probably hastened the widespread adoption of the use of envelopes for containing letters.

But you do not need to buy envelopes for your letters if you do not want to. Until fairly recently, official forms were often folded and posted in the following way. However, it is not a method of which the Post Office approves, because other letters can become trapped in the letter's open edges.

How to make a simple letter fold ★

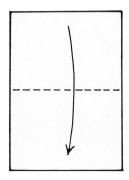

1

Fold the letter in half from top to bottom so that the edges meet.

2

Fold the left edge to the right about one-third of the way along the length of the sheet.

3

Fold in the right edge and tuck it into the pocket of the left flap.

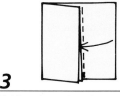

4

The completed fold.

Reproduced by permission of Punch

Punch *1844 takes a wry look at 'grahaming' (above)*

▶

Here is a way of folding a real envelope. The letter itself can be folded to form the envelope, in which case, when opened, the envelope will appear to be empty. It has been suggested that you can use it for sending a secret message: fold the secret message itself to form the envelope and send it apparently empty, or use it to carry a false or dummy message.

How to make an envelope ★

(John Cunliffe)

Use a rectangle of paper. First make a vertical centre crease.

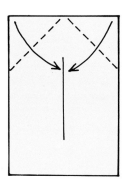

1

Fold the top two corners down to the centre crease so that they lie alongside it.

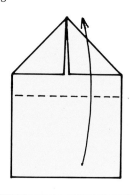

2

Fold the bottom edge up in a valley fold, so that the edge meets the top point.

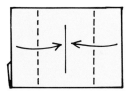

3

Take the left edge and fold it in to the centre. Repeat with the right edge.

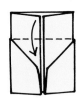

4

Fold the top edge down as far as it will go.

5

Fold the bottom edge up and tuck it into the pocket of the flap.

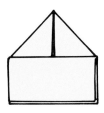

6

The completed envelope. Bring the top flap down after putting your letter into the envelope.

Clockwise from the top: Twist-folded boxes (page 178); Candles (page 54); Windmill (page 135); Heart (page 183); Stretched star (page 163)

EXHIBITIONS

The first public exhibition of creative origami ever held, as far as anyone can now remember, was a one-man show of the work of Michio Uchiyama, which opened at the Mitsukoshi Department Store, Tokyo, in 1931. Most big department stores in Tokyo now have floors which are used as galleries for temporary art exhibitions – sometimes major exhibitions of works loaned from the national collections of Europe and, of course, sometimes exhibitions of traditional Japanese arts.

Exhibitions of origami are now held regularly at these galleries and attract considerable interest. The First World Origami Fair, organized by the Nippon Origami Association at the Seibu Department Store, Tokyo, in 1976, was visited by Princess Michiko and other members of the Japanese imperial family. When the same organization took their Third World Origami Fair to Mexico in 1980, the president of Mexico attended the opening.

In America, the first opportunity for the public to see creative origami in a formal setting was the Plain Geometry and Fancy Figures exhibition held in 1959 at the Cooper Union Museum for the Arts of Decoration, now the Cooper-Hewitt Museum, New York.

Of course, a growing number of enthusiasts organize exhibitions of origami on a more modest scale, in such places as local schools and libraries. You may be among them. If so, remember that much of the interest in origami ▶

is in the folding of it – an origami model is not always a thing of interest to look at although you may have enjoyed folding it. After her experience of organizing a New York department store's exhibition in 1964, Lillian Oppenheimer said: 'We learned that origami figures are most interesting when they are grouped as though some action were taking place ... we had two kangaroos boxing, a half-dozen goslings waddling after their mother ... people seemed to find such groupings more interesting than larger, more elaborate single figures.'

So your displays may be more interesting if your models are grouped, but remember, this in itself will not allow the viewer an opportunity to perceive the pleasure of folding. It has been found that most successful exhibitions are organized in conjunction with classes where some of the models on display are taught or demonstrated. Other useful additions to exhibitions are wall charts that show instructions for folding models in diagrammatic form – or sets of partially folded models in series – and paper which visitors can take and fold as they study them.

Every visitor to a recent origami exhibition in Paris was asked to fold a candle (described right), using paper and instructions provided by the organizers. The visitors were then asked to add their candle to the ones already on display, so that ultimately everyone who attended the exhibition contributed to it.

How to make a candle ★★

(Jean-Claude Correia)

Use a small square of yellow paper, coloured side up. First find the centre point.

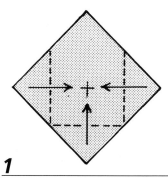

1

Fold in three corners so that they meet at the centre.

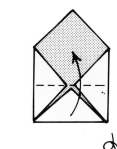

2

Fold up the bottom edge at the point where the three corners meet. Turn over.

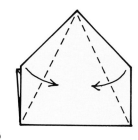

3

Fold in the sides of the front flap of the paper on crease lines which lie between the three corners on each side.

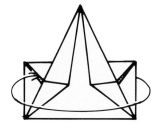

4

Curl the paper by running it between your thumb and forefinger. Then bring the right edge around and tuck it into the pockets of the flap on the left.

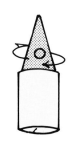

5

Take hold of the coloured section and give it a twist to form a flame.

6

The completed candle.

FANS

*I*nvented in Japan in the seventh century it is said, by someone who got the idea for the mechanism by studying the wing of a dead bat, the folding fan is the only type of paperfolded product to have reached the status of a major industry. By the nineteenth century, Japan was exporting millions of fans annually to the West; they were pleated by women who employed specially designed, serrated wooden blocks against which they pressed the paper to establish the creases.

In the West at that time the fan was used exclusively as a part of feminine costume. Spain developed fans which could be opened both ways to provide a change of colour or pattern. Spanish women developed a sophisticated 'fan language' of flirtation whereby the extent to which the fan was opened and the angle at which it was held carried great significance for the young man at which it was directed. But to the Japanese, the fan is a symbol of authority and it was carried rather like an officer's baton in pre-modern times. Because the rays of the fan are also said to symbolize the road of life widening out to a prosperous future, the fan has also become a traditional gift in marriages and coming-of-age ceremonies.

How to make a
fan ★

Use a rectangle of paper, about 1:3. Divide the length vertically into sixteenths. This can be done by folding the sheet – first into halves, then into quarters, and so on.

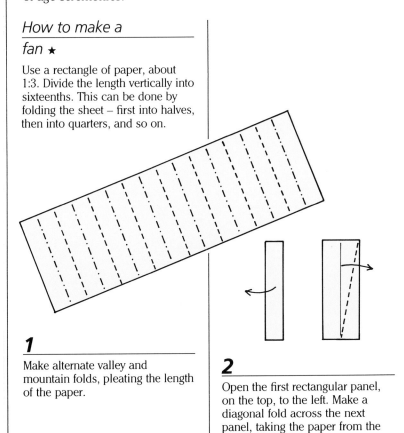

1

Make alternate valley and mountain folds, pleating the length of the paper.

2

Open the first rectangular panel, on the top, to the left. Make a diagonal fold across the next panel, taking the paper from the left to the right, in a valley fold.

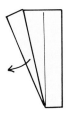

3

Open the third panel, to the left.

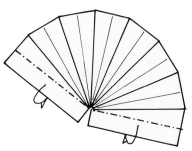

4

Repeat step 2. Then repeat step 3 and continue repeating these two steps.

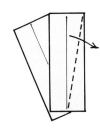

5

Mountain fold the bottom panels under and behind the structure so that they lie flat against the paper.

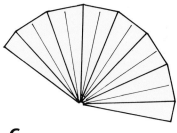

6

The completed fan.

Fans (page 55)

*F*LEXAGONS

A flexagon is a polygon which folds or 'flexes'. Usually made of paper or thin card, it has surfaces which comprise several smaller facets of identical shape. The polygon can be flexed so that the visible facets become hidden and the previously hidden facets become visible. If a pattern is applied to the visible surface it will disappear after flexing or, what is more remarkable, it will reappear as a *different* pattern.

The first flexagon was invented in 1939 by Arthur Stone, a young Englishman on a mathematics fellowship at Princeton University, after he had acquired a number of paper strips. Because of the difference between English and American standard paper sizes, he had found it necessary to trim off the edges of his sheets of notepaper so that they would fit his English loose-leaf folder; and by idly playing with these strips he discovered the basis of what he developed into the hexaflexagon described below. By the following day he had developed this into a more complex flexagon which he showed to his fellow-students. They were considerably inhterested and several of them joined Stone in the study of the structure. It was at this time that the name 'flexagon' was adopted, together with one prefix or another to describe the shape of the flexagon and the number of surfaces, or potential surfaces, which it comprised.

Martin Gardner describes the early history of flexagons and provides several examples in the opening chapter of his *Mathematical Puzzles and Diversions*, Pelican Books, 1965. He has written a further chapter on another aspect of flexagons in *More Mathematical Puzzles and Diversions*, which followed. A simplified version of the mathematical formula invented by Stone, which enables you to construct a flexagon which will flex any number of surfaces, together with examples and a short bibliography, appears in Paul Jackson's *Flexagons*, published by the British Origami Society in 1978. See also *M. C. Escher Kaleidocycles*, by Doris Schattschneider and William Walker, published by Tarquin Publications, Diss, Norfolk, in 1977.

Flexagons are frequently constructed from strips rather than squares or rectangles. Their ends are often glued in place and their surface decoration can be important to their effectiveness. For these reasons some flexagons can be regarded as a form of origami only if the word is interpreted to encompass all types of paperfolding. Two examples follow: the first is Stone's original flexagon, and the second is an example of a ring flexagon (or tetraflexagon). The latter may be treated as pure origami, but some readers may prefer to glue the ends and decorate the surface to make it both more stable and, perhaps, more interesting. ▶

exagons (page 58)

How to make a
hexaflexagon ★★★★
(Arthur Stone)

Use a strip of paper about 1:3. A 3cm-wide (1¼in) strip cut from the length of a quarto or A4 (8×11in) sheet is suitable.

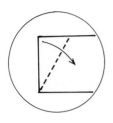

1

Take one end of the strip and fold it at an angle of 60° to the bottom edge. You can estimate the angle by observing that, when the left corner is folded, its edge bisects the lower corner angle.

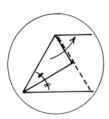

2

Fold the diagonal edge to meet the top edge of the strip.

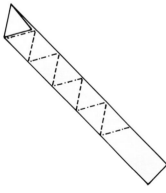

3

You have folded a little equilateral triangle. Fold the strip backwards and forwards in mountain and valley folds.

4

This will make a compact series of such triangles.

5

Open the folded strip of paper right out. Cut off the ends to provide yourself with a chain of ten equilateral triangles. This is the shape you need to make your hexaflexagon.

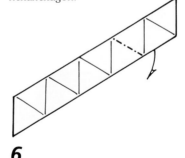

6

Mountain fold the paper on the right.

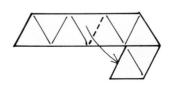

7

Valley fold on the left and tuck the long end underneath the projecting flap.

8

Fold up the bottom triangle and glue the two surfaces lightly together.

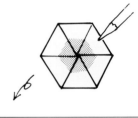

9

This completes the construction of the hexaflexagon except for surface decoration. Use coloured inks or crayons to decorate the top surface with a simple geometric pattern. Turn over.

10

Decorate this side too with a simple geometric pattern. Then fold it in half.

11

Swivel fold the front flap to the left.

12

You will find that the points at the top of the resulting shape can be separated.

13

The hexaflexagon can be opened out flat to present a blank surface. Decorate this with a third pattern.

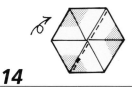

14

Then turn it over and you will find a fourth pattern – one that you did not draw yourself.

15

Fold paper in half and swivel the front flap.

16

Separate the points at the top and open the paper so that it is flat.

17

You will find a fifth pattern. Turn the paper over.

18

There is a sixth pattern on this side. 'Flex' again, by folding in half on different axes and swivelling, to cause the original patterns to reappear.

How to make a
ring flexagon ★★★★

Use a 1:2 rectangle of paper. Find the centre vertical line.

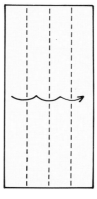

1

Fold the left edge to the centre, then fold it over again and again.

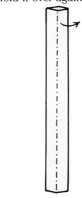

2

Squeeze open the paper into a tube and flatten it again so that the crease line lies at the vertical centre.

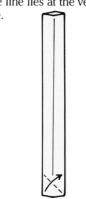

3

Fold the bottom edge to the right side.

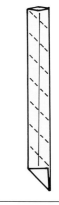

4

Now fold the horizontal edge to the right side so that it lies along the vertical edge on the right.

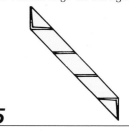

5

Continue folding until you reach this shape. Open out the paper.

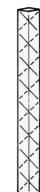

6

Fold the bottom edge to the left side. Repeat again and again.

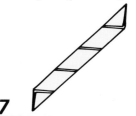

7

Continue folding until you reach this shape. Open out the paper. ▶

Ring flexagons (page 59)

ring flexagon continued

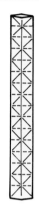

8

Fold horizontal crease lines wherever the diagonal crease lines meet.

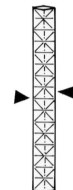

9

Press the edges to raise the form of the tube.

10

Start to make a series of concertina folds by pushing in the two top triangular areas down into the open tube.

11

Now press the tube flat and bring the two top points into a horizontal position.

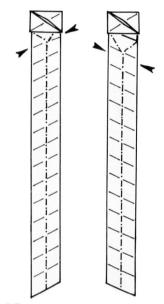

12

Watch point X. Press the edges to flatten the tube the other way.

13

Another concertina fold is created and point X is pushed to the edge.

14

Continue flattening the tube backwards and forwards, squeezing concertina folds into place. ▶

ring flexagon continued

15

Now bring the two ends together and tuck the two points of one end into the two pockets of the other end, one point in each pocket. A little glue will help to keep the ends in place, but it is not essential.

16

The construction of the ring flexagon is completed.

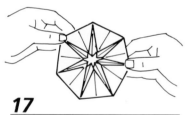

17

To operate the flexagon, take the outer edges back and push from behind, against the centre. This causes the star shape in the centre of the flexagon to expand and 'explode'.

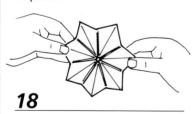

18

New surfaces appear and reappear in the centre as you continue to roll the sides back.

Having made a ring flexagon with plain paper, you may like to search out suitable printed patterned papers.

FLOWERS

There is a rich symbolism associated with flowers in Japanese culture, and they remain a popular subject in origami. In pre-modern Japan, when a woman sent her lover a maple leaf it signified the end of the affair. She was saying, in the flower language of the East, that her heart had changed like the colour of maple leaves in Autumn.

Another example is the lotus which has a strong association with Buddhism in the Far East: it is a symbol of purity because the flower blooming above the water remains unsullied by the mud in which its roots grow. And the iris, which has a narrow leaf that looks somewhat like a sword, symbolizes a strong, warrior-like spirit to Japanese people.

Most flowers are constructed from a preliminary base, but in this case it is a symmetrical structure consisting of four large triangular flaps. Step 1 of the frog base (page 25) is the preliminary base squashed to provide eight flaps. If you take either of these forms – the preliminary or frog base – or a similar one, and make a series of similar folds on each of the flaps, you are bound to create a form which has some repetitive feature and a rhythmic design. At some point you may discover that you have created your first origami flower.

The two following flowers, one traditional and one modern, are both constructed from the squashed preliminary base, but in the second example, by David Collier, the material is pre-creased and surplus paper is added by 'blintzing' before the base is formed. Collier has also devised a 'utility' stem and leaves which he uses to support this and other flower heads.

The most complete guide to origami flower making is Toshie Takahama's *Hana no Origami* (Flowers in Origami), published by Yuki Shobo, Tokyo, in 1973.

See also LEAF FOLDING and TISSUE FOLDING.

How to make an

iris ★★★

Use a square of paper. Start by completing the frog base (page 25) and turn it upside down.

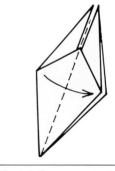

1

Fold up the small triangular flap at the front. Repeat on the three other sides.

2

Fold the left flap across to the right. Turn the paper around and fold the right flap across to the left.

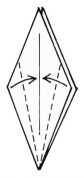

3

Fold the lower diagonal edges to the centre crease. Repeat on three other sides.

4

Fold down the top point. Open each flap and repeat on the three other sides.

5

Lift the front flap at right-angles to the body of the model. Repeat on the three other sides, raising the form of the flower.

6

The completed iris. Some people like to curve the petals by rolling each one around a pencil.

How to make a
flower ★★★
(David Collier)

Use a square of coloured paper, plain side up.

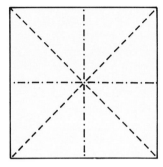

1

Make these valley and mountain folds by folding the edges and corners together.

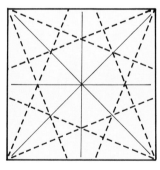

2

Fold each edge to the two diagonals in turn (eight folds in all) and open up the paper.

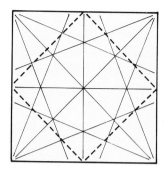

3

Fold the four corners in so that they meet at the centre.

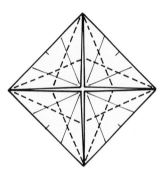

4

Fold the raw edges of each triangular flap to its outer edge and return.

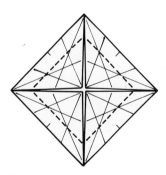

5

Fold each flap on a line between the outer intersections of the existing creases. ▶

flower continued

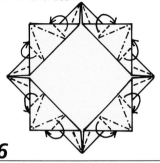

6

Make swivel folds on either side of each flap so that the flap edges meet the square edge.

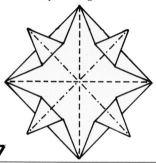

7

Collapse the paper into a modified preliminary base.

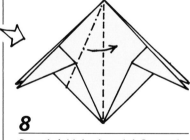

8

Squash fold the front left flap and open it out. Repeat on the three other sides.

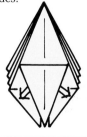

9

Pull out the edges concealed under the front flap. Repeat on the three other sides.

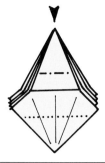

10

Sink fold the top point into the structure so that it meets the concealed horizontal edge. Repeat on the three other sides.

11

Fold the left and right corners to the centre line. Repeat on the three other sides.

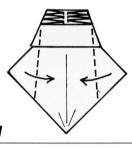

12

Fold down the top left and right corners. Repeat on the three other sides.

13

Take hold of the free flaps at the bottom and gently separate them.

14

Continue to separate the flaps, spreading the centre point and allowing the flower shape to appear. Fit the top point of the utility stem (below) into the centre hole at the base of the flower to complete.

How to make a utility leaf and stem ★★★
(David Collier)

Use a square of green paper similar in size to that used for the flower. Cut the square into three large 1:4 rectangles, marked (C); one 1:8 rectangle (B); and two smaller 1:4 rectangles (A). One of the larger 1:4 rectangles may be discarded.

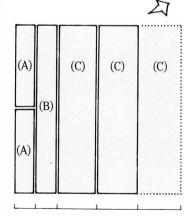

Leaf
Use one of the smaller 1:4 rectangles (A). Divide its length into quarters.

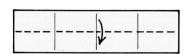

1

Fold the paper in half from top to bottom, in a valley fold.

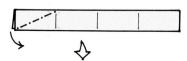

2

Inside reverse fold the paper at the left edge.

3

Fold the little flap in half. Then fold it again and tuck it into the structure. Open the paper by lifting the bottom edge from behind.

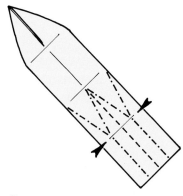

4

The left-hand end will rise into an upturned-boat shape. Flatten the paper at the right edge and form these new creases as shown. Pinch the top and bottom edges.

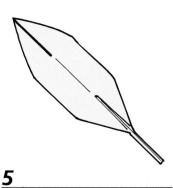

5

The completed leaf.

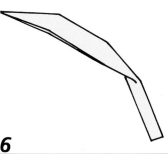

6

The leaf seen from the side. Use the other small 1:4 rectangle to make a second leaf.

Leaf stem
Use the 1:8 rectangle (B). Make a long central crease and divide its length into eighths.

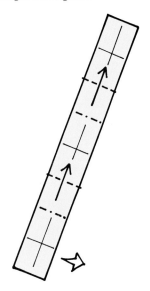

1

Make two pleats using the existing crease lines, as shown.

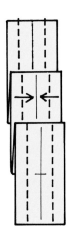

2

Fold in the left and right edges of the pleated strip so that they meet at the centre line.   ▶

leaf stem continued

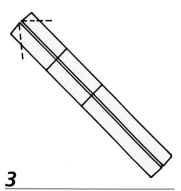

3

Fold in the left-hand corners to the centre line, in valley folds.

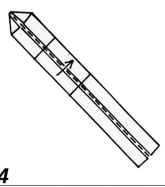

4

Fold the strip in half, from top to bottom, in a valley fold along the centre crease.

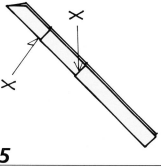

5

The completed leaf stem. Note the two pockets marked X in the diagram. Tuck a leaf into each of these pockets, one in front and one behind. It is much easier to do this if you first open the stem, reverting to fig. 4, then tuck in the ends of the leaves and fold the stem again.

Main stem and assembly
Use the large 1:4 rectangles (C). Make a horizontal centre crease in each.

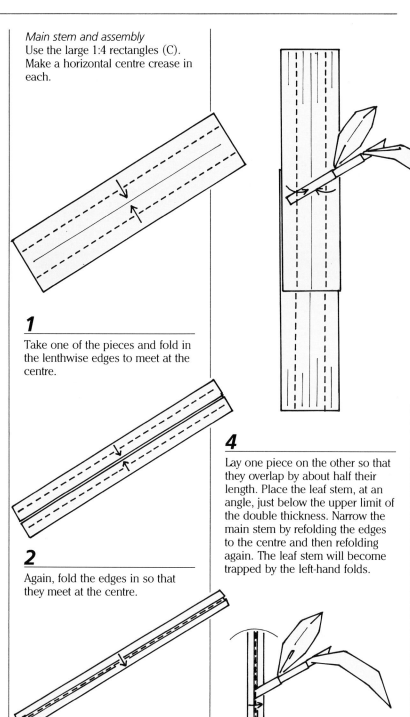

1

Take one of the pieces and fold in the lenthwise edges to meet at the centre.

2

Again, fold the edges in so that they meet at the centre.

3

Fold the strip in half. Repeat these steps on the other rectangle; then open them both.

4

Lay one piece on the other so that they overlap by about half their length. Place the leaf stem, at an angle, just below the upper limit of the double thickness. Narrow the main stem by refolding the edges to the centre and then refolding again. The leaf stem will become trapped by the left-hand folds.

5

Fold the main stem in half once more to complete the assembly.

*F*OIL

*B*y foil, most paperfolders mean the decorative gold or silver paper-backed foil that is obtainable from art and craft shops. Whether it is a good idea to use this as a material for origami is a matter of debate among devotees. Some paperfolders use nothing but foil, preferring it because it lacks the elasticity of ordinary paper. This means that when it is folded it stays folded, so a foil model tends to hold its shape better than one made from ordinary paper. On the other hand, its folded edges will be inclined to crack and it may quickly develop a well-thumbed look; it will not have the strength and tension in its lines and surfaces that a well-folded paper model has. Nevertheless, foil is generally accepted as a material for Christmas decorations.

Foil more generally means the unbacked aluminium foil used in cooking. Californian paperfolder Robert Lang makes what he believes to be a near-perfect origami material from this by bonding thin coloured tissue paper to either side of it (see LAMINATING PAPER). The foil can be partially seen through the tissue, an incidental effect creating an 'interesting iridescence'.

It is not surprising that origami enthusiasts have been known to apply their skills to the problem of making baking pans and other utensils from kitchen foil. Barbecue parties can provide opportunities for showing off the results.

The following box or dish can be made from a rectangle of any proportions, so it is suitable for making from an odd end of kitchen foil.

How to make a
foil box ★

Use a rectangle of foil (or paper). First find the centre.

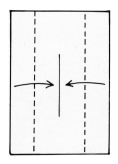

1

Fold in the longer edges so that they meet at the centre.

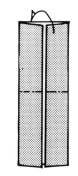

2

Mountain fold the paper rectangle from top to bottom, taking the upper half back behind the paper.

3

Fold down the right and left corners of the top edge so that they meet in the centre, and return.

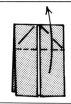

4

Fold up the front flap on a line where the existing creases meet the outer edges. Repeat behind.

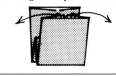

5

Take hold of the concealed edges behind the front flap and pull to left and right, in turn. Repeat behind.

6

Fold the left and right edges in to the centre. Turn the paper over and repeat.

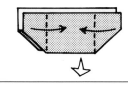

7

Fold the little top flap in half; then fold it over again. Repeat behind.

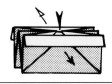

8

Pull gently on the narrow flaps at the front and back, and press down on the centre, to raise the form.

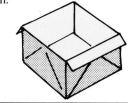

9

The completed box.

Flowers (page 63) with utility leaves and stems (page 64)

68

*F*ROGS

*I*n Japanese the word *kaeru* means both 'frog' and 'to return home'. Because of this, the folded paper frog had, at one time, a place in the folklore of Japan as a charm to ensure the safe return of a loved one. It is said that the wives of fishermen, in particular, made a practice of folding frogs to be placed in their household shrines while their husbands were at sea.

Japanese people still fold the same traditional frog, but nowadays only for play. By running a finger down the back of the frog, it can be made to jump, and if the paper is light and springy enough, it should turn a complete somersault.

The possibility of using paper to make jumping frogs is something which seems to have occurred independently to different people in different parts of the world. There are a number of different types of jumping frog, most of which operate by the pressure of a finger. Two are shown here: the traditional Japanese frog, and one collected by Bob Allen in America which he thinks may have originated there. It seems that the Chinese prefer frogs which are operated by blowing. The one shown below was introduced to the Reverend Philip Noble, a Scottish paperfolder, by the Anglican Bishop of Singapore, the Right Reverend B. I. Chin.

How to make a

Japanese jumping frog★★★

Use a square of paper, preferably green in colour. Start by completing the frog base (page 25).

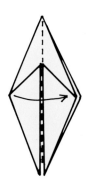

1

Take the front left flap across to the right. Turn the paper over and fold the front right flap across to the left.

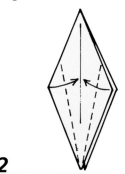

2

Fold the lower edges of the front flaps to the centre crease. Repeat on other three sides.

3

Return the top right flap to the left. Turn the paper over and return the top left flap to the right.

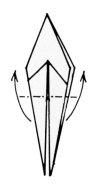

4

Inside reverse fold the front pair of bottom points up as far as they will go.

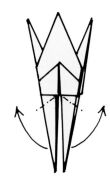

5

Now inside reverse fold the remaining pair of points out to the left and right.

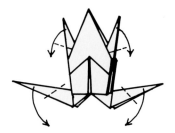

6

Valley fold each of the four points to form legs. ▶

Japanese jumping frog continued

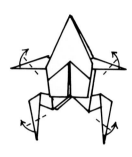

7

Fold each of the points again in valley folds, to form feet.

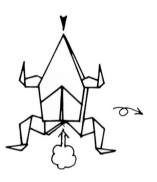

8

Blow into the hole at the bottom of the model and press down on the top point to raise the form of the body. Turn over.

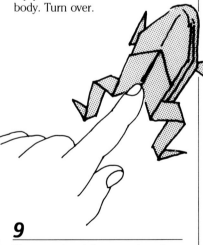

9

The completed Japanese jumping frog. Place on a flat surface and run your finger down his back, pressing firmly, to make it jump.

How to make a
Chinese jumping frog ★★

Use a small square of light paper. Start by folding the blintz (page 27).

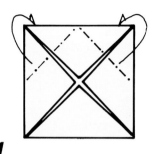

1

Mountain fold the top two corners by taking them behind the paper so that they meet at the centre.

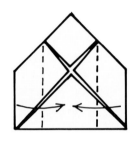

2

Fold in the right and left edges so that they lie in the centre.

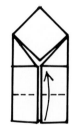

3

Fold up the bottom edge in a valley fold, to meet the horizontal line.

4

Fold down the top two corners of the front flap to meet at the bottom edge.

5

Take hold of the diagonal folded edges and pull the outer layers only to the left and right. Flatten them.

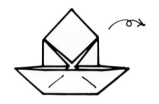

6

Now turn the paper over.

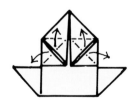

7

Separate the raw edges of the two central flaps and squash fold them to form eyes.

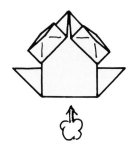

8

The completed Chinese frog. There are two schools of thought as to which is the better way to make it jump. Some say that you should blow down vertically, just behind the rear legs in short gentle puffs. Others say that you should get down on a level with the frog and blow under its rear legs.

How to make an
American jumping frog ★★

Use a small square of paper. First complete the waterbomb base (page 22).

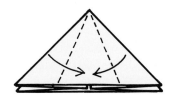

1

Fold the diagonal edges of the right and left front flaps to the centre crease.

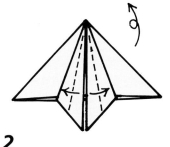

2

Fold them back to the new folded edges. Turn the paper over.

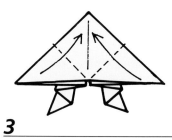

3

Fold up the left and right corners so that they meet at the top point.

4

Fold them back, in valley folds, to the new corners.

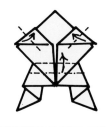

5

Fold up the points of the two top flaps, to make feet. Pleat the waist.

6

Turn the paper over.

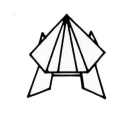

7

The completed American frog.

8

Run your finger down its back firmly. As with the Japanese frog it will jump.

GEOMETRY

*I*t is well established among educationalists that paperfolding can be useful as an aid in teaching geometry to children and articles on paperfolding often appear in specialist publications for mathematics teachers.

The first known text-book to exploit paperfolding in this way was a treatise by Dionysius Lardner published in 1840, according to Italian mathematician Giovanni Vacca in 'Della Piegatura della Carta applicata alla Geometria' (Paperfolding applied to Geometry), *Periodico di Matematiche,* vol. 10, 1930. But the most influential work of this kind has been Sundara Row's *Geometric Exercises in Paperfolding,* first published in Madras, India, in 1893 and reprinted in a revised edition by Dover Publications, NY, in 1966. In this book, 295 propositions are demonstrated by paperfolding. Another important work is D. A. Johnson's *Paper Folding for the Mathematics Class,* National Council of Teachers of Mathematics, 1971. The author recommends the use of heavy wax-paper because a crease then becomes a distinct white line.

English paperfolder John S. Smith, who has interested himself with this aspect of paperfolding in particular, believes that there are many advantages in folding paper to teach mathematics. Among them are: (1) no mathematical instruments are needed – the squares of paper themselves are simple substitutes for a straight-edge and a T-square; (2) several important geometric processes can be effected much more easily by paperfolding than by using a pair of compasses and ruler; (3) it is easier for students to fold neat diagrams than to draw them – as a result, they can appreciate so many more propositions directly.

GREETING CARDS

A model folded from a small square of brightly coloured paper makes a pleasing decoration when attached to a personal letter. Why not take this a step further and try making cards decorated with origami.

Jacques Justin has developed the idea of origami greeting cards by folding the card as well as the design from a single sheet of paper.

Flapping birds (page 12)

HANDKERCHIEF FOLDING

One way in which Lewis Carroll, author of *Alice in Wonderland*, used to amuse his young friends was to take a handkerchief from his pocket and fold it into a mouse. He would delight them by making the mouse appear to come alive, run up his arm and leap into the air.

The mouse is one of several stunts of unknown origin which uses a folded handkerchief as a prop and which is designed to entertain young children. Such tricks are part of a tradition of parlour magic and home entertainment. However, it is not enough simply to fold handkerchiefs – one should give some thought to their presentation or performance too.

Handkerchiefs can also be folded to make simple table decorations in the origami manner but, being folded from cloth instead of paper, the folds can be made softer and rounder. Such designs are interchangeable with those more often described as napkin folds. Indeed, the standard work on handkerchief folding in the English language remains Tom Osborne's *Napkin Folding*, published by D. Robbins and Co., New York, in 1972 (originally published as *Fun at Dinner with Napkin Folds* in 1943), which, despite its title, contains tricks more often associated with handkerchiefs.

Martin Gardner's *Encyclopedia of Impromptu Magic*, Magic Inc., Chicago, 1978, describes fifteen handkerchief folds and deals fully with the various ways in which the handkerchief mouse can be manipulated. In Frances E. Jacobs' *Out of a Handkerchief*, Hammond, Hammond and Co, 1943, the author introduces designs which need to be fastened with string or rubber bands to make them stable.

How to make a
banana ★

Use a plain handkerchief.

1

Fold in the four corners so that they all meet in the centre.

2

Take hold of the four corners with the fingers of one hand and lift the handkerchief.

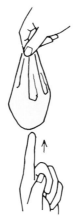

3

Push up the centre of the handkerchief with the forefinger of your other hand. Push it right up and let the fingers holding the handkerchief's corners grasp the handkerchief's centre between them.

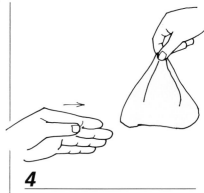

4

Now gather the base of the bundle with your free hand.

5

The banana is completed.

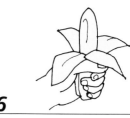

6

Your audience may not recognize it as a banana or as anything else but they should recognize it when you carefully fold down the four corners and solemnly take a 'bite' from it.

How to make a
bow ★

Use a plain or coloured handkerchief.

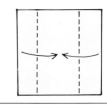

1

Fold in the left and right sides so that they lie along the centre.

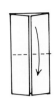

2

Fold the top half down to the bottom, in a valley fold.

3

Fold the bottom edge of the front flap up to the folded edge. Turn the handkerchief over and repeat.

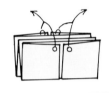

4

Carefully lift the four corners above the folded edges. Take the two left-hand corners between the finger and thumb of your left hand and the two right-hand corners between the finger and thumb of your right hand. Lift and pull apart.

5

The handkerchief will take the form of a hair ribbon with a large bow if placed on the head.

How to make a

mouse ★★

Start with a plain handkerchief folded diagonally in half.

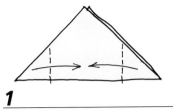

1

Fold the two corners towards the centre so that they overlap slightly.

2

Fold up the bottom edge and turn it over in a valley fold.

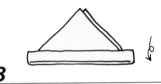

3

Turn the handkerchief over.

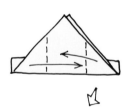

4

Fold in the left and right sides so that they overlap.

5

Fold up the bottom edge once more.

6

Tuck the top corner into the model, pushing it right in.

7

Put your thumbs into the base of the model and turn it inside out.

8

Keep turning it inside out (as one does a pair of laundered socks) until the two ends appear.

9

Hold one of the ends between your thumbs and forefingers. Let the model hang loose; swing it up and around a few times.

10

Two twisted projections will appear. Tie them into a knot to form a head with ears.

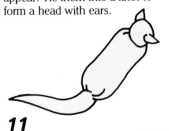

11

The completed mouse. ▶

mouse continued

Animating the mouse

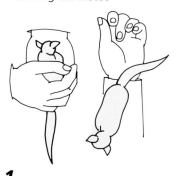

1

Hold the mouse in the palm of your left hand and stroke it with your right hand. Push it with the middle finger of your left hand (the stroking right hand will hide this movement from your audience) and the mouse will appear to run forward. Pull it back into your hand and repeat a few times. Then push it a bit harder and make it jump up your arm.

Place your hands in your lap, palms upwards, with the mouse lying across them. Wiggle your fingers to make it run from hand to hand. Alternate your hands to make it run indefinitely.

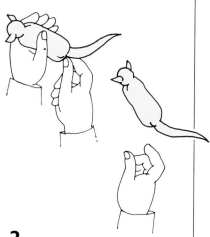

2

Finally hold it with its head towards your audience. With a flick of the forefinger you can make it jump into their laps.

HATS

Among the handful of origami techniques traditionally learnt by most westerners in their childhood is the pointed paper hat folded from a sheet of newspaper (although not everyone can remember how to fold it when they have children of their own). It serves as a warrior's helmet for children at play of course, but even adults have found it useful when they need to improvise something quickly to keep off sun or rain (wear it pointing back to front to keep the sun out of your eyes; wear it pointing sideways to keep the rain off your shoulders). Even Pope John Paul, has been seen to wear a paper hat on just such an occasion.

How to make a paper hat ★

Use a sheet of newspaper, preferably a doubled sheet for extra strength. First fold the two longer edges together to mark the horizontal centre line and open up.

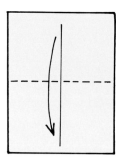

1

Fold the top edge down to the bottom edge in a valley fold.

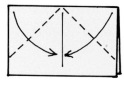

2

Fold down the left and right corners of the folded edge to meet at the centre line.

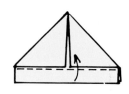

3

Fold up the front flap at the bottom over the horizontal edge. Do the same behind.

4

The completed hat.

Spanish children customarily decorate this kind of hat with a paper plume.

How to make a plume

Use any rectangular scrap of paper.

1

Roll up the paper quite tightly.

2

Cut or tear several slits in one end of the rolled up tube.

3

Fluff out the ends of the strips to complete the plume.

4

Decorate your hat by slipping the base of the plume into the pocket at the front.

The paper hat can be taken a few steps further to make a hat with a larger brim. It is sometimes known as a 'sailboat hat' because, if folded from a sheet of notepaper, it can be sailed in the bath as a boat, or, if folded to a larger scale from a sheet of newspaper, it can be worn on the head as a hat.

When there was a revival of interest in hats in the fashion world during the early seventies, London model Jenny Gaylor made herself a sailboat hat in black velvet, basing her design on drawings she found in a Rupert Bear annual. Her sailboat hats went on sale in a Chelsea boutique in 1972.

How to make a sailboat hat ★

Start by folding the paper hat (page 76).

1

Hold the front and back edges of the hat in either hand and pull them apart.

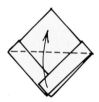

2

The hat will collapse into this new shape. Fold the bottom point of the front flap up to the top. Turn the hat over and repeat. ▶

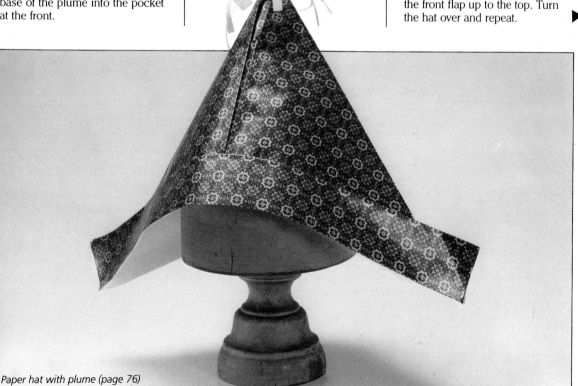

Paper hat with plume (page 76)

hats continued

3

Now pull the front and back edges apart as in step 1.

4

Fold up the bottom point of the front flap. Turn it over and repeat.

5

Take hold of the two side points and pull the outer layers to the left and right.

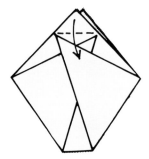

6

The completed hat.

HEADSCARF FOLDING

*I*n Europe, headscarfs were originally a part of peasant dress. They became acceptable to wear in England during World War II. Since then they have enjoyed periods of popularity in the early 1950s (when they were worn as turbans) and mid-1970s (when they were worn knotted at the nape of the neck).

Neither of these methods can be considered very imaginative (consisting as they do of one fold and a knot each). Why not take out one of your old headscarfs and use it to create something different? Here are two unusual techniques for folding headscarfs, collected by the Origami Center of America. You should use scarfs which are at least 60cm (23in) square and made of some non-slippery fabric.

How to make a

turban ★★

Start with the square folded in half diagonally.

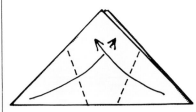

1

Overlap the two corners (how much they overlap will depend on the size of scarf).

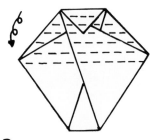

2

Fold the top point down in a valley fold.

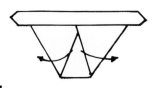

3

Roll down the material tightly starting from the top, and ending at a middle point.

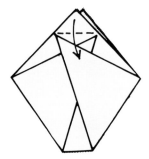

4

Now turn the whole thing inside out; grasp the ends of the roll while you do this.

5

The completed turban. Keep hold of the roll while you pull the turban down over your ears.

How to make a hood ★

Start with the square folded in half, from top to bottom.

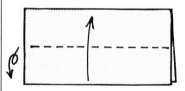

1

Fold the near bottom edge up to the folded edge. Turn the material over.

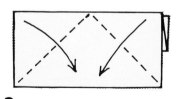

2

Fold the right and left top corners down to the bottom edge.

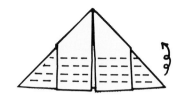

3

Roll up the material tightly, working from the bottom and stopping midway. Turn the material over.

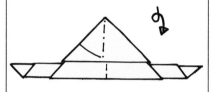

4

Fold the structure in half from right to left.

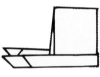

5

As you do so, lift the centre.

6

The completed hood. Tie the ends under your chin.

*H*INA

*T*he Doll Festival, which is celebrated annually in Japan on March 3rd in homes where there are young girls, is marked by the display of ceremonial dolls that represent the Imperial Court. These dolls are known collectively as *hina* or *o-hina*. A full set of fifteen can be seen in the Horniman Museum in London. The folding of paper versions is an activity commonly associated with the festival.

ITAJIME-SHIBORI

Decorating clothes and fabrics by means of tie-dyeing has become a popular pastime in the West in recent years. In Japan, where it is known as *itajime-shibori,* paper is often decorated in a similar way, the results being used as napkins for special occasions, or for purses and other containers.

Because paper holds its creases when folded, it is not necessary to tie it before you dye it. The resultant patterns have their own linear character which is rather different from that of tie-dyed fabrics. Dyeing folded paper is a good way of introducing children to fabric dyeing. All that is needed is a saucer, some cooking dyes and a few small sheets of paper. Try various kinds of papers, but for quick results use a very absorbent paper such as a paper napkin or kitchen towel.

Anne Maille's *Tie-dyed Paper,* Mills & Boon, London, 1975, gives a full account of the subject. As well as presenting many ways of folding paper before dyeing, the author suggests ways of using dyes to enhance the appearance of completed origami models.

How to make

tie-dyed paper ★★

Here is a simple exercise to introduce you to the possibilities of tie-dyed paper. Use a paper napkin or tissue. You will also need, as mentioned above, a small amount of at least one cooking dye in a saucer.

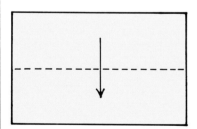

1

Fold the paper in half, from top to bottom, in a valley fold.

2

Fold the paper in half again, from top to bottom.

3

Fold the top left corner to the bottom edge. Then mountain fold in line with the vertical edge.

4

Repeat these moves until the folded strip appears as a bunch of folded triangles. Hold and compress the paper between your finger and thumb, and dip one corner of it into the colour. Remove immediately. Dip the other two corners to colour them too. Finally unfold the paper very carefully to find out what sort of pattern you have made, and lay it on an old newspaper to dry.

For samples of itajime-shibori, see the photograph on page 00.

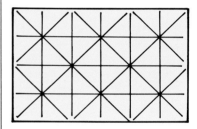

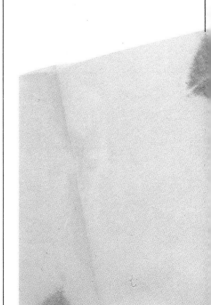

*Tie-dyed paper (left); Envelope
(page 52)*

JAPANESE TRADITION

The tradition of folding paper in Japan is a long and continuous one, probably going back to the sixth century A.D., at a time soon after paper was first introduced into the country from China. Since medieval times, paperfolding of a very formal kind has had an important place in both religious and secular life. Out of this formal use grew a tradition of paperfolding that was a decorative accomplishment and an amusement for girls and women. It is still regarded as such by many Japanese, but it is also finding respect as a valuable creative activity, receiving patronage from both Japanese industry and cultural institutions.

Japan, a country entirely without mineral resources, had to rely on her trees and forests for much of her raw material until modern times. It is from the bark of various trees that most Japanese paper has been traditionally made (see WASHI page 186) and the Japanese have exploited this paper for making many types of artifacts which, in other countries, are made from quite different materials.

There is perhaps another reason for the important place held by paper in Japan. The Japanese word *kami* can mean both 'paper' and 'God' (although the two meanings are distinguished by the characters, which are written differently). This has led to a tradition in which paper is regarded as something sacred; it has long been associated with the national religion, Shinto. Visitors to Japan are soon made aware of the connection by the many folded zig-zag streamers of white paper, called *o-shide*

which can be seen generally at the entrances to Shinto shrines. They are either suspended from straw ropes which are used to mark off sacred places, or else attached to branches of the sacred takaki tree. They are also sometimes worn in the hair of visitors to shrines or temples and often decorate the homes of ordinary people on festive occasions, such as those that take place during the New Year season.

There is a similar, sacred object, really a doubled form of *o-shide*, which is generally less evident. This is the *go-hei*, which takes the form of a pair of zig-zag streamers suspended from a rod or staff. *Go-hei* are to be found only inside Shinto shrines. Usually there is a single one in each shrine, placed in a commanding position, because it is in the *go-hei* that the temple deity resides, according to Shinto belief. It indicates the presence of the deity and also serves as a symbolic offering. The number of folds and the manner of folding are said to be of very great significance; more than twenty types are known to be used by various sects and only Shinto priests are permitted to make them.

Why the *go-hei* takes the particular form it does is not really known, but it may be that it was originally a symbolic substitute for the rolls of cloth that were once used as offerings to Chinese deities. It has also been remarked that the *go-hei* form has a certain resemblance to a cloaked human figure.

More naturalistic human figures, also folded from paper, are housed in some Shinto shrines

to receive the deity. They are called *katashiro*. Among them is a type known as *nagashi-bina*, or 'floating dolls', a full set of which comprises twenty folded paper figures, ten male and ten female. Traditionally, on March 3rd each year, one set was displayed in the household shrine while a second set was used for spiritual purification. This ritual was performed by breathing on the dolls, rubbing them against one's body to rid oneself of impurities, then throwing the infected dolls into a river to be carried away. The custom may well go back to prehistoric times when dolls became a substitute for human sacrifice. The purification ritual is said to be practised still in Tottori prefecture, but for most Japanese it survives in the Dolls' Festival *(o-hina matsuri)* only, in which elaborately costumed dolls are displayed in the homes of families with young daughters.

Go-hei have existed in Japan, in their present form, since the ninth century A.D. Probably as ancient is the custom of attaching folded paper butterflies to the long-handled wine cups that are exchanged in Shinto wedding ceremonies (see BUTTERFLIES). It also soon became customary always to decorate a gift with a folded paper wrapper, called *noshi* (see page 128), which contained a strip of dried sea food. There have been many attempts to explain the origin of this custom, but it seems most likely that it symbolizes the offerings of fish wrapped in straw that are made to Shinto deities on certain occasions. It is still obligatory in Japan to attach *noshi* (now containing a synthetic substitute for the sea food) to gifts for special occasions such as weddings and betrothals, but by 1930 commercial wrapping paper decorated with a printed *noshi* symbol had become available for use on less significant occasions.

There are also many traditional methods of folding paper containers for herbs, used in both cooking and medicine, which became formalized in the fourteenth century. Most of these wrappers were used regularly until the nineteenth century (see WRAPPERS). Mothers used to teach their daughters these traditional folds – things that the girl would need to know when she became a housewife herself. Fortunately she did not need to retain the techniques in her head; many families kept sets of origami patterns which they could refer to whenever necessary. They either took the form of completed models which had to be unfolded to discover their method of construction, or they were opened-up sheets with the crease lines marked by a series of pin pricks.

By the eighteenth century it was possible to buy sets of pre-folded origami samples. The earliest known set, available in 1728, was called *Go-hyaku Ori-bako* (Box of Five Hundred Folds). It is not known whether these were samples of functional and ceremonial origami only or whether play origami was included. Not for another fifty years was it possible to obtain information about origami, in the form of printed instructions, and by this time much of the material was clearly intended for

recreation and enjoyment.

The first such instruction book dates from 1797. Its title is *Ori-kata Tehon Chushingura* and it was published by Yoshino-ya of Kyoto. It contained a collection of woodcut prints illustrating scenes from the popular drama *Chushingura* (in which forty-seven loyal retainers of a feudal lord commit ritual suicide in order to protect their master's honour), and with these scenes were rudimentary instructions for folding the characters. Copies of this book still exist and it has been noticed that they contain announcements of the future publication of another origami book – one which would show how to fold flowers, animals, birds and fish. This untitled work, if it was indeed published, has yet to be rediscovered. The same house, Yoshino-ya, published *Sembazuru Orikata* (see SEMBAZURU) in the same year.

Almost another fifty years went by before the next major work appeared. Known as *Kan-no-Mado* (Window on Mid-winter), it is a collection of fifty small volumes of memoranda copied by Kazuyuki Adachi from earlier sources and finally compiled in 1845. One of the volumes contains illustrations for a total of forty-nine examples of ceremonial and recreational origami. The volume on paperfolding was derived from an earlier work called *Kayaragusa;* it is therefore sometimes known by this name too. It was used as the basis for a modern work entitled *A Japanese Paper Folding Classic: Excerpts from the 'Kan-no-mado'* by Julia and Martin Brossman, published in limited edition by

Pinecone Press, Washington, D.C., in 1961.

A full description of ceremonial origami is to be found in Sadatake Ise's *Tsutsumi-Musubi no Ki* (Notes on Wrapping and Tying) which appeared in 1865. An English language introduction to the subject is provided by Isao Honda's *Noshi: Classic Origami in Japan,* published by Japan Publications, Tokyo, in 1964.

In the 1890s, the Japanese government introduced a system of universal primary education based on Western lines. They adopted the educational practices of the German educationalist Freidrich Froebel and established kindergartens throughout the country. As Froebel's methods employed paperfolding (albeit of a very schematic kind) in the belief that it was an excellent method for bringing minds and hands into co-ordination, the curious result of this westernisation was the reinforcement of Japan's own tradition of paperfolding. Pre-school kindergartens are widespread in Japan, and the teaching of traditional origami continues therein. This has led to a broad base for the creative origami movement in Japan which is currently growing with the support of both industry and government.

JUAN ESCUDIRO

*A*merican magician Jay Marshall has a stage act centred on a hat of folded newspaper. He tells an involved and improbable story concerning a young Mexican, Juan Escudiro, and as each new character (and there are many) is introduced into the story, he partially unfolds the hat to transform it into a new one which he puts on his head to assume the new role. The hats become larger and larger until, with the final unfolding, it is revealed that they have all been made from an ordinary newspaper.

KASANE-ORIGAMI

'*K*asane-origami' is a Japanese term for 'layered paperfolding'. It is a technique in which several (five or more) sheets of differently coloured paper are overlayed so that 'ribbons' of different colours run along either one edge or two adjacent edges. These overlayed sheets are then treated as a single unit and folded together during at least part of the construction.

The technique is used particularly for folding stylized human figures, such as HINA (see page 79) dressed in the court costume of the Heian period (A.D. 794–1185). It was a striking characteristic of the costume of this period that layers of variously coloured undergarments were displayed as strips of colour at the edges of skirts and sleeves.

In America, Zoe Chiang has used several layers of differently sized coloured tissue papers to create a similar effect when folding flowers.

To gain a quick idea of the appearance of models which have been folded by this method, try the following trick, demonstrated by Japanese paperfolder Yasuhiro Sano.

1

Lay a pile of origami paper, neatly squared, on a flat surface. Rap the centre of the pile repeatedly with your knuckle.

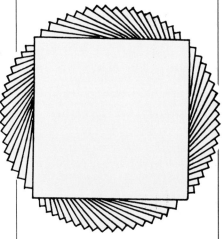

2

The sheets will rotate in a spiral to create this pretty effect.

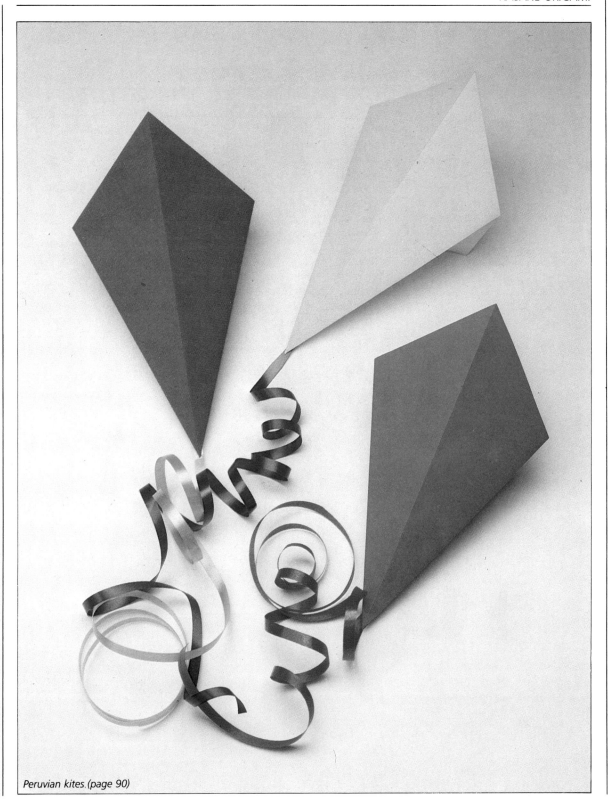

Peruvian kites. (page 90)

KIRIGAMI

The Japanese word for paper cutting, kirigami is an activity in which shapes are cut from paper, usually after it has first been folded. This results in a perforated pattern when the paper is unfolded. The manner in which the paper is folded naturally determines what form the pattern takes. Florence Temko introduced the word to the West in the first of her several books on the subject, *Kirigami,* published by Platt and Munk, c. 1960.

KIRIKOMI ORIGAMI

Most present-day practitioners of origami believe that it is wrong to destroy any part of their material (the original paper square or rectangle) by cutting it. They believe that any alteration to the paper should be made by folding alone. They will often fold with great complexity in order to create a shape which could be achieved more easily by cutting.

There is a school of origami, however, which allows cutting in the form of incisions. Its adherents accept that one should not discard any of the original material, but they have no objection to cutting into it. They would probably maintain that the original square or rectangle is not really being destroyed in this way.

The Japanese name for incised origami is *kirikomi* and much traditional origami is of this type. Here are instructions for folding two recent models, designed by young American paperfolders, in which incisions are crucial to the construction.

Both models start from traditional bases. In the sequences shown here, the antelope begins with a bird base (page 25) into which incisions are made without unfolding. You begin the spider by first folding a frog base (page 25), then unfolding it before making incisions. The methods are interchangeable, however.

How to make an

antelope ★★★

(Alice Blumberg)

Use a square of paper. First complete the bird base (page 25).

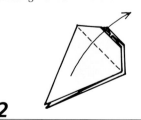

1

Sink in the top point on a line halfway between the point and the existing horizontal crease line.

2

Lift the front flap and fold up in a valley fold. Turn the paper over and repeat.

3

Fold the left flap to the right. Turn the paper over and fold the right flap to the left.

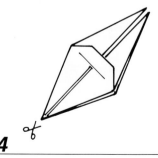

4

Cut the vertical centre line of both upper and lower flaps, from the bottom point to the existing horizontal crease line.

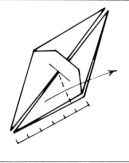

5

Fold up the bottom right flap.
(Note that the crease line starts
from a point one-sixth of the way
down the bottom right edge.)
Repeat behind.

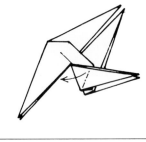

6

Squash fold the upturned flap.
Turn over and repeat.

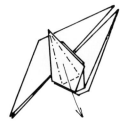

7

Petal fold the upturned flap, as
shown. Turn over and repeat.

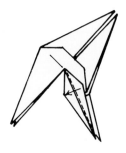

8

Fold the right flap in half, taking
the top edge to the bottom. Repeat
behind.

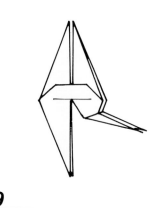

9

Turn the structure over.

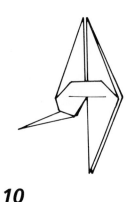

10

Repeat steps 5–9 on the flaps on
the right.

11

Inside reverse fold the four narrow
flaps.

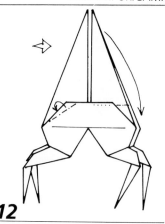

12

Inside reverse fold the top right
flap down. Mountain fold the left
edge as shown, and repeat behind.

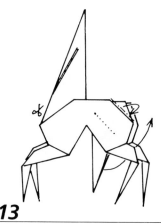

13

Mountain fold the flap on the right,
as shown. Inside reverse fold the
tail. Make a cut in the top left flap.

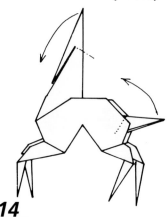

14

Inside reverse fold the top point to
form the head and ears. Outside
reverse fold the tail. ▶

Spider (below)

antelope
continued

How to make a

spider ★★★

(Bob Allen)

Use a square of paper, preferably
black. Start by completing the frog
base (page 25) and open up.

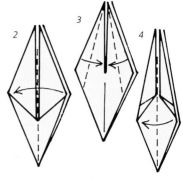

2

Fold the right flap across to the left
in a valley fold. Repeat behind.

3

Fold in the upper edges to meet at
the vertical centre line. Repeat on
other three sides.

4

Once more, fold the right flap
across to the left. Repeat behind.

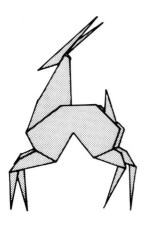

15

The completed antelope.

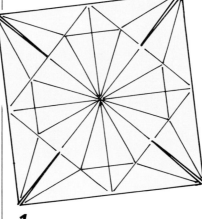

1

Make cuts from the four corners to
the 'blintz' lines. Then re-form the
frog base and place it with the
open ends at the top.

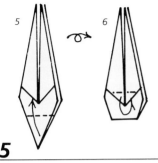

5

Fold up the bottom point and tuck it under the front flap. Turn the paper over.

6

Mountain fold the front corner, and tuck it under.

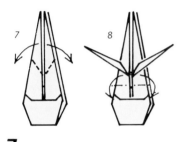

7

Fold down the front points to the left and right.

8

Now mountain fold the two flaps down into the model to form the rear legs.

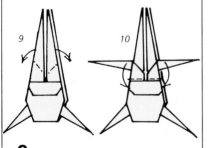

9

Mountain fold the next pair of flaps behind to the left and right.

10

Valley fold the two flaps down into the model.

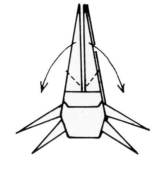

11

Valley fold the next pair of flaps down to the left and right.

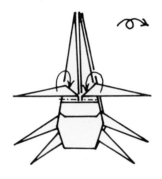

12

Mountain fold them down into the model to form a third pair of legs. Turn over.

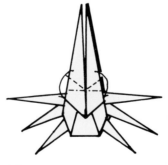

13

Swivel fold the remaining pair of flaps, as shown.

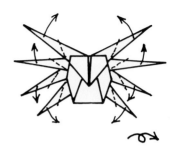

14

Valley fold all the legs as indicated. Turn over.

15

Pull up the concealed edges at the top in inside reverse folds and flatten them to form eyes.

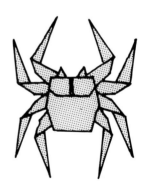

16

The completed spider.

KITES

Paper kites are generally kept rigid with a frame of light wood. However, simple kites can be made rigid without a frame by placing one or more folds in the paper. In many Latin countries, as well as in Japan, it is quite common for children to amuse themselves by making impromptu kites by tying threads to sheets of exercise paper which are folded in traditional ways.

A square of paper which has two adjacent edges folded to a diagonal crease is known to origami enthusiasts as a 'kite base' (page 24). When threaded as shown in the accompanying illustration, it makes a real kite.

A single fold is sufficient to make a sheet of paper quite rigid. If paper is pleated two or three times, then opened into a corrugated surface, we have the basis for many traditional kites. It is customary to make certain cuts across the pleated edges, which are then reverse folded to form stabilizers. Knowing where to place them – and where to attach the thread – is crucial to the success or failure of kite-making.

For a full account of the subject, see *How to Make and Fly Kites* by Saito, Hike and Modegi, published by Tokuma Shoten, Tokyo, in 1973, and T. Noguchi's *Origami Tako* (Origami Kites), published by the same company in 1976. Oliviero Olivieri's *Gli Aquiloni* (Kites), published by Sansoni, Firenze, in 1980, contains instructions for six or seven folded paper kites from Italy, Japan and Peru.

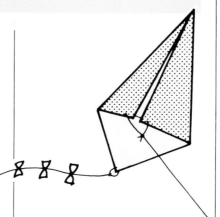

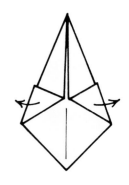

How to make a Peruvian kite ★★
(Olivero Olivieri)

Use a square of paper. You will also need thread, a paper streamer and some sticky tape. Start by making a diagonal centre crease.

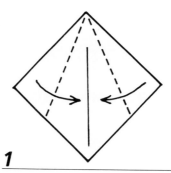

1

Fold two adjacent edges down to the centre crease to form a kite base.

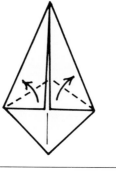

2

Fold up the horizontal edges so that they lie along the folded edges.

3

Open out the paper.

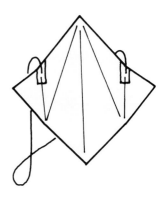

4

Stick the ends of the thread to the paper where the outer crease lines meet the edges.

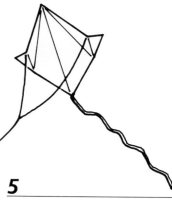

5

Complete the kite by forming a tail with the streamer and adding another length of thread.

KLINE-FOGLEMAN AEROFOIL

One day in 1968, Richard Kline, an art director in New York, folded a paper aeroplane for his six-year-old son. It was a task he had often undertaken before, but this time, without really knowing why, he tried something different. He folded the leading edge of each wing down so that it formed an 'open-ended wedge'. The result was a plane which flew farther and with greater stability than any he had folded before. So pleased was Kline with the plane's performance that he showed it to a pilot friend, Floyd Fogleman. He was intrigued – the model undoubtedly performed exceptionally well but, knowing something of aerodynamics, he could not understand why it should fly at all. The wedge-shaped wing seemed to be all wrong, flouting the first principles of flight. Fogleman realized that this needed serious investigation – perhaps his friend had stumbled on a completely new concept of aerodynamics.

All conventional aerofoils are based on the principle that the faster a gas or fluid flows, the less pressure it exerts. A conventional aerofoil is therefore constructed with a curved upper surface and a flat lower one – as it pushes forward through the air, the flow of air on the upper surface will increase in speed while on the lower surface it remains constant. This has the effect of increasing the pressure on the lower surface which, in turn, pushes the aerofoil upwards, giving it lift. Bearing this in mind, it could be expected that Kline's plane, with its 'upside down' wing, would crash on take-off.

Kline has not revealed the detailed design of his original paper aeroplane, but the two friends developed models in wood and metal from it and finally the Kline-Fogleman aerofoil was patented (US Pat. 3,706,430: the illustration shows a cross-section of the aerofoil as it appears in the patent records). When the aerofoil was tested at Notre Dame University with favourable results, it received considerable publicity. Reports appeared in the *Daily Telegraph* magazine, 10th April 1974, in the trade journal *OEM Design*, July/August 1974, and in *Time*, the weekly news magazine, 2nd April 1975.

However, paper plane folders have long used something of the sort instinctively. Note that the front part of the traditional aeroplane on page 14 drops, in effect creating a pair of wings which resembles the Kline-Fogleman aerofoil somewhat. A naval architect has expressed the view that the aerofoil is only an adaptation of a well-known principle of hydrodynamics. It works with extremely lightweight models such as paper planes, he says, because of the low speed of their flight. If this is so, it suggests that serious folders of paper aeroplanes should turn away from aerodynamics and acquire some knowledge of hydrodynamics instead.

KNIFE

A small square of paper, when folded diagonally in half, makes an effective impromptu paper knife. Having prepared your knife, fold the paper to mark the line you want to cut. Keep the paper folded and insert the paper knife between the two layers. Draw the knife at an angle across one end of the fold.

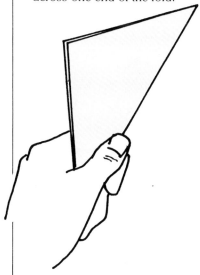

KNOTS

*I*f you are at all interested in knots, you may like to see what happens when you tie them in strips of paper instead of string. You will find that paper knots generally have an agreeable appearance, often in the form of regular geometric shapes. Mathematicians have taken some interest in their properties; the first known reference appears in Urbano d'Aviso's *Trattato della Sfera, etc*, which was published in Rome in 1682.

Strips about 1cm (⅓in) wide, cut from a sheet of writing paper, are sufficient for this project.

How to make a
thumb knot ★

Use one strip.

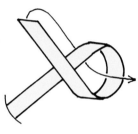

1

From a loop, as shown, and bring one end through it from behind. Tighten the knot gradually, allowing the paper to flatten.

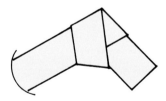

2

This is the result. If you cut off the ends, you will find that the knot forms a regular pentagon – a difficult figure to draw but so simple to fold.

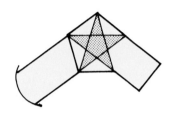

3

If the knot is held against the light, you will see the shadow of a perfectly formed five-pointed star.

How to make a
reef knot ★

Use two strips.

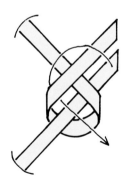

1

From a loop with one strip. Introduce the second strip from the front. Take it through and behind the loop, then bring it forward and thread it through the lower part of the loop. Tighten carefully, keeping the paper flat.

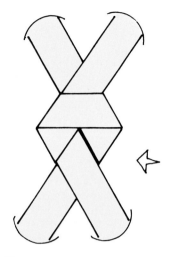

2

This is the result. If the ends are cut off in this instance, you will see that the knot forms a perfect hexagon.

How to make a
figure-of-eight knot ★

Use one strip.

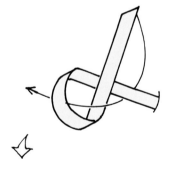

1

Form a loop as shown. Take the vertical strip down behind the horizontal one and then through the loop from the front. Gradually tighten and flatten.

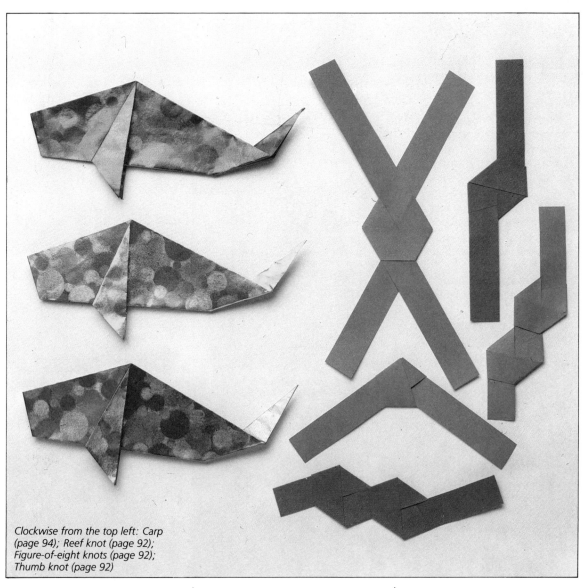

Clockwise from the top left: Carp (page 94); Reef knot (page 92); Figure-of-eight knots (page 92); Thumb knot (page 92)

2

This is the result. In this instance, if the ends are cut off the knot will form a six-sided figure with unequal angles.

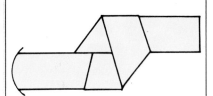

3

Try knotting a strip of paper repeatedly to make a decorative braid. To make longer braids, tuck the end of one knotted strip into the end pocket of another.

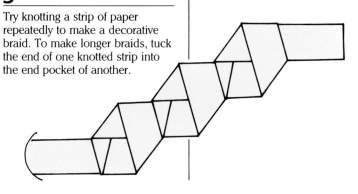

KOI-NOBORI

*B*ecause the *koi,* or Japanese carp, can swim upstream in the face of strong currents, it symbolizes the 'manly' virtues of perseverance and the will to overcome obstacles. It is therefore customary to hoist a paper streamer in the form of a carp, one for each son, on a pole outside the family home during Children's Day, which is celebrated annually in Japan on May 5th. Small origami versions of *koi-nobori* are commonly folded by children in preparation for this festival. The traditional method of folding a carp which follows, demonstrates one way in which a fish can be folded from a fish base (page 24).

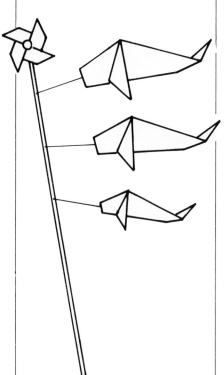

How to make a

carp ★★

Use a square of paper. Start by completing the fish base (page 24).

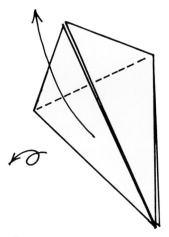

1

Fold up the front flap in a valley fold, as far as it will go. Turn the paper over.

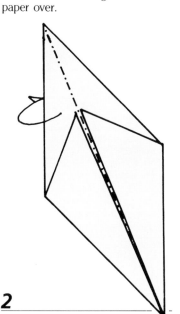

2

Mountain fold the paper in half, taking the left half behind.

3

Inside reverse fold the top and bottom points. Valley fold the front centre flap; repeat behind. Rotate.

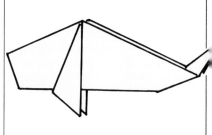

4

The completed carp.

KUSUDAMA
(Traditional Japanese Decoration)

*I*n pre-modern Japan, it was the custom to suspend a ball of sweet-smelling herbs above the bed of a sick person. These hanging balls, called *kusudama*, were also sometimes used as charms to ward off sickness. Nowadays they are used for their decorative qualities.

Instructions for making a traditional origami version (first carried in the Nippon Origami Association's journal *Origami,* April 1978) are given here. One ball is constructed from thirty-six squares of paper: these may be all the same colour or two or three matching colours, to suit your taste. Having made one ball, you may care to make a second and then a third, perhaps in different sizes, and suspend them above each other on the same thread. The Japanese like to attach streamers of paper or silk cord beneath them to catch the breeze. Complete kusudama-making kits are packaged by the art and crafts supplies firm Grimmhobby of Tokyo.

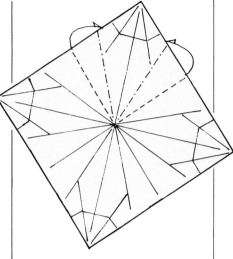

How to make a
kusudama ★★★★

You will need thirty-six squares of coloured paper, a needle and thread, and a little glue. To make one unit, take one square and start by completing step 1 of the frog base (page 25), but with the coloured side of the paper inwards. Repeat on three other sides.

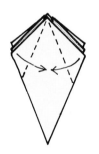

2

Fold in the raw edges so that they meet at the centre crease. Repeat on the three other sides.

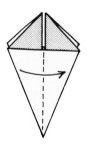

1

Take the left flap across to the right in a valley fold. Repeat behind.

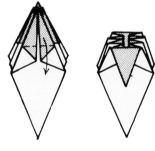

3

Fold the top point down as far as it will go. Repeat on the three other sides.

4

Now open out the paper. Take the centre of the top left and right edges behind to the centre.

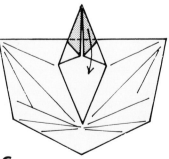

5

The form will begin to rise. Fold the raw edges to the centre crease, as shown.

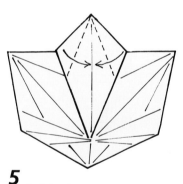

6

Fold the top point down along the line of the horizontal edge. ▶

Kusudama (page 95)

kusudama continued

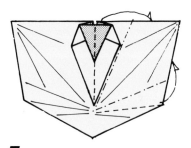

7

Take the centre of two edges to the diagonal centre crease line at right, in effect repeating step 4 on the adjacent corner of the paper.

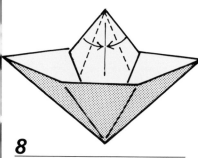

8

Fold in the raw edges to the centre crease of the newly formed flap.

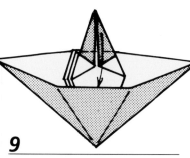

9

Fold the top point down along the line of the horizontal edge.

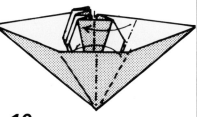

10

Crimp the right corner into the model, in effect repeating step 4 again.

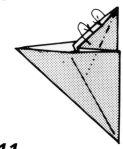

11

Fold in the raw edges, in mountain folds, to meet the right vertical edge.

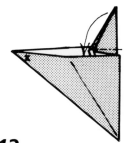

12

Inside reverse fold the top point down.

13

(New position) In effect, repeat step 4 on the remaining point X.

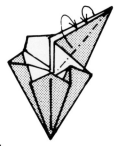

14

Tuck in the raw edges, in mountain folds.

15

Inside reverse fold the point down into the model.

16

The completed unit. Tie a long thread to its base. Repeat steps 1–15 on the remaining squares to make a total of thirty-six units. ▶

Assembly

1

Pass a thread through the base points of six units and tie them together.

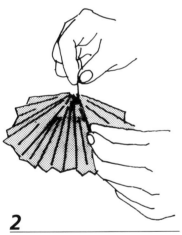

2

This will be the basis of the kusudama.

3

Slip the cluster over the thread to which a single unit has already been attached (step 16).

4

Now thread together eleven units, as in steps 1 and 2. Slip this cluster onto the main thread.

5

Thread together another eleven units and join this cluster to the kusudama which is now taking shape.

6

Thread together another six units and join this cluster to the others.

7

Finally, tuck in the last of the thirty-six units, after first dabbing a little glue to its side.

8

The completed kusudama.

*L*AMINATING PAPER

*T*here are papers available commercially which are remarkable for having a different colour on each surface. This is the result of laminating together two sheets of a different colour each.

Such two-coloured papers are useful for folding certain models, but it is not always possible to obtain a combination of the two colours you require in one sheet. British folder Mick Guy, finding it impossible to find the green and yellow combination he needed to fold a daffodil, decided to make his own laminated paper using the following method. And when another folder, Andrew Severn, wanted to use a design for an origami vase by Toshie Takahama to make a *real* vase – one which would hold cut flowers in water – he turned to this method to provide himself with the material. By substituting a thin polythene 'cling film' for tissue paper, he succeeded in making a waterproof material suitable for the project.

How to laminate

paper ★★

Materials: base paper (foil, gift-wrap paper, or other)
top paper (tissue paper)
glue: Spray adhesive
steel rule
craft knife or single-edged razor-blade
cardboard tube

1

Cut the base paper to the dimensions you require.

2

Cut the top (tissue) paper to the same dimensions, but allow a margin for overlap (this will be trimmed off later).

3

Lay out the base paper, white side up and, in a well-ventilated area, spray on a coating of adhesive. (Spray this as far away from you as possible so that you don't breathe in the droplets of adhesive.)

4

Having first rolled the top paper around a cardboard tube, gently unroll it, sticking it to the base paper and smoothing out any air bubbles as you go.

5

Allow the glued papers to stand for about two minutes.

6

Trim off the surplus tissue paper.

7

Check that all edges are stuck down.

*L*AMPSHADES

*P*leated paper lampshades are associated more often with the Scandinavian design movement than with origami, yet some of the techniques are similar and, what is more, designing lampshades is a good exercise for those people who would like to fold creatively but claim they do not know how to start.

A pleated lampshade is basically constructed by combining reverse folds with pleats. One way of doing this is first to pleat your paper and unfold it, then to fold a variety of parallel crease lines across the pleats and finally to collapse the paper into whatever form results.

To design a lampshade, or similar structure, you will need a rectangle of paper. Use a foolscap or A4 sheet and start by folding it into a series of pleats of equal width. Bring the ends together with the pleats lying vertically. Do the pleats retain their form as pleats? If not, there are not enough of them and you may have to double their number. Is the cylinder absurdly long and narrow for a lampshade? Then open the paper and cut off one edge to improve the proportions.

Now place a series of one or more similar reverse folds into the pleats, then bring the ends together again to see what form you have created. Consider whether you like it and, if necessary, how you can improve it. This can be done either by altering the direction of your reverse folds or by increasing (or decreasing) their number.

Here are three basic designs for you to explore and develop. In each case the opened paper with its pattern of creases is shown with the raised form which can be achieved from it.

Wire supports for lampshades are available from suppliers of craft equipment. When you have created a design you are pleased with, repeat it on a larger scale to fit around a wire support. The two ends of the paper should be stapled together. Thoki Yenn, a Danish paperfolder who has designed many lampshades, says that wire supports are not necessary: a cardboard disc, with a hole in the centre for the wire, is sufficient, provided that it is large enough to keep the paper away from the light bulb.

Authentic Swedish lampshade designs can be found in B. Schussler's *Lampskarmer,* published by ICA, Vasteras, Sweden, in 1968.

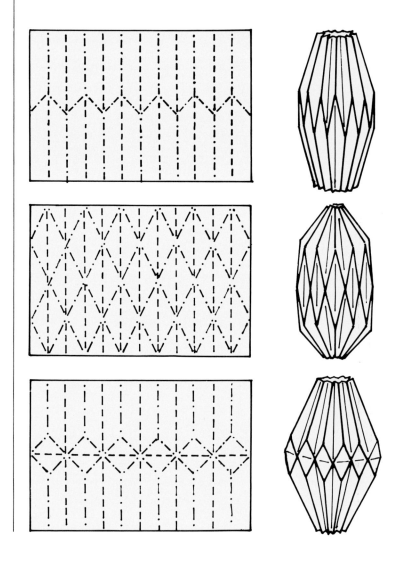

Lampshade (left)

LARGE-SCALE MODELS

While working as origami consultant on the production team of a BBC television play, Birmingham paperfolder Ray Bolt happened to mention to a colleague that he wished he could try folding a life-size version of George Rhoads' Elephant (a model which appears in Samuel Randlett's *The Best of Origami,* Faber, 1964), but he had never possessed a big enough sheet of paper, nor the space to work in. This conversation led to his being given the paper and the space in front of the television cameras. Bolt, with the aid of four assistants, folded an elephant from a 78 square metres (841sq ft) sheet of paper on the BBC programme *Pebble Mill at One,* on April 19th 1979. It may have been the largest origami model ever folded from a single sheet.

Working on such a scale presents unexpected problems, Bolt discovered. In effect, it requires a team of folders to work together as a giant hand, each one using his entire body as a finger.

See also SMALL-SCALE MODELS

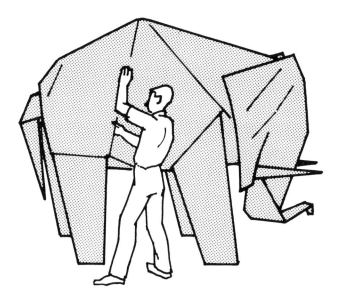

LAUNDRY FOLDING

There is a correct way to fold various garments during and after ironing, according to such sources as *The Art and Practice of Laundry Work* by M. C. Rankin, published by Blackie, probably during World War I. For example, whereas a plain handkerchief should be folded simply in half and in half again (as shown in fig. 1), a lace-trimmed handkerchief requires a final diagonal fold on the top layer (fig. 2) so that the trimming appears on all sides (fig. 3).

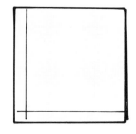

1

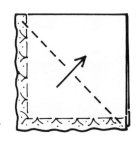

2

3

LEAF FOLDING

*I*t may be that people folded leaves in Japan at a time before paper was generally available. Certainly there is a long tradition among country people there of making simple playthings in this way. Here are two examples.

How to make a long-leaf boat ★

Use a long, tender leaf (Japanese children use bamboo). Do not remove the stalk.

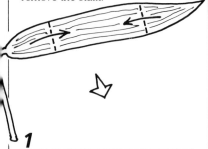

1

Fold in the two ends, towards the centre.

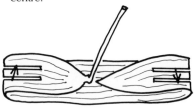

2

Make pairs of cuts or tears at each end to form three looped flaps. Lift the outer flaps and thread one through the other at each end in turn.

3

The leaf is raised into the form of a boat with a standing mast. Float in a running stream.

How to make a flower doll ★

Use a suitable wild flower and several tender leaves.

1

Fold the leaves in half by taking the top half and folding it down to the bottom half, in a valley fold.

2

Wrap one leaf, folded edge upwards, around the flower stem.

3

Overlap this with another leaf. Continue wrapping the leaves around the flower stem until you have something which looks rather like a figure wearing an elaborate Japanese dress. Pierce the stalk of the final leaf through its tip to hold the doll together.

LINDBERGH CASE

*B*ecause a banknote – part of the ransom money in the Lindbergh kidnapping case – had been folded in an unusual way (once lengthways and twice across), the filling station attendant who received it recalled who had given it to him and this led to the arrest, trial and execution of Bruno Hauptmann in 1936.

That, in brief, is the received account of the manhunt that followed one of America's most widely publicized crimes of this century. However, Anthony Scaduto, in *Scapegoat: The Truth about The Lindbergh Kidnapping* (Secker and Warburg, London, 1977), suggests that the folded money clue was not a pointer to Hauptmann's guilt but quite the reverse.

It is true, the author says, that during 1933 and 1934 ransom money folded once lengthways and twice across turned up in stores in the Bronx district of New York, and the police, believing they had discovered an idiosyncracy of the kidnapper, were on the look-out for such folded notes. But later, other notes from the ransom money were passed unfolded and it was one of these that led to Hauptmann's arrest.

Hauptmann maintained until the end that he was innocent of kidnapping and murder, that he had taken the incriminating money from a cardboard box which a friend had left with him for safekeeping and which he had only opened after the friend failed ▶

to return and reclaim it. He did not convince the jury with this story, but Scaduto's investigations have provided some very belated corroboration. He has shown that all the money that had been passed between the payment of the ransom money and the summer of 1934 (when Hauptmann claimed he had discovered the cache) without exception had been folded into eighths, but not one of the notes which Hauptmann was known to have passed was folded in this way.

LOIN CLOTH

A long scarf can be transformed into a loin cloth by folding it around yourself in the manner traditionally used by Japanese wrestlers. It is much easier, however, if you have someone to tie it for you.

How to make a loin cloth ★

Use a long scarf.

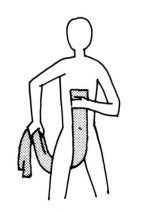

1

Hold one end of the scarf against the midriff and pass the other end between your legs.

2

Take the free end across behind you and then in front of you across the waist, and pass it through the loop already created. Pull tight.

3

(Back view) Tuck the free end around and around the waistband.

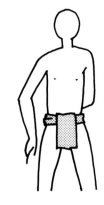

4

(Front view) Let the other end of the scarf drop to form an apron.

Japanese wrestlers wearing loin cloths
(left)

MAP FOLDING

What is believed to be the oldest folding map in existence can be seen in the City Museum, Milan. It dates from ancient Egyptian times, is drawn on papyrus and has a grid of cracks and creases across it which seems to indicate that it was originally folded in the way that maps have continued to be folded down the centuries.

Such folded maps, in which pleated folds cross others at right-angles, are always liable to tear with use. In recent years, attempts have been made to design folding maps which will not tear. Most notable among these is the Japanese Miura-ori map, which is distinguished by the fact that its crease lines are placed so that they are interdependent, one pushing against another. It can be unfolded in one movement and it suffers much less stress than a traditional map does. The principles behind this invention are described in an article in the *New Scientist,* 23rd October, 1980. It is not something which can be easily adapted for use by amateurs, however.

The simple map folding technique described below can be used by everyone. Adapted from small maps produced by a Dutch cartographic company, it, too, allows the folded item to be opened in one movement and collapsed instantly. The technique is particularly useful for folding a page of notes into an inconspicuous and convenient form. Shoppers can use it for their shopping lists; public speakers can fold their notes in this way and slip them into their pockets.

How to make a
map fold ★★

Use a rectangle of paper. First mark the vertical centre crease.

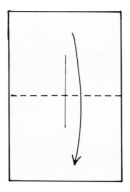

1

Fold the paper from the top to the bottom, in a valley fold.

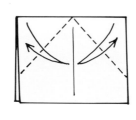

2

Fold the top corners down to the centre crease and return.

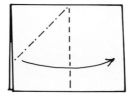

3

Squash fold the top left corner to the front and open it out.

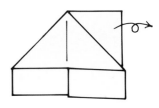

4

Now turn the paper over.

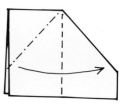

5

Squash fold the left corner again, and open it out.

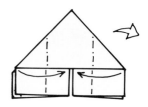

6

Inside reverse fold the uppermost left and right flaps so that the edges overlap at the centre. Repeat behind.

7

The completed map fold. Take hold of the front layer between the thumb and forefinger of one hand. Similarly, take hold of the rear layer and pull apart.

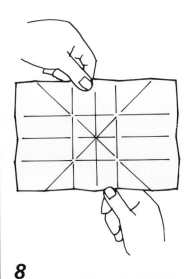

8

The opened map.

MIZUHIKI

Mizuhiki is coloured string, made of paper and stiffened with paste, which is used in Japan to tie up wrapped gifts or offerings on special occasions. The string may be coloured gold and silver (for wedding gifts), red and white (for other happy events) or black and white (for condolence offerings at funerals).

The string usually comes in bundles of five and is traditionally tied with a single-, double- or triple-looped knot. In recent decades, however, methods of tying mizuhiki have become much more elaborate. The illustration shows mizuhiki knotted and tied to represent a crane – a symbol of good fortune. The two knots form a head and body and the large loops form a tail.

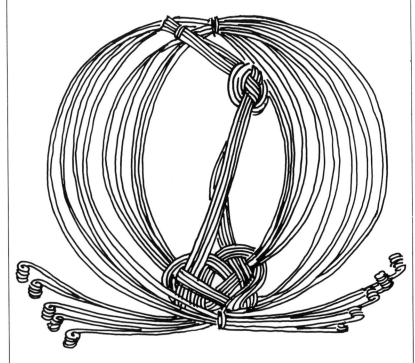

MOBILES

Origami models are particularly suited to the construction of mobiles, says American paperfolder Alice Gray, because they are so light that every breath of air sets them stirring, and they put no strain on lamp fixtures and other improvised supports.

The sort of models most appropriate to this treatment are representations of things that fly, float or swim naturally, but there is no reason why you should not try other subjects too. In addition to a number of models, you will need scissors, a needle and thread (heavy-duty nylon sewing thread is recommended, but nylon monofilament is stronger and you may want to use this for the upper part of a very large assembly), and light-weight rods (either fine bamboo slats, taken from an old mat perhaps, or wire, in which case you will need a cutting tool). A little glue is useful for sealing knots when you are quite sure that you have everything in the right place.

Writing in the spring of 1967 in *The Origamian,* the journal of the Origami Center of America, Alice Gray gave useful advice on mobile-making based on her own experience. The essence is balance, she says, and you achieve it by balancing each element in turn, from the bottom up, beginning with the individual models. In theory, each model must have a centre of gravity and a single thread attached at that point should suspend it in a balanced position. In practice, it is often difficult to find this point and it is simpler to attach two or three threads in places which allow you to control the attitude of the model. Adjust these several threads so that the model hangs properly and knot them together. Cut off all but one of the threads at the knot. For most models, threads 30cm (11¾in) long are ample.

When all your models are threaded and balanced, you will need somewhere to hang the completed elements of the mobile temporarily while you measure and adjust. One solution is to use a clothesline and pegs for this purpose.

Prepare your first rod and tie a short piece of thread to the middle of it; this should be tight enough to hold, but loose enough to allow you to slide it along the rod. Tie the thread of one model to each end of the rod, adjusting the relative lengths of the threads so that the relationship between the models is pleasing. Check that there is sufficient clearance between the models when they turn. Then slide the knot of the central thread along the rod until the models balance one another.

Make up as many pairs of models as you want in this way, attaching one rod to the next, reserving some models to be balanced singly against pairs, for variety. Avoid the temptation to make the structure absolutely symmetrical. An asymmetric mobile will generally look more attractive. Indeed, you can make a dramatic contrast between one element of a mobile and others. Imagine, for example, a single eagle circling around a flight of herons.

Finish the mobile with a loop of thread or a little wire hook (depending upon the available support) on which you can hang it.

Another idea, a very simple one, is to make a standing mobile of elements that will bend backwards and forwards rather than circle. For this you will need a block of polystyrene (of the kind often used as packing material) and rods similar to those described for the hanging mobile. Just mount the models on the rods and insert them into the block in a suitable arrangement. If the rods are supple enough, the models should sway in the wind.

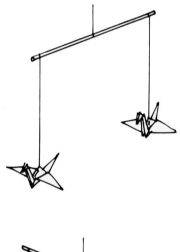

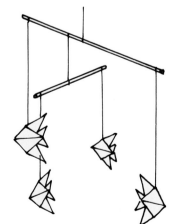

Antelope mobile (left and page 86)

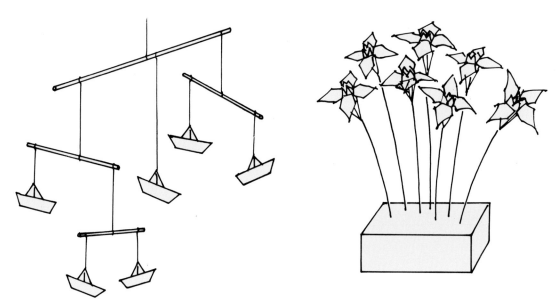

MODULAR ORIGAMI

Modular origami consists of folding several similar and comparatively simple shapes (modules) and fitting them all together to make a more complex construction. With a dozen or so modules, it is not too difficult to build a solid geometrical figure. This is a satisfying achievement, in spite of, or perhaps because of, the fact that you cannot always be sure what figure will result until all the pieces are fitted together. In the hands of a specialist, such as retired architect Norishige Terada of Osaka, it can also be the means of constructing authentic architectural models using many hundreds of sheets of paper.

Traditional examples of modular origami, such as the KUSUDAMA (page 95), may be glued together, but most modern paperfolders prefer their modular constructions to be held together by interlocking, if possible. The examples which follow are of the latter type.

Several books devoted to modular origami have appeared in Japan where it is more often called 'unit origami'. These include Kunihiko Kasahara's *Yunitto Origami to Yasashii Sakuhin* (Unit Origami and Easy Models), published by Subaru Shobo, Tokyo, in 1976. A smaller volume, *Atarashii Yunitto Origami* (New Unit Origami), by the same author, and Tomoko Fuse's *Yunitto Origami* (Unit Origami), was published by Chikuma Shobo, Tokyo, in 1983.

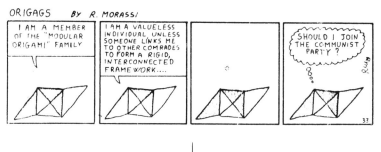

ORIGAGS   BY R. MORASSI

| I AM A MEMBER OF THE "MODULAR ORIGAMI" FAMILY | I AM A VALUELESS INDIVIDUAL UNLESS SOMEONE LINKS ME TO OTHER COMRADES TO FORM A RIGID, INTERCONNECTED FRAMEWORK.... | | SHOULD I JOIN THE COMMUNIST PARTY? |

How to make a

sunburst ★★

(David Collier)

Use eight small squares of coloured paper. Take one of the squares and fold two opposite edges together. Make a firm crease and open up. Place it coloured side upwards.

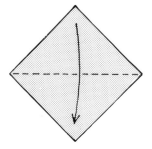

1

Fold the two opposite corners together in a valley fold.

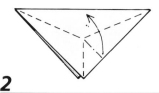

2

Rabbit-ear fold the upper layer of the folded triangle.

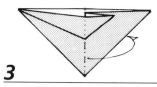

3

Mountain fold the paper in half, taking the right half behind, but leaving the flap in front.

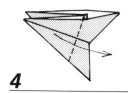

4

Bring the top left point down on a crease at right-angles to the folded edge of the rabbit-ear flap.

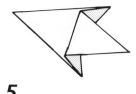

5

Turn the structure over.

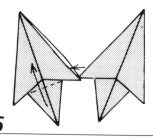

6

Repeat the above on the remaining squares to make a total of eight modules. Working on a flat surface, tuck the corner of one module into the side pocket of another, then fold up the bottom point.

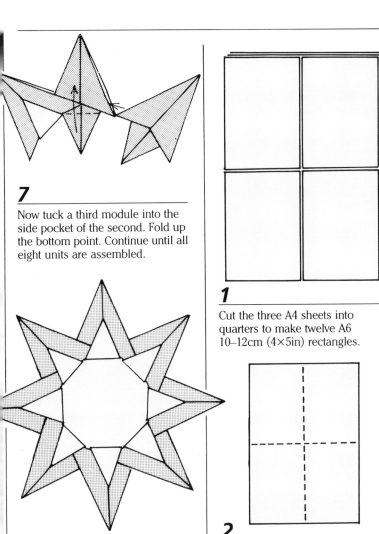

7

Now tuck a third module into the side pocket of the second. Fold up the bottom point. Continue until all eight units are assembled.

8

The completed sunburst.

How to make a dodecahedron★★

(Dave Brill)

Use three sheets of A4 paper.

1

Cut the three A4 sheets into quarters to make twelve A6 10–12cm (4×5in) rectangles.

2

Take one of the rectangles and crease the centre lines vertically and horizontally.

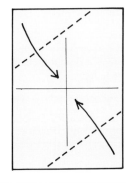

3

Fold in two opposite corners, in valley folds, so that they meet at the centre.

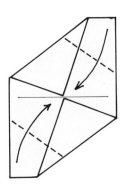

4

Fold the other two opposite corners to the centre, in the same way as above.

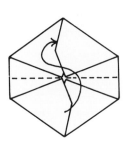

5

Fold the paper in half in a valley fold, interlocking the two inside flaps.

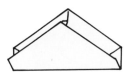

6

Flatten.

7

Fold point B in to the centre line so that AB is parallel to CD. ▶

Dodecahedrons (page 111)

dodecahedron continued

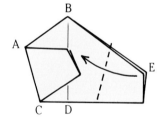

8

Fold point E in to the centre line overlapping the left flap.

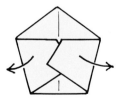

9

Then open the two flaps.

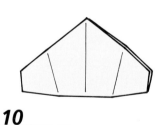

10

This will complete one module. Repeat steps 2–9 on the other eleven rectangles.

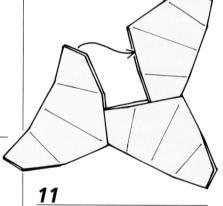

11

Take three modules and join them by tucking the flap of one into the pocket of the other (the diagram shows this in progress). When the third flap is tucked in, the form of the final structure will start to emerge. Make a total of four triple-module units by joining the others similarly.

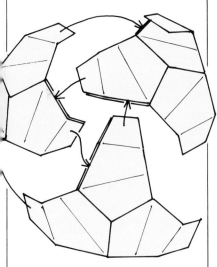

12

Link three triple-module units by tucking flaps into their pockets.

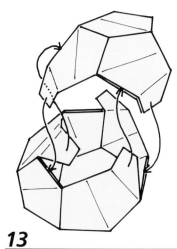

13

Add the remaining unit.

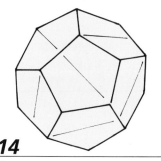

14

The completed dodecahedron.

MONEY FOLDING

Money folding is more popular in America then elsewhere, probably because all American banknotes, of whatever denomination, are of the same size, with sides in the ratio of 3:7. In Britain and elsewhere, banknotes change their shape over the years. This is not always a disadvantage, however. The English £1 note, until its demise, had sides in the ratio 1:2 (as near as made no difference) and so could be used for folding many standard 1:2 origami models. Norwegian 50 krone and 100 krone notes are almost square in shape.

Non-Americans who wish to fold designs intended for dollar bills, but who are without access to any, may like to note that they can obtain correctly proportioned material quite easily from A4 paper. Fold a short side to a long side, and cut along the horizontal edge. This produces two pieces of paper: the folded part, when opened, forms a square, and the remaining part is of dollar bill proportions.

The first collection of designs for folding money to appear in one volume was Al O'Hagan's *Bill Folds,* published by Snyder's Magic Shop, Cleveland, Ohio, in 1945. Subsequently Magic Inc., Chicago, published *The Folding Money Book* by Adolfo Cerceda in 1963, and *The Folding Money Book Vol. 2* by Samuel and Jean Randlett in 1968; these have recently been reprinted.

An international money-folding exhibition, which displayed designs submitted by enthusiasts from four continents, was held at the Central Bank and Trust Company of Lexington, Kentucky, in the autumn of 1980. This was the first exhibition of its kind.

How to create dollar bill-sized paper

Use a sheet of A4 paper.

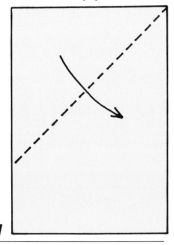

1

Fold a short side of the paper down to meet the edge of a long side.

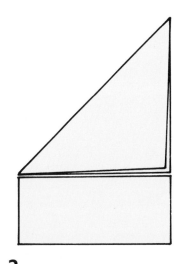

2

Cut along the newly created horizontal edge. The small rectangle will be of dollar bill proportions.

▶

113

How to make a portrait ring ★★

(Max Hulme)

Many foreign banknotes can be used to make portrait rings of famous characters from history or mythology. The first step provides margins for the top and bottom of the portrait (in some instances you need to mountain fold above, as well as below, the head), while those in step 2 provide margins at the sides of the portrait. The folding method shown below can be adapted easily to make a ring from a £10 note, which carries the portrait of Florence Nightingale.

Use an English £5 note with the portrait of the Duke of Wellington facing upwards (or any other note of your choice, see above).

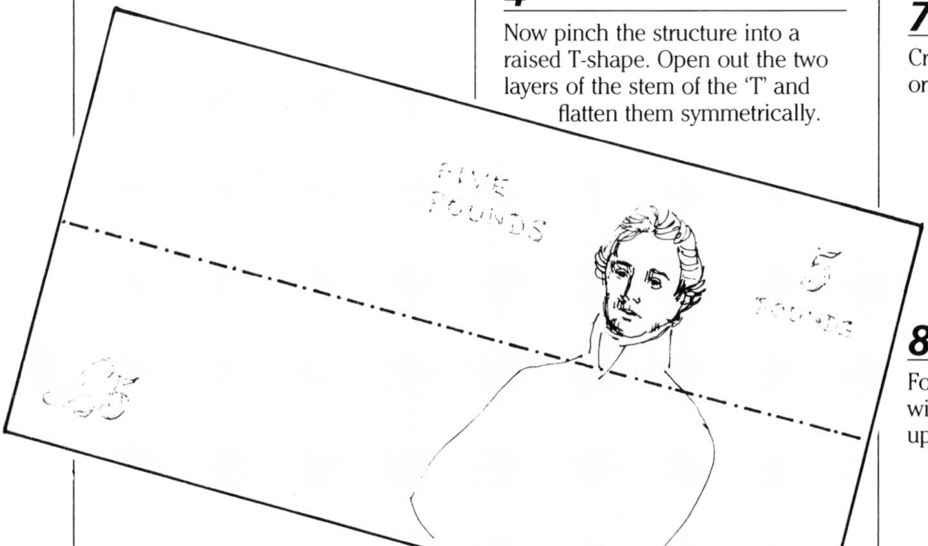

1

Mountain fold the note in half, tucking the top half down behind the bottom half.

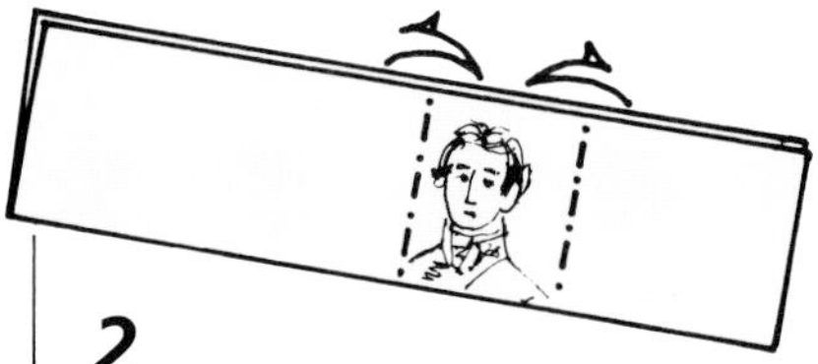

2

Make firm mountain folds on either side of the head, and return. Turn the paper over.

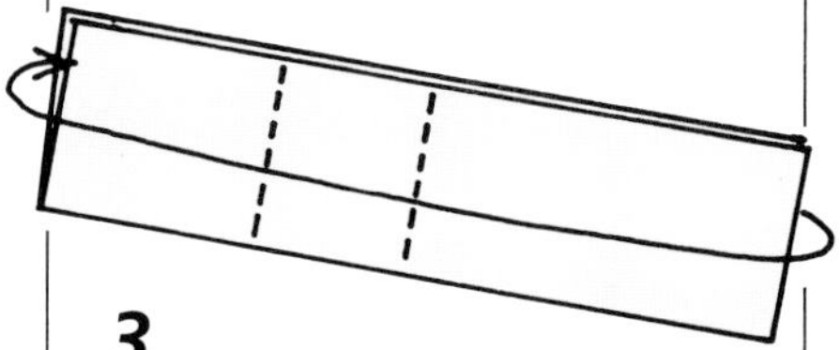

3

Take the right edge and tuck it right into the left edge.

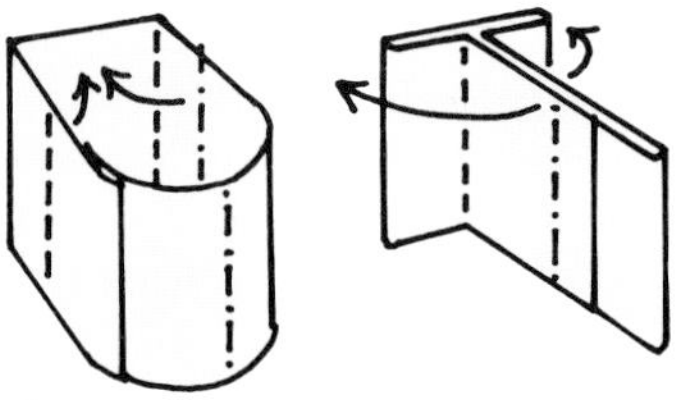

4

Now pinch the structure into a raised T-shape. Open out the two layers of the stem of the 'T' and flatten them symmetrically.

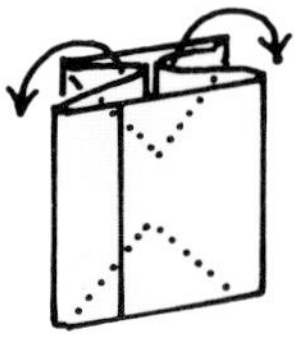

5

Make four inside reverse folds – two at the top and two at the bottom.

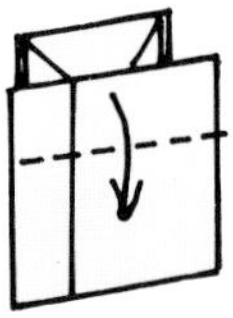

6

Fold the upper edge down in a valley fold, as far as it will go.

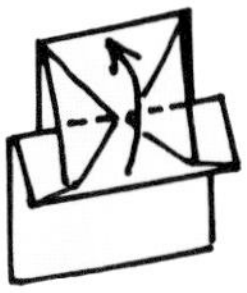

7

Crease the fold then return it to original position.

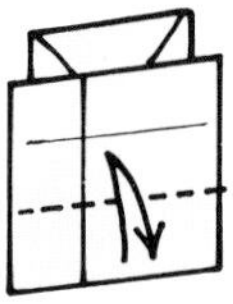

8

Fold the lower edge up as far as it will go. Crease and return. Open up the front flap.

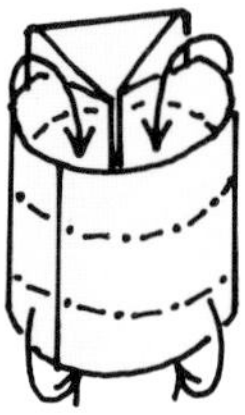

9

Mountain fold the upper and lower edges inwards to form the ring.

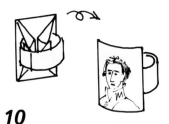

10

Turn over to produce the completed ring.

How to make a
Borgia ring ★★★
(Kenneth Kawamura)

Use a US dollar bill. First divide it into eighths lengthways.

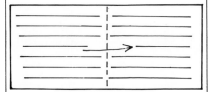

1

Fold it in half, joining the left edge to the right, in a valley fold.

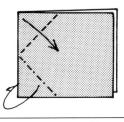

2

Valley and mountain fold the folded edge to the centre line, as shown.

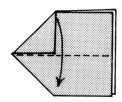

3

Fold in half, bringing the top edge down to the lower edge at the front. Take the bottom edge behind.

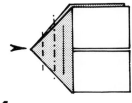

4

Double sink the left point.

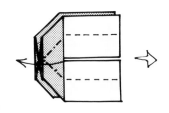

5

Take the raw edge of the left flap to the left, allowing the top and bottom edges to meet in a sort of petal fold. Repeat behind.

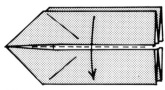

6

Fold down the top flap. Fold the bottom flap up behind the paper.

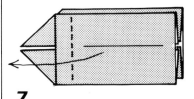

7

Fold the top flap to the left as far as it will go. Repeat behind.

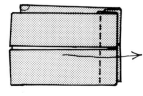

8

Fold the flaps to the right.

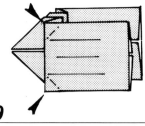

9

Inside reverse fold the top and bottom corners of the front folded edge. Repeat behind.

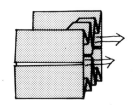

10

Fold the front flap to the left. Repeat behind.

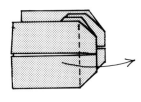

11

Pull out the raw edges and flatten them.

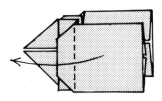

12

Fold the top flap to the right in a valley fold. Repeat behind.

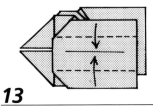

13

Fold the top and bottom edges of the front flap to the centre. Repeat behind. ▶

Borgia ring continued

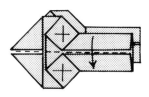

14

Bring the top flap down in front, to the bottom edge, and take the bottom flap up behind.

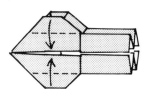

15

On the left, fold the top and bottom edges in so that they meet at the centre. Repeat behind.

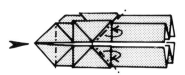

16

On the left, push in the point of the upper layer to make a pocket. Mountain fold the loose corners and tuck them in. Repeat behind.

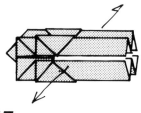

17

Open up the paper so that the pleated flaps on the right are brought into a new plane.

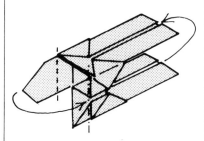

18

Curve the flaps on the right and tuck them into each other to form a ring. Tuck the point on the left into the pocket.

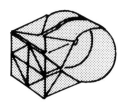

19

The completed Borgia ring. The front has four corner pockets which can be used to hold a miniature picture about 1.5cm (½in) square. Remove this and open up to reveal the 'secret' compartment inside.

*M*ULTI-PIECE MODELS

*W*hen several dissimilar types of units are assembled, the result is sometimes called a multi-piece model.

See MODULAR ORIGAMI.

How to make Bluebeard's Castle ★★★★

(Ed Sullivan)

This is made by assembling three types of folded unit: basic units (to build towers and walls), turret supports and roofs. Use squares of paper, all the same size and coloured the same on both sides. Select paper of one colour for the basic units and turret supports and paper of a contrasting colour for the roofs. Fold at least thirty basic units to build the framework of the castle first. Then add towers and turrets in any way which pleases you.

Basic unit
Use paper about 10cm (4in) square.

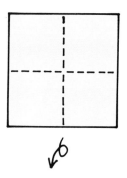

1

Fold the opposite edges together in turn in valley folds. Crease and open up. Turn the paper over. ▶

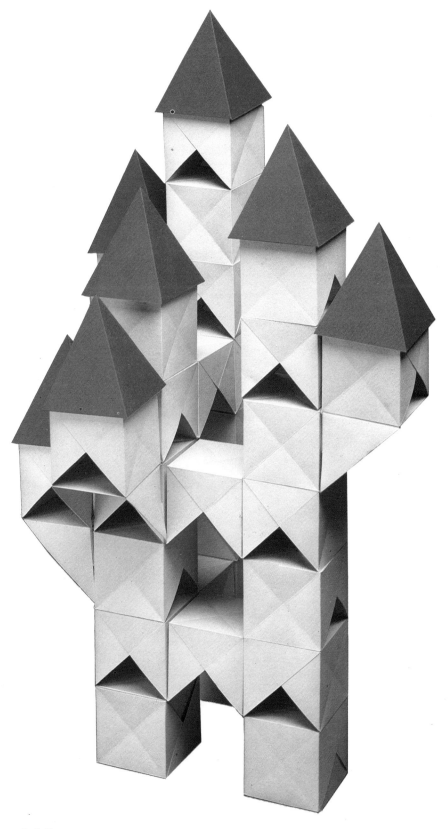

Bluebeard's castle (left)

Bluebeard's castle continued

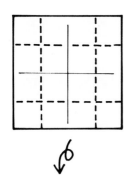

2

Fold each edge to the centre in turn, in valley folds. Crease and open up. Turn the paper over.

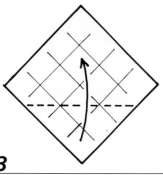

3

Fold up the bottom corner in a valley fold, to where the creases intersect at the top.

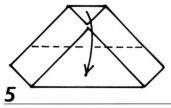

4

Fold the top corner down to meet it.

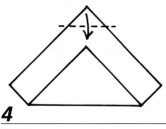

5

Bring the folded edges together, taking the edge down to the bottom edge.

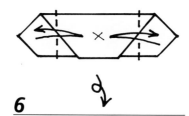

6

Fold the left and right corners to the centre, crease and return. Turn the paper over.

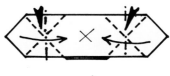

7

Press down on the centre of each vertical crease in turn as you bring the side corners in to the centre of the paper. This action allows a pair of inside reverse folds to form on each side.

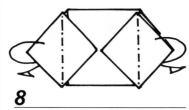

8

Mountain fold the left and right corners behind to the centre and return.

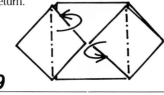

9

Tuck the left and right front corners behind the concealed vertical edges. Turn the paper over.

10

Raise the uppermost layer right up. As you do so, the ends will pull in.

11

Pull on the flap inside to raise the inside layer.

12

Pinch the corners to make a neat box-like form. Mountain fold the front triangular flap into the box. This completes one basic unit.

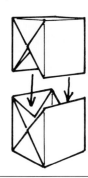

13

Slide one basic unit into another to make a block for the base of a tower.

14

To build a tower, pull out the two triangular flaps from a third unit; tuck them into the side pockets of the base block.

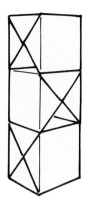

15

Continue building the tower with more units, by tucking their flaps into the pockets.

Turret support
Use paper about 10cm (4in) square. Complete steps 1–8 of the basic unit.

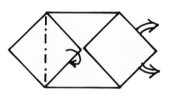

1

Tuck one of the front corners behind the concealed vertical edges. Open up the other end.

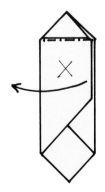

2

(New position) Take the front flap across to the left, allowing the top point to flatten.

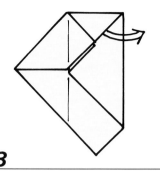

3

Take the right-hand flap and open it to the right.

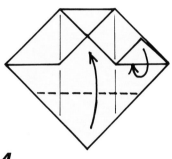

4

Mountain fold the little triangular flap on the right and tuck it into the model. Fold up the bottom point.

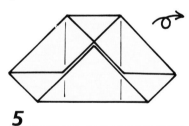

5

Turn the paper over.

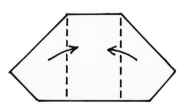

6

Fold up the sides so that they are at right-angles to the base.

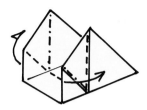

7

Swivel fold the front edge to raise it into a new plane. Triangular flaps will form on the left and right.

8

Turn the model upside down. Raise the little flap at the top. Open the paper on the far side.

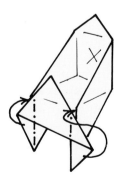

9

Mountain fold and tuck in the side flaps. Refold the paper that you opened in step 8 to complete a turret support. ▶

Bluebeard's castle continued

10

To join it to a tower, fold down the top triangular flap and tuck it into the pocket of one of the basic units that forms the tower.

Roof
Use paper 10cm (4in) square. First make the diagonal crease.

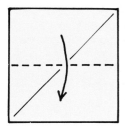

1

Fold the paper in half from top to bottom, in a valley fold.

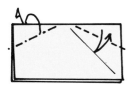

2

Valley fold the top right edge to the existing crease line on the right. Mountain fold the top left edge behind to the existing crease line on the left. Then open up the paper.

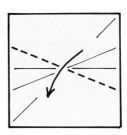

3

Refold the paper on the existing diagonal crease line, as shown.

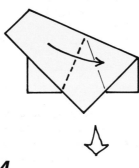

4

Fold the paper in half, bringing the outer corners together, as illustrated.

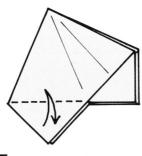

5

Fold up both layers of the bottom triangular area, and return.

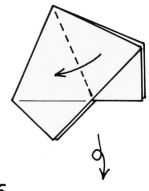

6

Fold the uppermost right flap to the left in a valley fold. Turn the paper over.

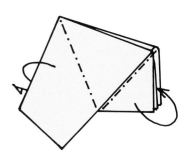

7

There are now three layers of triangular flaps on the bottom right. Tuck the front two back into the rear pocket. Mountain fold the left section, make a firm crease and return.

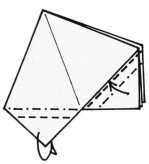

8

Form two pleats as shown. Tuck pleats into the pockets so that little triangular flaps project.

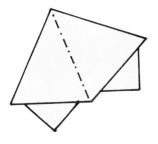

9

Separate the layers at bottom to raise the form.

10

The completed roof. When assembling the structure, tuck the triangular flaps into the side pockets of a basic unit.

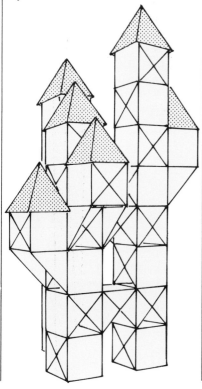

NAPKIN FOLDING

*I*f table napkins are folded into decorative shapes, then the meal is marked as a special occasion. Many people think so, and there is some evidence that the ancient art of napkin folding, which fell into neglect between the wars with the decline in domestic service and the fashion for understatement, is now enjoying a revival.

Napkins were first folded decoratively in the princely palaces of Renaissance Italy, and the first book to contain illustrations of them was Matthia Geiger's *Li Tre Trattati*, published in Italy in 1629. The designs therein are elaborately pleated treatments of difficult subjects, such as double-headed eagles and three-masted yachts in full sail, and one cannot easily imagine how to reproduce them. The first English reference appears in a treatise by Giles Rose: *Perfect School of Instructions for Officers of the Mouth* (1682), which contained advice directed at the banqueting staff at the court of King Charles II. Here, too, the designs are virtually impossible to reproduce.

Folded napkins started to decorate the tables of middle-class families in the nineteenth century, and Mrs Beeton included a section of designs in an edition of her *Household Management*, which appeared in the 1880s. The designs she favoured were still quite elaborate but less so than those of the seventeenth century. Today, it is considered unhygienic to handle napkins overmuch and simple designs are usually preferred.

Recent publications include Linda Hertzer's *Fancy Folds*, Hearst Books, 1980, which contains ninety-four designs; this book is the most comprehensive guide to the subject. James Ginder's *A Guide to Napkin Folding*, Northwood Publications, reprinted in 1980, contains forty-four designs and is used as a text-book by the catering trade. Lillian Oppenheimer and Natalie Epstein's *Decorative Napkin Folding for Beginners*, Dover Publications, 1979, contains twenty-two well-taught designs and many full-page colour plates.

Here are three simple napkin folds for you to try. Either cloth or paper napkins may be used, but remember that a cloth napkin must be sufficiently starched for it to retain the creases that are put into it. The first of the folds, often known as a mitre, functions as a receptacle for bread rolls or Melba toast. The second fold, the fan, is included simply for its decorative effect. The third, the buffet server, is designed to hold cutlery and is particularly useful for self-service parties.

▶

How to make a
mitre ★

Start with the napkin folded in half, with the folded edge at the top.

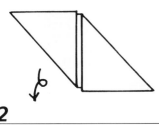

1

Fold the bottom left corner up to the top centre. Fold the top right corner down to the bottom centre.

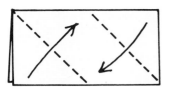

2

Turn the napkin over and rotate it.

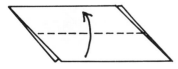

3

Fold up the bottom edge to the top in a valley fold.

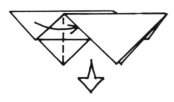

4

Fold the left point in and tuck it under the right flap.

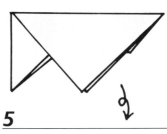

5

Turn the napkin over.

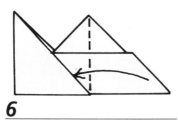

6

Fold the right point in a valley fold, and tuck it under the left flap.

7

Open out the structure slightly to form a container for rolls or toast.

How to make a
fan ★

Start with the napkin folded into quarters. Arrange as shown.

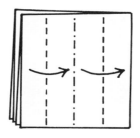

1

Pleat the upper doubled layer, as indicated.

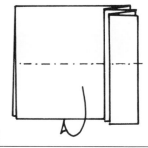

2

Mountain fold the napkin in half, taking the bottom half back behind the napkin.

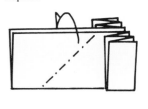

3

Mountain fold the left edge back and down.

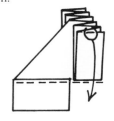

4

Take hold of the top edge of the front pleat; pull it forward and down through 180°.

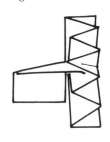

5

The pleats will fan out, like this.

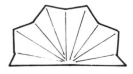

6

The completed fan (front view).

How to make a
buffet server ★

Start with the napkin folded into quarters. Arrange as shown.

1

Fold the napkin diagonally in half, in a valley fold. Make a firm crease and return.

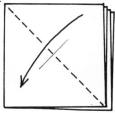

2

Fold the top left corner of the upper layer down to the bottom right corner.

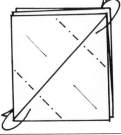

3

Mountain fold the two corners behind to the centre. Rotate the napkin.

4

The completed buffet server. Use the front pocket to hold cutlery.

NAPPY FOLDING

*I*n continental Europe, disposable nappies have taken over from the traditional sort – all Swedish mothers use them, as do at least four out of five mothers in France and West Germany. But some mothers still prefer the traditional squares of white towelling; they consider them to be both cheaper and more absorbent.

Although they have remained faithful to the traditional nappy, these same mothers have, for the most part, given little thought to the many alternative ways in which a nappy could be folded around a baby. A nappy suitable for a boy will not necessarily suit a girl, and a nappy suitable for young babies may not suit them when they have grown bigger and become more active. Here are three possibilities to consider.

How to fold a
nappy ★

Dr Spock's Method
Dr Spock introduces a simple nappy fold (in his *Baby and Child Care*, Bodley Head, 1969), half of which has three layers and the other half six layers. 'A boy needs the double thickness in front; a girl needs the thickness in front if she lies on her abdomen, at the back if she lies on her back,' says Dr Spock. The nappy needs to be fastened with a pin at either side.

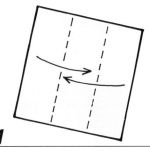

1

Fold the nappy into thirds, as indicated.

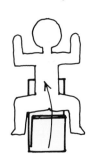

2

For a boy, fold up the cloth about one third from the bottom. For a girl, fold down the top third.

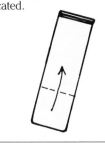

3

Place the baby on the nappy and bring the lower edge up between its legs.

4

Pin the nappy at the sides. ▶

nappy folding continued

German Pinless Method
German mothers have expressed shock and surprise that mothers in other countries should fasten their babies' nappies with pins, says Marlene Stroud. They consider it to be a dangerous practice. In Germany, the traditional method is to wrap the nappy in such a way that pins become unnecessary.

First fold the nappy in half diagonally. Place the baby on the nappy.

1

Bring the right point down across the baby's thigh and tuck it in under the baby's leg.

2

Bring up the bottom point.

3

Hold it in place then bring the left point across and tuck it under the fold on the right.

4

The completed nappy fold.

Japanese 'Origami' Method
Japanese mothers have a slightly more complex nappy folding method, one which is clearly related to origami techniques, says Toshie Takahama. Because the folding reduces the nappy to a comparatively small shape, it is suitable for younger babies only. This nappy fold provides seven or eight layers where the thickness counts – more than any other method.

First fold the nappy into a waterbomb base (page 22).

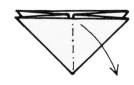

1

Pull the centre of the upper edge down to the right, in a mountain fold.

2

Pleat the two layers of the square flap together as indicated.

3

Place the baby on the nappy as it is shown here.

4

Fold the three corners in front of the baby's stomach.

5

Pin the nappy at the front.

NEWSPAPER FOLDING

Most homes have an untapped supply of folding material in the form of old newspapers – suitable, of course, for making practical items rather than decorative objects. For more things to fold from newspaper, see BANGERS and HATS.

How to make a
pair of slippers ★★★

Use two double-page sheets from a large-size (broadsheet) newspaper.

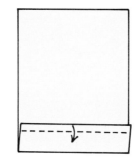

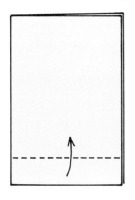

1

Take one double page, still folded, and fold up the bottom edge so that it lies somewhere below the centre.

2

Fold down three or four centimetres (one to one-and-a-half inches) of the same edge to form a hem. Turn the paper over.

3

Fold the left edge across on a line one-third of the way from the left. ▶

Pair of newspaper slippers (above)

slippers continued

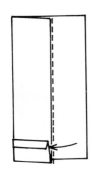

4

Fold the right edge similarly to the left, tucking the bottom corner into the left flap.

5

(Detail) Lift the hem behind the front hems over the front section.

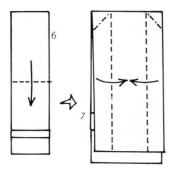

6

Fold the top edge down so that it lies somewhere above the bottom edge.

7

Fold the left and right edges of the front flap towards the centre, squash folding the top corners.

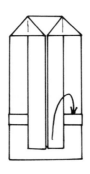

8

Tuck the bottom of the front flap into the pocket behind it.

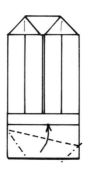

9

Fold up the bottom edge at an angle, like this, squash folding the corners on the left and right. Tuck the paper under the hem.

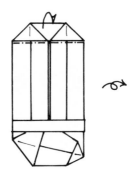

10

Mountain fold the paper at the top and turn the structure over.

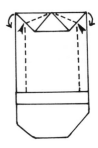

11

Fold the sides and raise them. Form the heel by bringing the two top corners forward in turn.

12

Bring the top layer of each flap down, push against the inner edge with your thumbs as if to turn the corner inside out.

13

(Detail) The heel of one slipper (for the left foot) completed. Make a slipper for the right foot by completing steps 1–8, then in step 9 form a mirror image of the folds shown here, and finally complete steps 10–13.

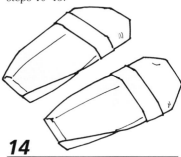

14

The completed pair of slippers.

NO-SEW CUSHION COVERS

The American magazine *Women's Day* carried an item on making cushion covers in September, 1974. The designs, one for a square cushion and one for a round one, appear to be based on traditional origami designs, using felt instead of paper as the material, and knotting threads to hold the folds in place. These two projects illustrate yet another way in which traditional origami can be adapted to modern living.

How to make a square cushion cover ★★

3

Bring the pairs of opposite corners together in turn and knot them in the centre.

4

The completed cushion cover.

1

Measure around the cushion to be covered, starting and ending at the centre of one side, to find the full girth. Using this measurement as the length of one side, mark and cut a square from the felt. With a needle, tie eight pieces of strong thread, about 20cm (8in) long, to points around the square – one at each corner and one at the centre of each edge. Place the cushion in the centre of the square. Bring the two pairs of opposite edge threads together in turn and knot them.

2

Pull the four corners of the square outwards and arrange them to make the sails of a windmill. Turn the cushion over.

Round cushion cover ★★

1

Measure from the centre of one side of the cushion to the centre of the other. Using this as your radius, draw a circle on the felt with an improvised pair of compasses. These can be made by tying a pencil to a pin with a length of string cut to 5cm (2in) longer than the radius of the circle. Holding the pin upright and steady on the fabric, carefully draw a circle to the full extent of the string. Cut out the circle.

▶

*round cushion cover
continued*

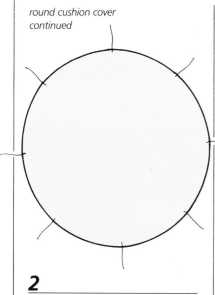

2

Fold the circle in half and, with a needle, tie a piece of strong thread, about 20cm (8in) long to either end of the fold. Unfold and refold at right-angles to the first fold so that the two threads come together. Tie a piece of strong thread to either end of this new fold. Unfold and refold twice more to divide the circumference into eighths, tying threads to either end of the fold in each instance. You should now have eight threads tied to the circle equidistantly around the circumference.

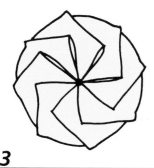

3

Place the cushion in the centre of the circle. Bring any two opposite threads together and knot them. Next, bring together and knot the pair of threads that lie at right-angles to the first pair. Then knot the remaining two pairs. Arrange the folds neatly to complete.

NOSHI

Japanese people customarily attach a little open-ended wrapper which contains an exposed strip of yellowish material, a few centimetres (just over an inch) long, to the top right corner of any special gift. These symbolic objects are called *noshi*, but their full name is *noshi-zutsumi*, the latter part of the word meaning 'wrapper'. The most common explanation of their use is that it derives from the thousand-year-old practice of adding some kind of raw fish or game to a gift to signify its freshness and, by implication, freedom from spiritual impurities.

Gradually the fish was replaced with abalone or sea ear and by the twelfth century this was stretched and dried and the number of strands reduced. Very finely sliced whale meat was also widely used. But in modern times, a synthetic paper-like substitute replaces any real foodstuff. In fact, the contents of the wrapper gradually lost importance over the centuries and the wrapper itself, in one of its prescribed forms, took on the significance.

Noshi wrappers which resemble those seen today were already in use by the latter part of the twelfth century, and standardized folding methods had become firmly established by the fourteenth century. In essence, the folding methods consist of laying together two sheets of paper, one red and one white, taking opposite corners across each other, turning them outwards and pleating them once or twice at prescribed angles. In fact, a modern Japanese is less likely to fold a *noshi* himself than to buy one in a shop or department store where they can be obtained complete with knotted *mizuhiki* (see page 107). They may also use a wrapping paper on which the wrappers appear in printed form.

For more about this type of origami, see Isao Honda's *Noshi: Classic Origami in Japan*, Japan Publications, Tokyo, 1964.

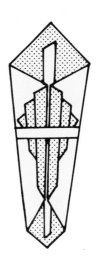

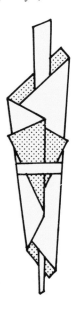

Tato (page 167)

OFFSET-CENTRE BASES

*I*f you displace or offset the centre point of one of the classic bases, you can fold a structure with flaps of unequal length, and by varying the degree of offset, you can create flaps of different proportions. This is something which readers who want to fold creatively may like to bear in mind. For example, American paperfolder James Sakoda folds the traditional crane (page 156) from an offset-centre bird base which, he believes, has the effect of giving the crane more pleasing proportions.

The accompanying illustrations show a preliminary base in which the centre has been offset to a point one quarter of the way down the vertical centre line. The resultant form, with a small flap at the top and a much larger flap behind and extending below, can be developed into stylized human figures.

How to make an
offset-centre preliminary base

Use a square of paper. Start by making the centre diagonal crease and mark the centre point.

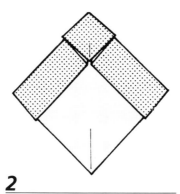

2

The completed offset-centre preliminary base.

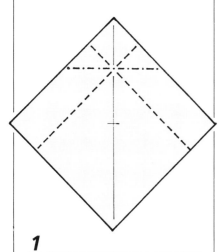

1

Fold the top left and right edges in turn to the centre point and return. Mountain fold the top point behind to the centre and return. Press against the point where the crease lines intersect, and bring down the top point to the centre in front this time. Allow the folds to re-form.

ONE-FOLD ORIGAMI

*I*t is interesting to consider what can be achieved by placing just one fold in a sheet of paper. As the following two models demonstrate, it is possible to make both an action model and a sound-producing model by employing this minimal method. It proves that you do not necessarily have to struggle with complex procedures to create interesting origami.

How to make a
flapping bird ★
(Ricky Wong)

Use either a square or rectangle of thin paper.

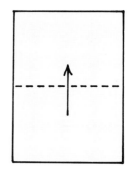

1

Fold the paper in half, taking the bottom edge up to the top in a valley fold.

2

Open; push up against the fold to 'break' it, at a point about one third along its length.

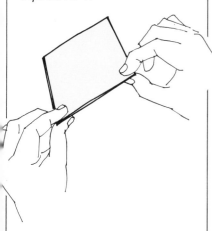

3

The completed bird. Hold the two layers of paper at each end above the fold between your forefinger and thumb. Pull and lift, bringing your forearms in to play, to make the wings flap.

How to make a squeaker ★

Use either a square or rectangle of paper. Fold the paper in half. Hold the paper with the folded edge at one side and separate the near edges very slightly by moving your finger. Place your lips lightly to these edges and blow. This should result in a loud squeak.

ORIGAMI

Origami may have a long history but the word itself is comparatively modern. Contrived from the root of the Japanese verb *oru*, 'to fold' and *kami*, 'paper', it was introduced into the Japanese language by Mr S. Konishi of Ochanomizu Kindergarten in 1880, according to Sumiko Momotani. Before then, alternative words such as *orikata* and *orisue* were used.

Origami became recognized as a part of American English when it was given an entry in the 1961 edition of Webster's Dictionary. After the English publication of books by Robert Harbin and Samuel Randlett in 1963, which contained 'origami' in the titles, the word soon became accepted as part of the Queen's English, too. Since then it has been adopted into other European languages. But French paperfolders remain resistant to its use, preferring their own *pliage de papier*, and Spanish paperfolders continue to use the word *papiroflexia*, a word coined by Vicente Solorzano Sagredo.

ORIGAMIANS and ORIGAMISTS

When Lillian Oppenheimer founded the New York Origami Center (now the Origami Center of America), in 1958, and wanted a title for the Center's journal, she chose *The Origamian* because the name was redolent of the distinguished American newspaper *The Oregonian.* The result, unanticipated by her, was that readers of the journal started to call themselves, and other paperfolders, 'origamians'. The word persists in the origami community, although it now has to compete with a rival English coinage 'origamist'. I prefer to avoid both.

Pajarita (page 134)

*P*AJARITA

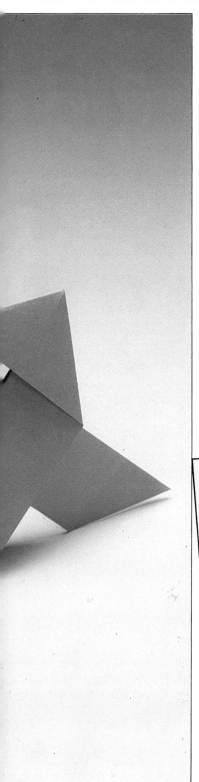

*P*ajarita is Spanish for 'little bird'. It is also the word that Spaniards use for folded paper models in general. Most Spanish people regard folding paper as synonymous with making little paper birds because this is something that nearly all of them learn to do as children. The fold they learn is the traditional 'pajarita' shown below.

The model may have originated in Spain but it is known throughout Europe. In France, Emile Zola coined the expression *'faire des cocottes à longeur de journée'* to describe the work of people employed in government offices. The hens he accused them of making all day were folded paper hens – in fact, the same traditional model that Spanish children fold.

To many German children it is known as a crow, although it sometimes also serves as a horse in their play. In Britain it used to be called a hobby-horse, but it is no longer widely known and seems never to have won children's affection to the extent that it has in France and Spain – countries where the little paper bird is recognized as a symbol of childhood. Indeed, there is an old-established sweet shop called 'La Pajarita' in Madrid which sells pajarita-shaped chocolates, and in the northern Spanish town of Huesca, there is a monument to the pajarita in a local park.

Vicente Palacios devotes sixteen pages to methods of folding the pajarita in his *La Creacion en Papiroflexia*, Miguel A. Salvatella, Barcelona, 1979. In an earlier book, *Papirogami* (1972), the same writer lists references to the bird in Spanish literature, which he has traced back to 1793.

▶

How to make a

pajarita ★★

Use a square of paper. Start by creasing the vertical centre line and marking its centre.

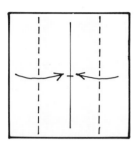

1

Fold the left and right edges in to the centre line, in valley folds.

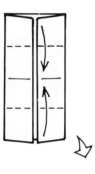

2

Fold in the top and bottom edges so that they meet at the centre.

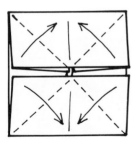

3

Fold the corners of the front top flap to centre top, and the corners of the front bottom flap to centre bottom.

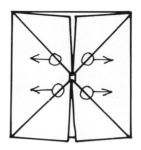

4

Take hold of the sides of the triangular flaps in turn, freeing the outer layers from the inner layers and pulling the points outwards.

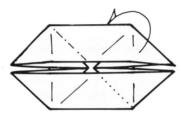

5

Now mountain fold the top half diagonally letting the points swing into position.

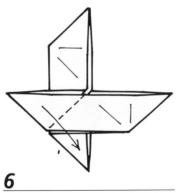

6

Fold down the left flap.

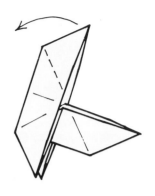

7

Outside reverse fold the top point. Open the model partially, separating the two layers of the top flap so that the point can be taken to the left.

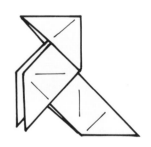

8

The completed pajarita.

TRADITIONAL TOYS FROM THE PAJARITA

Step 5 of the pajarita, shown here as fig. 1, can be treated as a base. In fact, if you squash fold the four front flaps so that the corners of the paper meet in the centre, the result is a multiple of four pre-liminary bases which is sometimes known as the windmill base.

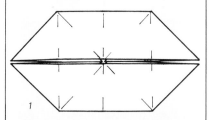

1

The windmill which is commonly developed from this base is shown in fig. 2. If it is constructed from stiff paper and pinned to a stick, it can be made to spin when caught by a breeze. When the base is turned over and all four flaps are extended, it can be made into a table (fig. 3).

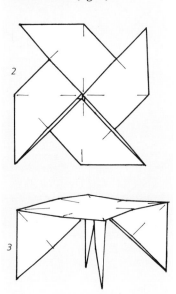

*P*APER

You can go a long way in origami without recourse to any special or exotic papers. The most useful thing to say about paper is: just make sure you have plenty of it.

However, it is convenient, though not essential, to have some ready-cut squares of paper always to hand. Such paper, brightly coloured on one side and white on the other, packaged and sold as 'origami paper', can be obtained from the suppliers listed on page 00. They can sometimes also be found in art and craft shops, stationery shops, toy shops and oriental gift shops. 12cm (5in) and 15cm (6in) squares are the most common sizes, but smaller and larger sizes are also available.

Try using some of the various kinds of notepaper which are manufactured in all sorts of colours nowadays. As a general rule, the lighter, thinner papers – even airmail paper – are more suitable for folding than the heavier ones; flimsy paper becomes quite rigid once a few folds have been placed in it.

On the other hand, heavy papers such as cover paper have a place, too, and they are particularly suitable for making com-paratively simple large-scale models. They can be obtained from art and craft shops as can, in many instances, surface papers, flint papers and poster papers, all of which are coloured on one side only and are sold in single sheets about 50×75cm (20×30in). Plain brown wrapping paper, as well as fancy wrapping paper, which can be found in many corner shops, should not be over-looked. If you intend using much of these larger sheets of paper, you should consider buying a cutter and metal rule, or perhaps a guillotine.

Other types of paper are discussed, in relation to folding, throughout the book. See FOIL, ITAJIME-SHIBORI, LAMINATING PAPER, MONEY FOLDING, NAPKIN FOLDING, NEWSPAPER FOLD-ING, PRINTED PAPER FOLDING, TISSUE FOLDING and WASHI.

PERFORMANCE ART

'*P*erformance art' is a term currently used in the art world to describe artistic experiments which involve human activities that cannot be fitted comfortably into the established categories of dance, music, drama and so on. Characteristic of much performance art is the involvement of the audience in the creative process.

It is doubtful whether many teachers and demonstrators of origami consider themselves to be engaging in performance art, but American writer Samuel Randlett has described it as such, and in England, Paul Jackson has presented it as such (see BANGERS). In France, where Jean-Claude Correia has referred to 'the choreography of paperfolding', the treatment of origami as performance art is much more common; the Mouvement Français des Plieurs de Papier has instigated several attempts at demonstrating origami in ways other than a simple exposition of how a model is constructed, employing light and sound effects.

PICTORIAL ORIGAMI

*S*ome people like to create montages, or pictures of origami, by mounting models, suitably arranged, onto paper or card. This is rather like painting with origami, using models as areas of colour. You could try making wall decorations in this way, or greeting cards.

An entirely different approach to pictorial origami has been developed by Bob Allen, one which is more comparable to drawing than painting. By 'drawing' with folded edges of paper he creates original, highly stylized, linear landscapes, one of which is described below.

How to make a seagull and surf ★★★
(Bob Allen)

Use a rectangle of white or lightly tinted stationery paper. Start by dividing the width into thirds and marking the creases.

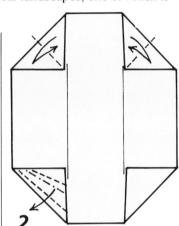

2

At the top, bisect the two corners by folding them in valley folds, and return. At the bottom left, double swivel the point down, as illustrated.

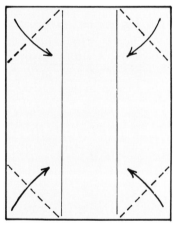

1

Fold in the top and bottom corners to the one-third lines.

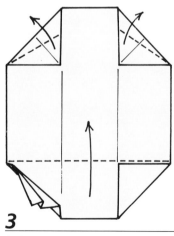

3

At the top, fold up the two corners at an angle of about 30° from the folded edge. Fold up the bottom edge along the raw edge of the right flap. ▶

Seagull and surf (left)

seagull and surf continued

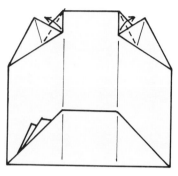

4

Make two folds at the top – each fold lies between the base of an existing crease and one end of the top edge.

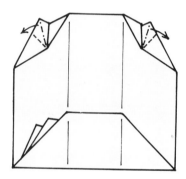

5

Turn the existing crease lines on each of the top flaps into mountain folds. Pull the points down.

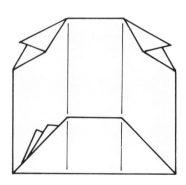

6

Flatten the paper.

7

(Detail of top right corner) Squash fold the pointed flap and open it right out.

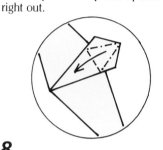

8

Petal fold the flap by folding back the two corners in mountain folds, and then folding the top point down, as indicated.

9

Fold up the point in a valley fold, on a line between the two corners of the flap.

10

Turn the paper over.

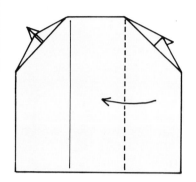

11

Fold the right edge across to the left on the existing crease line.

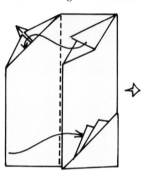

12

Fold the left edge to the right, tucking the bottom left corner into the bottom right pocket and hooking the flap above into the pocket on the left.

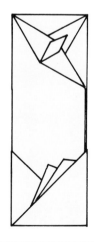

13

The completed panel.

PICTURE FRAME

*U*nlike many methods of folding origami picture frames, the following can be adapted easily to frame a picture of any reasonable size and proportions. For a photograph about 8×12cm (3×5in), use an A4 sheet of writing paper or similar. Start by making the vertical centre crease.

How to make a

picture frame ★★★
(Larry Hart)

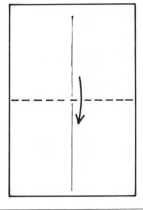

1

Fold the paper in half, taking the top edge down to the bottom edge.

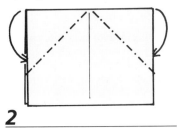

2

Inside reverse fold the two corners of the folded edge to the vertical centre line.

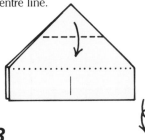

3

Fold the top point down to where the corners are concealed, then turn the paper over.

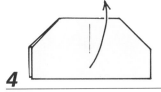

4

Lift the front edge right up.

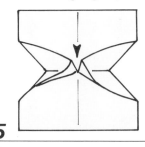

5

The two inside flaps will start to rise. Flatten the folded edge of each flap to form squash folds.

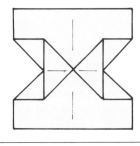

6

Place the picture in the centre of the inner square.

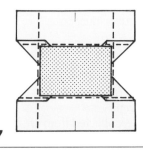

7

To establish the inner limits of the frame, fold all the edges of the paper in turn over the picture and return. Put the picture aside.

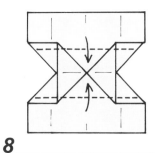

8

Refold the top and bottom edges of the frame on the crease lines just made.

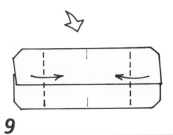

9

Refold the left and right edges similarly.

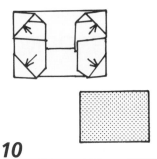

10

Tuck the corners of the picture into the four corner pockets of the frame to complete.

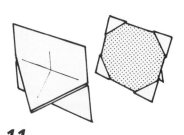

11

Adjust the large flap behind so that the framed picture can be made to stand on a desk-top or dressing table.

▶

Talking foxes (below)

PLAYGROUND FOLDS

*E*nglish paperfolder Dave Brill has observed that there are certain types of model which might be classified as 'playground folds'. They are models which have not appeared in books – at least not in any of those known to the origami world – and yet they are known to children who show each other how to make them. Eventually a child will introduce one of them to an adult origami enthusiast who will consider it worth recording.

Some models, such as the salt cellar construction (page 153) and the waterbomb (page 184) may be taught to children by adults, but surely not some of the uses to which children put them. Such interpretations of well-known models must be considered as part of this tradition.

A playground fold may appear naive. It may be constructed in breach of the rules, happily including cuts and tears, which some devotees of pure origami will deplore. But if it is an action model with an unusual effect, as it often is, it will probably excite sufficient admiration for its faults to be forgiven.

Three examples follow. The talking fox was collected from an eight-year-old French boy who learnt it from his school friends in Paris. The camera (which looks nothing like a camera but certainly *sounds* like one) was collected from an eight-year-old Japanese girl in Tokyo. The crawling beetle was introduced to an English children's nurse by a Mauritian.

How to make a talking fox ★★
(collected by Julien Correia)

Use a rectangle of fairly thin paper (e.g. a page from a magazine). Start by cutting the rectangle into a square and a surplus strip. Find the centre of the square by folding.

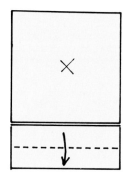

1

Fold the strip in half, lengthways, by taking the top edge down to the bottom edge.

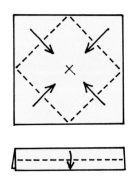

2

Fold the four corners of the square to the centre. Fold the strip in half again, from top to bottom.

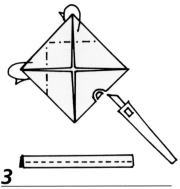

3

Mountain fold two adjacent corners of the square behind to the centre. Cut, or tear, a small hole in the opposite edge. Fold the strip in half for the last time.

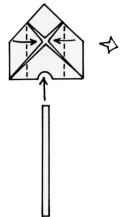

4

Insert the folded strip into the hole and push it inside right up to the opposite corner. Fold the two sides in to the centre.

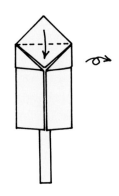

5

Fold down the top point (thereby also folding down the top of the strip inside). Turn the paper over.

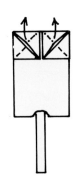

6

Lift the raw edges of the two little square flaps and squash fold.

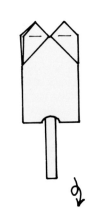

7

Turn the structure over.

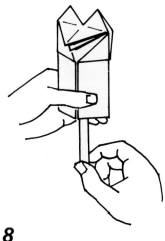

8

The completed talking fox. Hold the body with one hand and move the handle up and down with the other. The fox's jaw will open and close.

How to make a camera

(collected by Rika Taguchi)

Use a square of paper. Start by completing step 6 of Yakko-san (page 190).

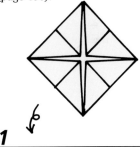

1

Turn the paper over.

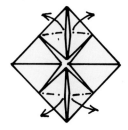

2

Separate the raw edges at the centre of the top and bottom flaps in turn, and squash fold them. ▶

141

camera continued

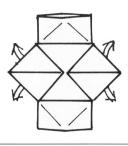

3

Open up the paper. (This completes a traditional figure sometimes called a Japanese lantern)

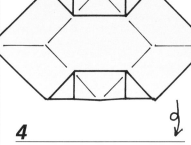

4

Continue opening the paper until it looks like this. Turn the paper over.

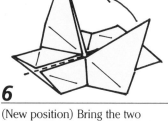

5

Pinch the left and right corners together to form 'rabbit ears'.

6

(New position) Bring the two standing flaps towards each other so that the two points cross over just a little.

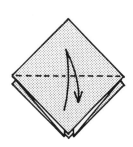

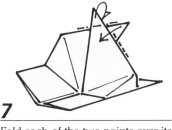

7

Fold each of the two points over its neighbouring edge to lock the model in this form.

8

The completed camera.

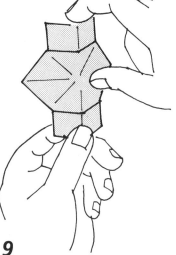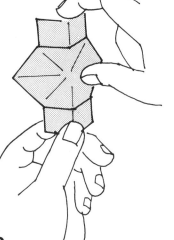

9

Hold as shown, with one thumb resting on the back of the camera at its centre. Raise and point the camera at your subject; press with your thumb and the two locked points should separate with a satisfying 'click!'. Some children like to conceal a tiny drawing, in the top of the camera, which can be produced as the photograph.

If your camera fails to click, it is most likely because you took the points too far across each other in step 6.

How to make a crawling beetle ★★

(collected by Fiona Caldwell)

Use a square of paper, preferably coloured. Start by completing the preliminary base (page 20).

1

Fold the bottom point up to the top point, and return. Repeat behind.

2

Fold the bottom point of the upper flap up to the newly-formed centre crease. Repeat behind.

3

Take the folded edge up to the centre crease and then fold it over again. Repeat behind.

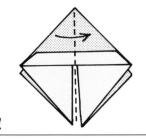

4

Take the uppermost left flap and fold it across to the right. Repeat behind.

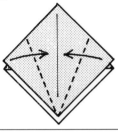

5

Fold the bottom left and right edges of the uppermost flaps to the vertical centre crease. Repeat behind.

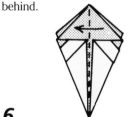

6

Take the uppermost right flap and fold it across to the left. Repeat behind.

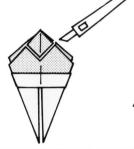

7

Remove the top point. You may cut neatly at right-angles to the outer edges (which makes a neat little preliminary base) or simply tear it off. This separated point is the beetle; the remaining structure is the track along which the beetle will crawl.

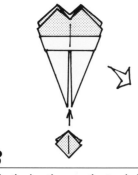

8

Slip the beetle onto the track. The pointed ends of the track should lie one on either side of the beetle's axis, between the triangular flaps.

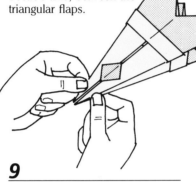

9

Take hold of the two points and agitate them by moving your hands back and forth rapidly. If you are doing it correctly (and you may not get it quite right immediately) the beetle will start to crawl along the track.

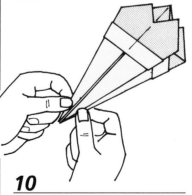

10

Keep on agitating the points and the beetle's route will take him 'under the carpet'. Watch the hole on the far side until you see him show his nose there and finally drop through.

*P*OSTAGE STAMPS

*F*or Christmas 1981, the Swedish Post Office issued a special stamp which featured a cut-out paper dove with a pleated paper tail. At the same time, the Post Office produced instruction leaflets which showed children how to make the dove depicted on the stamp. The bird in that design was only half origami, but the traditional paper crane (page 156) that appears regularly on Japanese 40 yen and 60 yen stamps, typifies origami.

Jennifer Toombs designed a set of four 'origami' stamps for the British Solomon Islands in 1974, the centenary year of the Universal Postal Union. In these stamps, the folded figures of a postman, a pigeon (pigeon mail was used between the Islands during World War II), the winged horse Pegasus, and Saint Gabriel (the patron saint of telecommunications and philately) are each depicted against a section of a map of the Islands.

For Christmas 1982, the same designer returned to origami sources to represent figures of Joseph, Mary and the Angel Gabriel in a set of three stamps issued by Christmas Island.

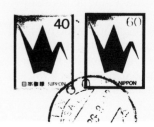

Picture frames (page 139)

FOLDING

*I*nstead of folding a bird from an ordinary sheet of plain or coloured paper, as most people would do, the late Guiseppe Baggi would fold one from a sheet of music and call it a 'song bird', and Canadian folder Gar Low once folded a snail from a postcard to express his opinion of the postal service.

This type of paperfolding, in which printed matter is exploited with amusing effect, is an interesting genre. Many examples of money folding belong to it. You do not need unusual folding skill to succeed in it, just an ability to recognize printed matter which will lend itself to this kind of treatment.

boy wearing a newspaper hat ★★★

(Eric Kenneway)

You will need a square, cut from a newspaper or magazine, on which there is uninterrupted small print in the top quarter of one side (side A) and blank space in the bottom quarter of the other (side B). What appears in the remaining three-quarters of each side is immaterial.

It is a good idea to look for a page which contains a large advertisement with a lot of blank areas. Check whether there is small print suitably placed on the reverse side, and if so, cut your square from this. Start by dividing the square into eighths by pleating.

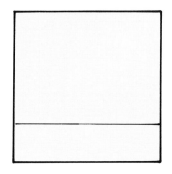

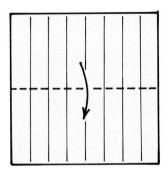

1

With side A uppermost, fold the top edge down to the bottom edge.

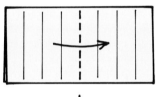

2

Take the left edge and fold it across to the right edge, in a valley fold.

3

Fold the top left corner to the nearest pleat crease; make a firm crease and return. Then open up the paper.

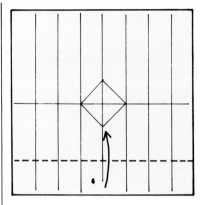

4

Fold the bottom edge up to the bottom point of the centre diamond. Turn the paper over.

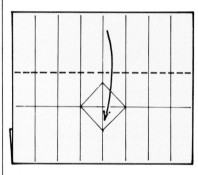

5

Fold the top edge down to the bottom of the centre diamond. Turn the paper over again.

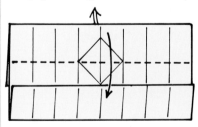

6

Fold the top part down on the existing horizontal crease line in the centre of the diamond, letting the paper swing up from behind.

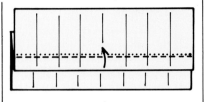

7

Fold up the bottom edge of the front flap on a line just below the concealed raw edge. Turn the paper over.

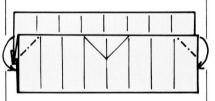

8

Inside reverse fold the two top corners of the front flap down to the first vertical creases on either side.

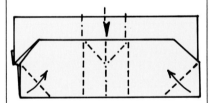

9

First fold up the two bottom corners; then press down on the centre of the folded ridge to make a trough.

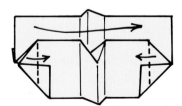

10

Fold the left and right corners inwards; then fold the structure in half by taking the left half across the right. ▶

boy with a newspaper hat continued

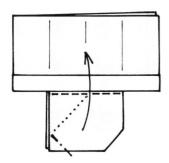

11

Lift the top layer of the bottom edge.

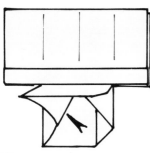

12

Push against the inside ridge to form a squash fold with a long 'lip' lying vertically at its left.

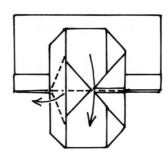

13

Pull the edge of this lip to the left while bringing the top flap down.

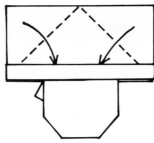

14

This will form a face in profile. Finally tuck the two top corners behind the rim to form a paper hat.

15

The completed boy wearing a newspaper hat.

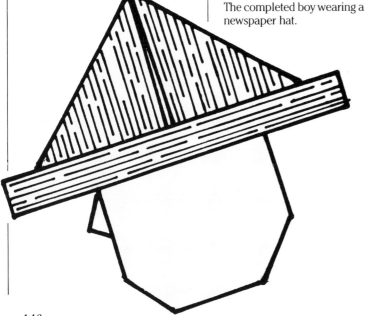

PURE ORIGAMI

Sometimes paperfolders refer to 'pure origami'. They generally apply this term to models which are constructed by folding alone, to emphasize that other technical aids, such as cutting or gluing, have not been used. Some creative folders impose further limitations on themselves and will not contemplate folding anything other than a square.

English paperfolder John S. Smith is of this mind. He has developed a technique of folding which does away with the necessity of using most of the traditional procedures. Called 'pureland origami', it is a technique which grew out of a desire to simplify paperfolding for beginners and to create a body of work suitable for teaching. He found that reverse folds, in particular, present problems to inexperienced folders, and so he invented alternative procedures which have similar results. Now he has dispensed with all folds other than valley and mountain folds. In effect, because mountain folds are made by turning the paper over, valley folding and turning the paper back again, this means that only valley folds are used.

Look at the following diagrams for folding a swan. You may be able to discern that the final model, or something very similar, can be achieved by first folding figure 3, mountain folding the vertical centre line and then making a series of reverse folds. This would be the traditional method. The method shown here is the 'pureland' one, however, and will give you some idea of the technique.

How to make a

swan ★

(John S. Smith)

Use a square of white paper, not too small. Start by folding opposite corners together to mark the centre crease. Unfold.

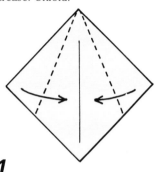

1

Fold two adjacent edges in to lie along the centre crease.

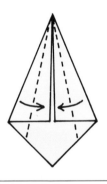

2

Bring the folded edges in to meet at the centre crease.

3

Fold the top point down so that it extends slightly beyond the bottom point.

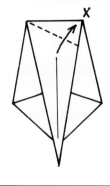

4

Fold the front flap up so that the centre crease meets corner X (turn the paper over to check this).

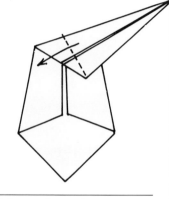

5

Fold the top flap to the left on a line at right-angles to the flap's centre crease.

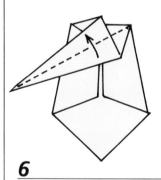

6

Fold the top flap in half, taking the bottom edge up to the top edge.

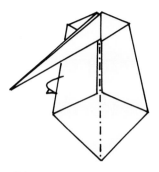

7

Mountain fold the bottom flap in half, taking the left half behind.

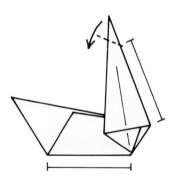

8

(Rotated to new position) Open the uppermost layer of the right-hand flap to the left.

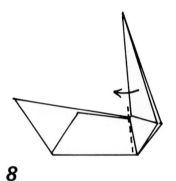

9

Fold the top point down to the left, as shown. (Note the point where the fold line meets the right edge of the triangular flap – the distance between this and the flap's bottom right corner equals the length of the base line.) ▶

147

swan continued

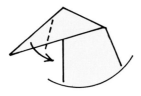

10

(Detail) Fold the point down to the right in a valley fold.

11

Then fold it up on a line along the horizontal edge.

12

Fold it down again, across to the left, as shown.

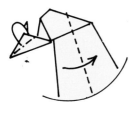

13

First mountain fold the little flap in half. Finally, close the larger flap which was opened in step 8, in a valley fold.

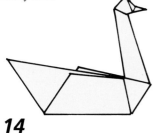

14

The completed swan.

Left to right: Swan (page 147);
Cluster puzzle (right)

PUZZLES

Because origami can be considered a form of puzzle-solving, it is not surprising that there are many people who enjoy both origami and other kinds of puzzles. Among them are some who try to combine their interests by folding paper replicas of traditional puzzles. One folder, Wayne Brown, has made a tangram set by folding each of the seven tangram pieces from squares of paper. (A tangram is a puzzle square which has been cut into seven pieces. These pieces can be recombined to create a variety of forms.) Another paperfolder, Anthony O'Hare, has succeeded in making origami jigsaw puzzle pieces which lock together.

Peter Ford collects construction puzzles – those that are usually made up of several interlocking blocks of wood which you are meant to dismantle or reassemble. He designs origami versions of them which, being made of paper, are even more of a challenge because the pieces must be handled with considerable gentleness. Here is an example.

How to make a
cluster puzzle ★★★★
(Peter Ford)

To make one of six pieces, use a 5:8 rectangle of paper-backed foil. First divide the paper into forty squares by folding; then make the diagonal folds at either end and the two short vertical folds at centre left and right.

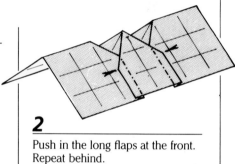

2

Push in the long flaps at the front. Repeat behind.

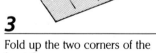

3

Fold up the two corners of the front flap.

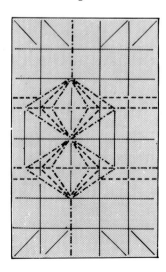

1

Fold the crease lines as shown; then collapse the paper.

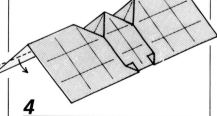

4

Fold in the edge of the far side and turn the paper over. ▶

149

cluster puzzle continued

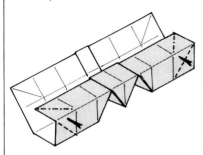

5

Push in the edges on the left and right.

6

Tuck in the pointed flap. Repeat at the other end. Look ahead to steps 7 and 8; try to integrate these two moves.

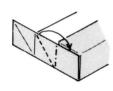

7

Swivel fold the edge to raise the rear edge of the paper. Repeat at the other end.

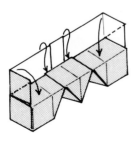

8

Tuck in the edge of the vertical flap, making small pointed flaps at either end.

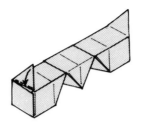

9

Fold the pointed flap in a valley fold and tuck it in. Repeat at the other end.

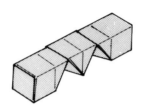

10

One completed block. Make five more in the same way.

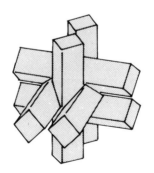

11

Then try to assemble them into this design.

QUILLING

There is a form of paper craft in which paper is rolled or curled instead of folded. Narrow strips are wound into tight coils and allowed to spring open partially. The coils may then be pinched or moulded into a number of standard shapes which are assembled to make decorative filigree patterns. Indeed, the traditional designs used in this technique are based on the designs of metal filigree work.

The craft was known in England in the fifteenth century, when it was used as a substitute for metal in the construction of decorative church screens. It is believed that, at this early date, the coils were prepared by winding paper strips around quills – hence the name 'quilling'.

There was a revival of interest in quilling in the late eighteenth century when it became popular as an accomplishment for young ladies, being used by them mainly to decorate the surfaces of cabinets and boxes. It became a popular creative hobby once again in the early 1970s, particularly in America where 'quilling kits' started to appear in craft shops. See Betty Christy and Doris Tracy's *Quilling: Paper Art for Everyone*, Henry Regney Co., Chicago, 1974, and Elizabeth Aaron's *Quilling: The Art of Paper Scroll Work*, Batsford, London, 1976.

RESIN

*T*here are many kinds of synthetic resin which can be applied to models in liquid form and then allowed to harden to give them a glazed appearance and to render them permanent. Look for them in shops that sell such things as marine supplies and model aircraft kits, as well as art and craft shops. When using resin, do follow the instructions carefully; it can be highly flammable.

Models can also be embedded in sheets or moulded blocks of clear resin. Moulding kits which contain small moulds are available, as well as those containing resin and coloured pigments, and it can be amusing to use these to fix small-scale origami into translucent jewel-sized blocks, then mount the results on rings, pendants and other dress accessories. For more about this technique, see K. Zechlin's *Setting in Clear Plastic*, published by Mills & Boon, London, in 1971.

For another way of rendering models permanent, see WAXING MODELS (page 186).

RULES

*M*ost people who enjoy origami casually will not concern themselves over-much with the 'rules' – but Alice Gray has formulated the following code to which, she believes, most contemporary paperfolders instinctively subscribe. It appeared in the journal of the Origami Center of America, *The Origamian*, vol. 12, issue 2.

A model made from one sheet of paper is better than an equally successful model of the same subject made from two or more sheets.

If several sheets are used, it is better to lock them together in the folding than to paste them.

A model without cuts is better than an equally successful model of the same subject in which cuts are used.

Other things being equal, a model from a square sheet of paper is better than one of the same subject made from paper of any other shape.

When the finished models are equally pleasing, a simple one is better than a complicated one.

RUPERT ANNUALS

Reproduced by permission of Express Newspapers p.l.c.

*C*an you remember the circumstances of your first encounter with paperfolding? Perhaps for you, as for many people, it took place somewhere between the yellow covers of a Rupert Annual, all of which have featured paperfolding regularly since World War II. The early postwar annuals even introduced paperfolding into the stories themselves.

The publishers of this annual were faced with increasing competition from other children's publications after the war, and they thought it no longer sufficient just to reprint some of the Rupert Bear cartoons which had ▶

been appearing in the *Daily Express* since 1920. They wanted new ideas, and Alfred Bestall, who wrote and illustrated the Rupert stories, suggested paperfolding. His own experience of paperfolding went back to 1899 when, at the age of seven, he and other children had been taught to fold a paper boat by an entertainer at a Christmas party.

So instructions for the flapping bird (page 11) were featured in the 1946 annual, and other traditional models appeared in the following issues – a paper kettle in 1947 and the PAJARITA (page 133) in 1948. In 1948, the Rupert book achieved sales which were a record for a children's annual, although still short of the one-million-plus it was to reach in later years. By then, children from all over the world had started to send in their own origami creations, some of which Alfred Bestall included with his own designs.

Alfred Bestall maintained his interest in paperfolding. He was President of the British Origami Society when he died in 1986 at the age of 93.

For more about Rupert Bear and Alfred Bestall, see George Perry's *Rupert, a Bear's Life*, published by Pavilion Books, London, in 1985.

Alfred Bestall paperfolding (above)

SALT CELLAR

*T*his structure is the only example of paperfolding reported by the Opies in their *Lore and Language of Schoolchildren* (Clarendon Press, 1959), a book which contains many of the traditional forms of play passed on by children in Britain. Although it is usually described only as a salt cellar in books, it can be used as a container for other things – and children have found their own uses for it, which are described below.

How to make a
salt cellar ★

Use a square of paper. Fold the opposite edges together in turn to mark the centre creases and then open up.

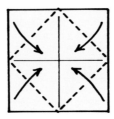

1

Fold all four corners into the centre.

2

Turn the paper over.

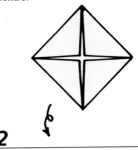

3

Again, fold each of the corners into the centre.

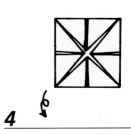

4

Turn the paper over again.

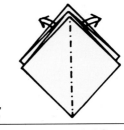

5

Form a preliminary base.

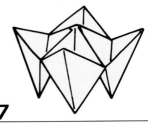

6

Pull out the concealed flaps on both sides and raise the final form.

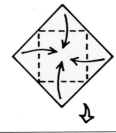

7

The completed salt cellar. Made from a fairly large square of coloured paper it can be used as a container for sweets or biscuits at party time.

▶

How to make a
cootie catcher ★

To American children, the salt cellar construction is traditionally known as a 'cootie catcher'.

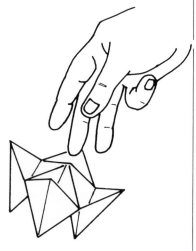

1

Complete the salt cellar (page 153). Pick it up with your thumb and three fingers, one in each pocket.

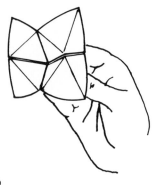

2

You will find that by spreading your fingers the front of the model can be opened two ways: this way. One way is demonstrated here.

3

And this is the second way. Draw a lot of little black spots on the surfaces revealed when the structure is opened one way.

Martin Gardner says that the trick is to hold the model with the spots concealed, as in step 2, and ask someone to cough into it. As he or she does so, quickly move your fingers so that the opening is reversed, and show all the 'germs' you have caught. In former times, children would grab at their friends' hair with cootie catchers and show them filled with 'lice'.

How to make a
fortune teller ★

To children in many countries, this construction is used as a fortune teller. It is usually prepared for this purpose in a way similar to the following. Start by returning the model to its flat form, as in fig. 5, page 153.

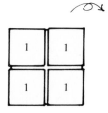

1

On each surface marked 1 on the diagram, write the name of, say, a football team or pop star, a different one for each surface. Turn the paper over.

2

On each surface marked 2, write the name of, say, a colour or flower. Open up the four corners.

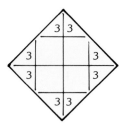

3

On each surface marked 3, write a brief 'fortune,' one for each surface. Return the model to its completed form and hold as stage 2 for the cootie catcher. Ask a friend to choose his or her favourite football team (or pop star) and then open the front of the model, this way and that way, as you spell out each letter of the chosen subject. Next, ask your friend to choose one of the four alternatives revealed on the surfaces marked in step 2 – then lift the chosen flap to discover his or her fortune.

SCENIC ROUTE

There is more than one method of folding most origami structures – more than one sequence in which the folds can be placed; and if other people are to find pleasure in the act of folding your origami designs, then the folding method should be chosen with care. The way a model is taught may be quite different from the way in which the creator constructed it originally.

As in narrative story or a piece of music, one step should follow another naturally – but not always predictably. Some origami teachers try to organize folding methods so that they contain what the Japanese call *igai-sei:* the element of surprise. Such a method is not, in every instance, the shortest or most direct one. It is comparable, in the happy phrase of John. S. Smith, to taking the scenic route.

SEMBAZURU
(thousand cranes)

Two of the oldest-known Japanese origami books have both dealt exclusively with one and the same subject – how to fold the crane, a long-necked bird which was adopted as a Chinese Taoist symbol of long life and good fortune. The crane symbol appears in many Japanese folk arts over the centuries, and folding paper cranes has been a popular activity there for at least two hundred years. But since World War II, the crane has gained a special significance – as a symbol of peace.

This significance originated with a twelve-year-old girl called Sadako Sasaki, who was orphaned by the bomb which fell on Hiroshima and also became a victim of radiation sickness. As she lay in her hospital bed she used the little pieces of paper in which her powdered medicine was wrapped to fold cranes. Her hope was to fold one thousand cranes in the belief that if she succeeded her prayers would be answered. At first she prayed for her own recovery, but later, as she saw other children in the ward die and began to suspect that she was not destined to recover, Sadako changed her prayer to one for universal peace. She managed to ` complete 644 cranes before she died.

Her story was publicized in Japan and soon other children began to follow her example, folding cranes as symbolic prayers for peace and sending them to Hiroshima. In 1958, a monument was erected in Hiroshima Park; at its summit

stands a bronze statue of a young girl holding up a folded crane. Many thousands of the paper cranes that had been sent to Hiroshima were hung from this monument in the form of streamers.

Karl Bruckner, an Austrian, wrote about these events in a book, *Sadako Will Leben,* which was published in Vienna in 1961; the English version, *The Day of the Bomb,* was published in London the following year. In its many translations, this book brought Sadako's story to the notice of peace-movement sympathizers throughout the world. Many of them folded cranes for peace, sometimes forming clubs for that sole purpose, and sent them to Hiroshima to join the cranes already hanging from the Peace Tower there. ▶

How to make a
paper crane ★★★

Use a square of paper. First
complete the bird base (page 25).

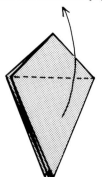

1

Raise the front flap and fold it on a
line between the two top corners.
Repeat behind.

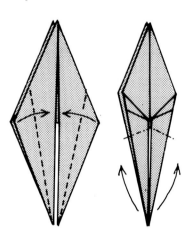

2

Narrow the lower points by folding
the sides into the vertical centre
line. Repeat behind.

3

Inside reverse fold the lower left
and right points.

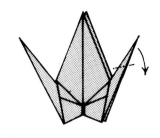

4

Inside reverse fold one of the
points to form the bird's beak.

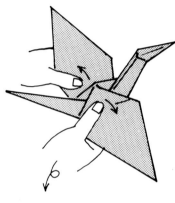

5

Take hold of the wings and bring
them down, spreading the central
point slightly. This will keep the
wings in a horizontal position.

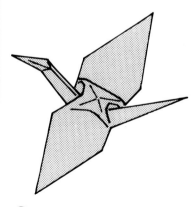

6

The completed paper crane.

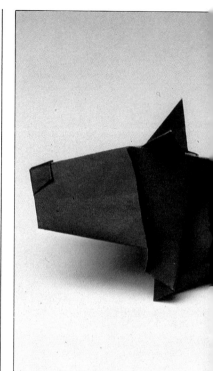

*Black and white Scottie dogs (page
159) .*

Having folded one paper crane,
you may like to fold some
traditional combinations of
cranes, which are collectively
known as 'a thousand cranes'.
These figures are made with
squares or rectangles of paper
which are cut into smaller
squares, except for certain
corners which are left uncut. In
this way a chain of squares is
created. If a crane is folded on
each of these squares, the
result will be a chain of paper
cranes. According to the
placing of the folds on the
squares, the cranes may all be
linked beak to tail, or they may
alternate, one pair beak to beak
and the next pair tail to tail, or
they may be joined wing to
wing, and so on.

How to make
kissing cranes ★★★

Use a 1:2 rectangle of paper. Form two squares by cutting along the centre line, leaving a join about 3mm (¹⁄₁₀ in) wide at one end. Fold the cranes (page 156) so that they are joined beak to beak.

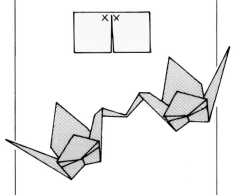

How to make a
quartet of cranes ★★★★

Use a square of paper. Cut along the centre lines to make four smaller squares joined at the centre. Fold them into four cranes (page 156) joined by their tails. Then try folding four cranes which are joined by their beaks or wing tips.

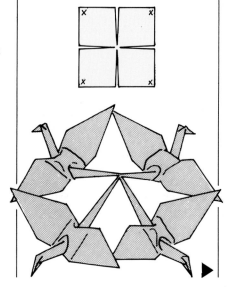

You will see that if the two end squares of a chain are superimposed and folded as one, it is possible to make a closed circle of cranes. Indeed, you can make several closed circles if the chain has sufficient squares and some of them are superimposed.

Many such designs first appeared in a book called *Sembazuru Orikata* (How to Fold a thousand Cranes), which was originally published in Kyoto in 1797, and is now regarded as a classic of origami literature. A facsimile edition was published by the Nippon Origami Association in 1977. However, the diagrams and text are not easy to understand, even for a Japanese, and well-illustrated modern Japanese commentaries on the 'thousand cranes' have appeared in recent years. Among these is Yutaka Yamagata's *Sembazuru wo Orimashō* (Let's Fold a Thousand Cranes), published by Reimei Shobo, Nagoya, in 1971.

In the following examples, an X in the corner of a square indicates that, when a crane is folded, this corner should form the head. In all but the simplest projects, you will find it worthwhile to mark these corners before cutting into the paper.

How to make a mother
crane and young ★★★★

Use a 1:2 rectangle of paper. Find the horizontal centre line; then find the quarter lines and make cuts on them, as shown. Make two horizontal cuts from the quarter line cuts towards the outer edges of the rectangle.

Place square A onto square A¹, with the corners marked X together, and fold them as one (page 156). Then fold the other squares.

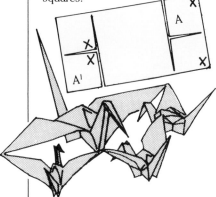

How to make a
circle of cranes ★★★★

Use a 1:2 rectangle of paper. Find the centre lines and quarter lines and cut as shown. Place square A onto square A¹ and fold together. Place square B onto square B¹ and fold together. Then fold the other squares.

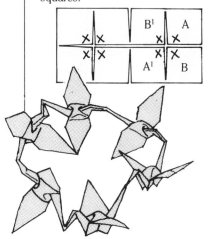

How to make a hanging
boat of cranes ★★★★

Use a square of paper. Divide the sides into fifths, then cut as shown to form one large square and sixteen smaller squares. Place squares A, B and C onto squares A¹, B¹ and C¹ in turn, and fold together. Then fold the other squares.

This procedure results in a chain of small cranes which divides into two chains of cranes from which the larger crane is suspended. The woodblock illustration, taken from *Sembazuru Orikata* (1797), shows a young woman holding the 'hanging boat' construction in her hand. One of the kneeling women has just completed a mother crane with two young cranes linked by their beaks to her tail.

USING THE 'THOUSAND CRANES' APPROACH WITH OTHER MODELS

Some modern paperfolders enjoy the complexity of the 'Thousand Cranes' approach and adapt it to make compounds of other models. For example, you can fold elephants and line them up in a row or circle joined trunk to tail. You may be able to think of other things that would be suitable for this approach.

Giles Gautherin, a French painter and designer, has adapted this approach to create the Scottie dog, described below.

How to make a
Scottie dog ★★★
(Giles Gautherin)

Use a square of paper. First complete the fish base (page 24).

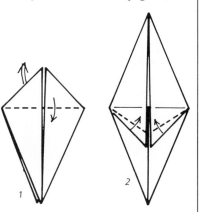

1

Fold the two small top flaps down on the line indicated, at the same time bringing up the rear flap.

2

Crease the two small front flaps by folding them up in valley folds.

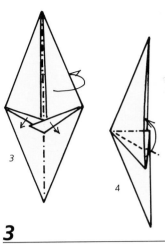

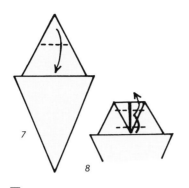

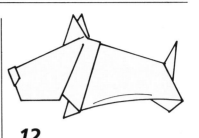

12

The completed Scottie dog.

How to make black and white Scottie dogs ★★★

(Giles Gautherin)

Use a 1:2 rectangle of paper, black on one side. Cut along the centre line to form two squares, leaving a join about 3mm (¹/₁₀in) wide at the top. Twist this so that one square has its reverse side facing upwards. Then fold a fish base (page 24) on each square. Complete the folding as shown on the left, to make a pair of Scotties, one black and one white.

  Giles also uses a square of paper, patterned with a black and white check design, which he cuts as for the Quartet of Cranes (page 157) and folds into a litter of black and white checked puppies.

3

Return them to their former position, then mountain fold the model in half.

4

Take hold of the front flap and bring it up into the model, forming a crimp. Repeat behind.

7

Fold down the top point, so that it meets the horizontal line.

8

Fold the same point back in valley folds, over and over.

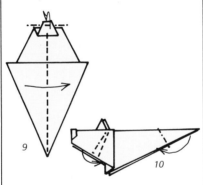

9

Mountain fold the tip behind. Then fold the model in half, in a valley fold.

10

(New position) Inside reverse fold the right point. Crimp on the left.

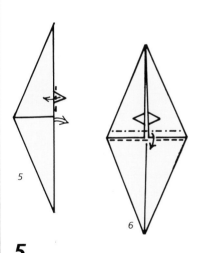

5

Valley fold the little point. Repeat behind. Open up the paper by bringing large rear flap round to the front again.

6

Pleat across the centre, as shown. Turn the paper over.

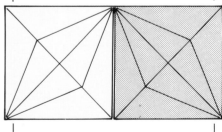

11

Inside reverse fold the right point to form both rear legs and tail. Shape the body.

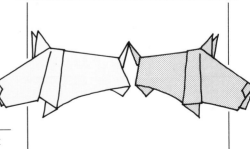

SHAPE AND SURPLUS

*T*he traditional approach to creating a new origami figure is to select one or other of the bases (pages 20–26) as the point of departure. Other approaches are described under BOX PLEAT- ING, CROSS PLEATING and elsewhere in this book. All these approaches have a common factor, something that was recog- nized by John S. Smith in 1968 when he wrote a paper introducing his simple concept of 'shape and surplus'.

The basis of origami technique, according to Smith, lies in these two elements. At each stage of its development an origami figure will, of necessity, possess a shape, but to be capable of development the figure must also have surplus, in the form of one or more extra layers of paper. Without surplus a figure cannot retain its shape when a fold is placed in it, let alone be expanded – it can only be reduced.

The accompanying illustrations show that an unfolded square of paper (fig. 1), has no surplus; it cannot therefore be folded without the shape being reduced. You can provide yourself with a figure which has an exactly similar shape and yet which has surplus too, by folding it in certain ways. For example by folding a square in half and in half again (fig. 2), or by folding a blintz (fig. 3), or by folding a preliminary base (fig. 4). Each of these figures has the same shape, but the surplus is differently distributed in each one and they are therefore capable of being developed differently.

With such figures you can modify the shape not only by reduc- ing it (which incidentally provides you with extra surplus) but also by expanding it (by taking some of the surplus beyond the limits of the shape). So you see, the shape and surplus of a figure are not fixed; they are constantly being transformed into each other as the figure is developed. To create successfully it helps to be aware of this interchange in your material.

SMALL-SCALE MODELS

*I*n response to a 'smallest flapping bird' competition, A. Naito of Japan folded a model from paper a mere 2.9mm (about ⅒in) square. To display his model, which measured only about 2mm from beak to tail, Naito mounted it on the point of a needle and enclosed it inside a transparent globe. It was nonetheless difficult to see with the naked eye. Nigel Keen, an ophthalmic op- tician, solved the problem by fitting a contact lens to the outside of the globe through which viewers could study the model properly.

The winning model in a 'world's smallest crane' competition, held in 1986, was folded from aluminium- coated paper a mere 1mm (¹⁄₂₅in) square. The compe- tition was organized as an exercise in improving the skills of medical specialists who were engaged in sewing individual blood vessels. The winning model was folded by Assistant Professor Y. Watanabe (Anatomy Depart- ment of Sapporo University), by using a needle under a microscope.

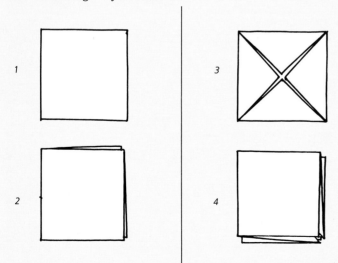

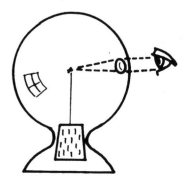

SOCIETIES

Societies based in English-speaking countries only are listed here, but the British Origami Society, which has members throughout the world, can provide information about societies in other countries if required.

Australian Origami Society
c/o Clare Chamberlain
806/112 Goderich Street
Perth 6000
Australia

British Origami Society
c/o Dave Brill
12 Thorn Road
Bramhall
Stockport
Cheshire
England

Friends of the Origami Center
of America
c/o Michael Shall
15 West 77th Street
New York
NY 10024
USA

New Zealand Origami Society
c/o Kim Hunt
79 Dunbar Road
Christchurch 3
New Zealand

West Coast Origami Guild
c/o Robert Lang
PO Box 90601
Pasadena
CA 91109
USA

SOUND-PRODUCING ORIGAMI

You will have discovered that folded paper can provide the means of making a very loud noise (see BANGERS, page 18) or a quiet click (see Camera, page 141). You can even make it squeak or shriek by blowing into it (see ONE-FOLD ORIGAMI, page 130). It is rather surprising how many different types of sound can be produced.

How to make a
tumbling toy ★
(Seiryo Takekawa)

Use a square of paper. Start by folding opposite edges together in turn to mark the horizontal and vertical centre creases.

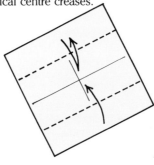

1

Fold the top edge to the centre; crease and unfold. Fold the bottom edge to the centre and leave folded.

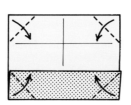

2

Fold in the four corners to the newly formed horizontal line.

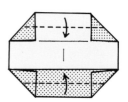

3

Fold in the top and bottom edges to the horizontal lines.

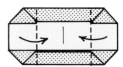

4

Fold the left and right edges to the centre; crease and then raise the sides.

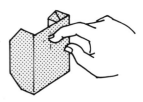

5

The completed toy. Stand it on a flat surface; tap it lightly with a finger and, as you would expect, it will fall forward.

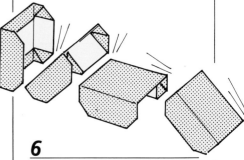

6

But if you turn it upside down and tap it as before, the toy will fall forward and turn a complete somersault with a 'rat-tat-tat'.

SQUARE

The square has consider-
able symbolic signifi-
cance in the Far East, through
the influence of Taoism. This
is the philosophy in which
opposing forces in nature are
seen, not as entities, but as
qualities inherent in all
things.

These opposing forces, *yin*
and *yang,* are most com-
monly represented by com-
plementary tear-drop-shaped
segments of a circle. But they
may also be represented by a
square *(yin)* containing a circle *(yang)* which in turn contains a square which contains
a circle and so on *ad infini-
tum,* to demonstrate the belief
that everything in nature contains the seed of its opposite.
In Taoist writings, the square
has been described as the
First Form, and also, as a symbol of the undifferentiated
void from which the duality of
opposing forces originated.

Whether for this reason –
that the square is a metaphor
for something fundamental in
nature – or for other reasons,
there are purist paperfolders
who will use paper of no other
shape for folding. However, it
must be said that there are
others who prefer to use rectangles on the grounds that
they have a more 'natural'
shape. It is certainly easier in
most homes, to lay one's
hands on a rectangular sheet
of paper than a square one.

STARS

Try making four- and eight-pointed star shapes by using the
windmill base as a point of departure. To make this base, use
a square of paper and complete steps 1–4 of the PAJARITA, page
134 (fig. 1). Squash fold the two pairs of front flaps so that the
corners of the paper meet in the centre (fig. 2).

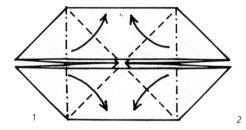
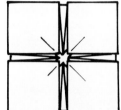

If you petal fold each of these four corner flaps, you will see a
star shape emerging which you should be able to develop in your
own way.

The star described below, however, is unusual because it has
five points, although folded from a square. It is not geometrically
accurate, it is true, but it will serve usefully as a Christmas tree
decoration or as a sheriff's badge for a child.

Other stars are described under STRETCHING and TRIANGLES.

How to make a
five-pointed star ★★

Use a square of paper, plain side
up. Start by folding opposite edges
together in turn and opening them
up to mark the two centre lines.

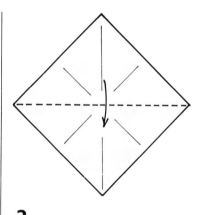

2

Fold the top corner down to the
bottom corner and leave folded.

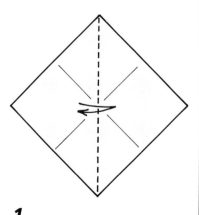

1

Fold the right corner over to meet
the left; make a crease, and return.

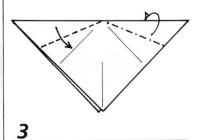

3

Take the folded edge down to the nearest crease lines: valley fold the left corner forward and mountain fold the right corner back.

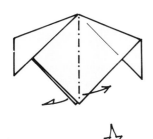

4

Now separate the two layers at the bottom, extending the front points to the right and the back one to the left.

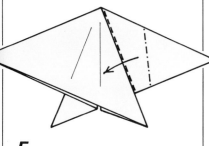

5

Take the right flap across the folded edge, returning the point outwards.

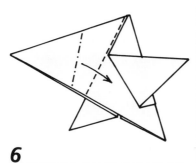

6

Do the same with the left flap.

7

Turn the paper over.

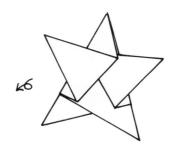

8

The completed five-pointed star.

STRETCHING

Partially opening a folded structure by taking hold of two points and pulling them apart is generally known as 'stretching'. The effect is to remove some of the folds, while retaining others. Stretching can also have the effect of making the structure rigid, as takes place in the final stage of making the following decoration.

How to make a stretched star ★★

Use a square of paper or, for a more decorative effect, use two squares of differently coloured paper placed together with the coloured surfaces outwards. Start by folding the corners to the centre to form a blintz.

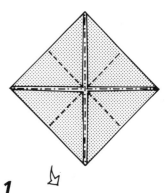

1

Form a preliminary base (page 17) on the blintz.

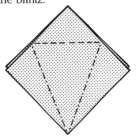

2

Form a bird base (page 15). Now turn it upside down. ▶

stretched star continued

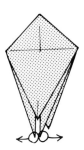

3

Take hold of the two inside flaps between the finger and thumb of both hands. Pull apart.

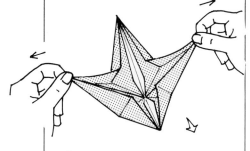

4

Continue pulling apart until the radiating folds in the centre of the paper disappear with a 'pop' and the structure maintains a partially opened, rigid form.

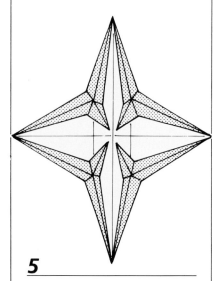

5

The completed stretched star.

Tape-folded chrysanthemums (right) with leaves (page 166)

TAPE FOLDING

Some of the effects which result from stretching pleated paper can be seen in the dish (page 47) and the fan (page 55). By folding a long strip of paper in a somewhat similar way, you can arrive at some interesting and unexpected shapes. When you have folded the set of three chrysanthemums, described below, try increasing the number of flowers by using longer paper. Try also narrowing the pleats and increasing the number of pleats in a set to alter the angles at the perimeters of the flowers.

Used rolls of tape from adding machines and certain types of ticket machine will provide you with material for experimental folding, but if you intend to mount your results for display, you may like to cut your own tape from sheets of coloured paper.

How to make a

Chrysanthemum ★★★★

(Yoshihide Momotani)

Use paper tape, coloured on one side, with sides in the ratio of 1:16.

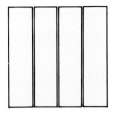

1

You can make a suitable tape by dividing a square of paper lengthwise into quarters, and joining them end to end with sticky tape.

2

(Detail) Divide the length of the tape into sixteen square areas by folding it, first into halves, then into quarters and so on.

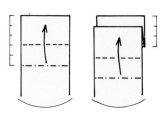

3

With the white side up, form every crease line into a mountain fold. Then take up the mountain fold below the topmost square to a line about one-fifth of the way from the top.

4

Repeat this step in the next square.

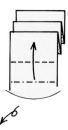

5

Repeat again in the third square. Repeat these steps along the entire length of the tape. ▶

chrysanthemum continued

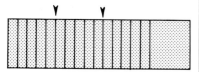

6

Turn the tape over and ensure that the top is on the left. Count five mountain folds from the left and open the next pleat (i.e. the sixth mountain fold). Count four more mountain folds and open the next pleat.

7

Fold up about one-third of the width of the tape.

8

Take hold of the tape on the left between your finger and thumb. Pull the corner of the first pleat down, stretching the paper.

9

Flatten the new folds to fix the shape. Pull the bottom corners of the next four pleats in turn.

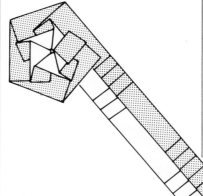

10

This will produce this flower shape. Do the same with the next set of pleats.

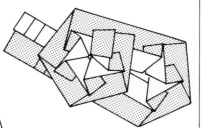

11

This will produce another, partial, flower shape. Make a third flower shape in the same way from the remaining set of pleats. Now swivel fold or pleat the paper between the flowers, to make them appear separate, and overlap one flower with another.

Leaf
Use a square of green paper. The length of its sides should be about twice the width of the tape. Start by marking the diagonal crease line.

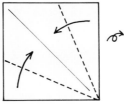

1

Fold two adjacent edges in to the diagonal crease line. Turn over.

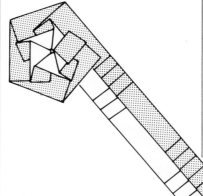

2

Take the folded edges into the crease line, letting the paper kick out from behind. Turn over.

3

The completed leaf.

Mounting
Mount the flowers, with the leaves, on paper or card to complete.

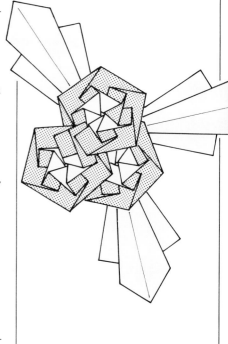

*T*ATO

A *tato* is a traditional type of folded paper purse in which a Japanese housewife keeps small items such as needles, ends of thread, buttons and so on. Some people consider them to be useful for keeping postage stamps, too. *Tato* often take the form of hexagonal or octagonal stylized flower patterns. The late Michio Uchiyama used them as a basis for developing many hundreds of stylized flower designs which are now housed in a museum of folk art in Tokyo.

How to make a

tato ★★

Use a square of paper. Start by folding the fish base (page 24).

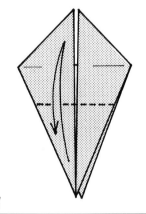

1

Fold the bottom point up to the top and return. Turn the paper over and repeat.

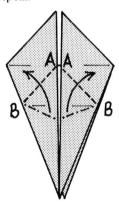

2

Using points A and B on the creases as markers, separate the centre edges as you bring up the bottom point again. Repeat behind.

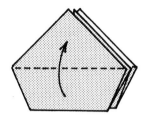

3

Fold up the bottom edge of the front flap at a point between the two middle corners.

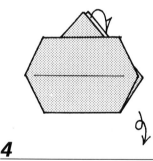

4

Mountain fold the rear flap down. Turn the paper over.

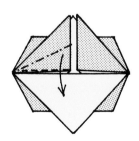

5

Squash fold the top left flap.

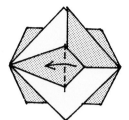

6

Fold its point to the left.

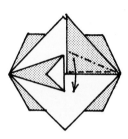

7

Squash fold the top right flap.

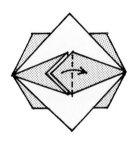

8

Fold its point to the right.

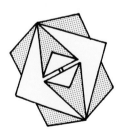

9

The completed *tato*. As with most of these purses, it has a large flap on each side. Pull them apart and the purse will open; release them and it will return to its original form.

TEACHING

For a model lesson, see 'Teaching Origami' in Samuel Randlett's *Art of Origami*, Faber, London, 1963. Here are some preparations which you can make if you are invited to teach or demonstrate origami for the first time before a group of people.

1

Before all else, try to find out how many people are expected to attend and for how long you are expected to teach (there may be other things you would like to know too: how will the seats be arranged; do the members of the audience belong to any particular age group and so on), because without this minimum information you cannot make adequate arrangements.

2

Taking the expected size of the audience and available time into account, make sure that you have enough paper for everyone to fold – preferably more than enough. You can always use the left-over paper on some future occasion.

3

Prepare paper to use yourself during the demonstration. This should be much larger than standard-size origami paper if your audience is likely to contain more than a handful of people.

4

Decide what models you intend to teach, then make sure that you not only *know* how to fold them but that you can *explain* how to fold them. You can practise this by talking aloud while working through the stages of folding the models.

5

As a rule, it is better to choose a lot of very simple models for teaching, rather than one or two more complex ones. This will not only give every member of the audience a greater chance of folding something successfully, it should also give them a variety of things to take home – something practical, something decorative, and a toy or two perhaps.

THERAPY

In 1914, when the Englishman Charles Gibbes became tutor to the ill-fated nine-year-old tsarevich, youngest child of Nicholas II, he had difficulty in communicating with the withdrawn boy whose history of illness is well known. Gibbes won the child's confidence by a method used probably many times before and certainly many times since – he showed him how to make something from a piece of paper. A paper hat was the first fold the tsarevich learnt and this encouraged him to speak, so Gibbes recorded in his diary.

Speech therapist Gwyneth Radcliffe has had similar experiences but, she writes, 'I also use origami as part of therapy itself in many different ways. Because of the inherent attractiveness of the subject to children of a wide age range, it is useful to improve attention skills, as a tool for improving language development, and is particularly useful in improving sequencing skills. It can also be useful in articulation therapy (e.g. paper puppets can be useful in demonstrating lip movements). Finally, I have used origami most successfully in overcoming the embarassment some children feel in being taken out of class to receive therapy. I have found that by providing a child with a paperfold to take back into school with him, this has given him such kudos with the other children that a reluctant patient has become one eager to work to 'earn' his origami to show off to his classmates.'

It is worth noting that, because origami in its purest

form requires absolutely no equipment other than one small sheet of paper, it is both safe and manageable; it can be enjoyed by the mentally disturbed and by patients confined to bed. It is also thoroughly tactile and can be enjoyed by the blind and partially sighted.

Japanese paperfolder Saburo Kase, who has been blind since early childhood, is a gifted creator of origami designs. He regularly teaches origami both to the blind and people with other handicaps. His method of teaching the blind, which he does on a one-to-one basis, is to guide their fingertips across the paper with his own fingertips. In 1981, the International Year of the Disabled, he was invited to make an American tour; he taught origami to handicapped groups and others in eight cities.

*T*HUMBNAIL FOLDING

*M*argaret Campbell describes a curious method of pleating a narrow strip of paper in her book *Paper Toy Making*, first published by Pitman, London, in 1937 and reprinted by Dover, New York, in 1975. She suggests that paper pleated in this way can be used to decorate an origami umbrella or placed in a paper dish to represent flowers. In fact, it is worthwhile trying this technique purely for the experience and with no other aim in mind.

How to make an accordion-pleated paper ribbon

Prepare a strip of paper about 0.2cm (1/10in) wide and about 10cm (4in) long. Take the end of the strip between the finger and thumb of one hand. Bring your thumbtips together, turned upwards, allowing the length of the strip to lie along the opposite thumb. With the paper between your thumbnails, click each thumbnail over the other in turn and continue doing this. It should make the regular sound of a clock ticking and the paper strip should swing from side to side rather like a metronome. The paper will become accordion pleated as it moves down between your thumbs.

*T*ICKET FOLDING

*T*ickets provide ready-to-hand material for improvised paperfolding which can relieve the tedium of long bus and train journeys (Leo Tolstoy was a ticket folder of this sort). In London, bus tickets are no longer the brightly coloured, tempting things they once were, but some other towns are more fortunate.

All Paris Metro tickets, for example, are bright yellow with a brown stripe through the centre; because tickets do not have to be handed in at the barriers, there are always plenty of discarded ones to be found around the exits of Metro stations. This has encouraged Parisian paperfolders to explore the possibilities of folding tickets, and they have found them well suited to making modular and multi-piece models in particular. In 1983, Le Mouvement Français des Plieurs de Papier edited and published *Le Ticket Plié*, a book devoted to ticket folding, in which the following model appeared.

How to make a palm tree ★★
(Didier Boursin)

Use eleven Paris Metro tickets or similar small rectangles of paper or card. Six will form leaves; three will be used for the trunk and two will form collars which hold the rest together.

Fold all the tickets in half by taking the bottom edge up to the top. Put three aside for the trunk.

▶

palm tree continued

Leaves

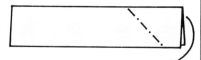

1

Take three tickets. On each one form an inside reverse fold towards one end.

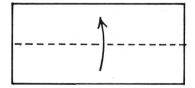

2

This will produce a flat-edged projection.

3

Take three more tickets and curve them by running them between your finger and thumb.

Collars
Open up one ticket.

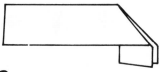

1

Fold in the top and bottom so that they meet at the centre crease.

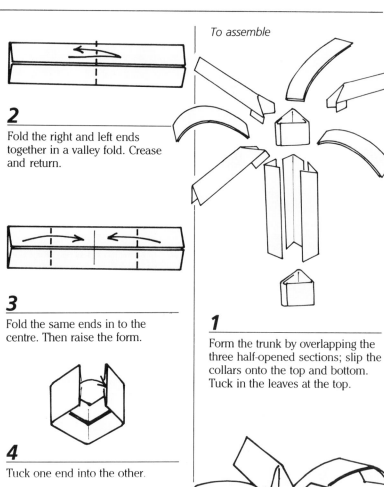

2

Fold the right and left ends together in a valley fold. Crease and return.

3

Fold the same ends in to the centre. Then raise the form.

4

Tuck one end into the other.

5

This will produce a triangular collar. Repeat steps 5–9 on one more ticket to make another collar.

To assemble

1

Form the trunk by overlapping the three half-opened sections; slip the collars onto the top and bottom. Tuck in the leaves at the top.

2

The completed palm tree.

*T*ISSUE FOLDING

*B*oxes of paper tissues in a variety of colours can be bought in many chemists' shops and large stores. They will provide you with an opportunity to make decorative flowers of the kind described below. Their making demands a soft and gentle style of folding in which your own judgement can be brought into play. You may find them quite easy to make – but not at all easy to make really well.

How to make a

rose ★★★
(Megumi Biddle)

You will need a minimum of four pink (or white or yellow) tissues and one green tissue.

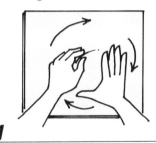

1

Lay two pink tissues together on a flat surface. Pick at the centre with the finger and thumb of one hand. Rotate the paper around the centre with your other hand.

2

Arrange the paper into neat furrows with the fingers of your left hand while still holding the centre and continuing to rotate the paper.

3

Still holding the centre, lift the paper.

4

Rotate the paper to make an ice-cream cone shape.

5

This completes the core. Lay it aside for the moment.

6

Lay two more pink tissues together and divide them vertically into quarters by cutting or tearing.

7

Take each of the double-layered strips in turn and fold them in half.

8

Gather together about one-third of the free ends of each. These will become outer petals; put them aside for the moment too.

9

Lay two green tissues together and divide them vertically into quarters.

10

Take one of these and run it between your fingers.

▶

Paper tissue roses (page 171)

rose continued

11

Arrange the four outer petals around the core.

12

Place the prepared green tissue around the flower.

13

Tie the green tissue in place with a single knot.

14

Separate the four layers of green tissue and curl the edges tightly between finger and thumb, shaping the tissue into leaves.

15

Step 14 in progress. This completes the rose.

16

Make one or two more, ideally, and display them together in a brandy glass or something similar.

172

*T*RIANGLES

*A*s a relief from folding squares and rectangles, try folding triangular paper. The triangle is a shape particularly suitable for folding sitting birds – one corner can be used to form the neck and head, and the other two corners can be used to form a pair of wings. Triangles can be prepared in the following ways.

How to make a right-angled triangle ★

Use a square of paper.

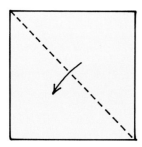

1

Fold it diagonally in half so that the two opposite corners meet.

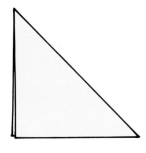

2

The resultant shape is a double-layered right-angled triangle. Cut along the fold to make two equal triangles.

How to make an equilateral triangle ★

Use a rectangle of almost any proportions (but not a square). Start by folding the longer edges together to mark the centre crease.

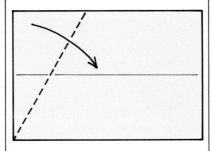

1

Fold the left edge down, taking the top end of it to the centre line while making sure that the bottom end of the fold starts in the corner.

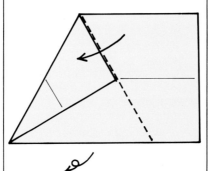

2

Fold the paper across the raw edge. Turn the paper over.

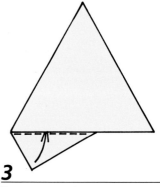

3

Tuck in the surplus paper at the bottom.

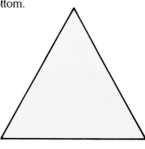

4

The completed equilateral triangle. Use this folded shape or open it and cut along the crease lines.

Larry Hart likes to make a triangle by folding a banknote in the above way from which he then folds a six-pointed Star of David.

How to make a Star of David ★★

Use an equilateral triangle of paper.

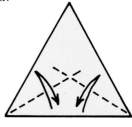

1

Fold two pairs of adjacent edges together in turn, crease and unfold. The point at which the creases cross marks the centre of the triangle.

▶

Star of David continued

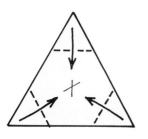

2

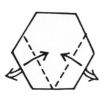

Fold the corners into the centre. Turn the paper over.

3

Fold two alternate edges to the centre in turn, letting the points kick out from underneath.

4

Fold the top edge to the centre, similarly tucking one corner under the right flap to hold it in place. Turn over.

5

The completed Star of David.

*T*ROUBLEWIT

*T*roublewit is, or appears to be, an ordinary sheet of pleated paper. It is held by a performer who manipulates it rapidly to represent a variety of objects. To be truly entertaining, the performer needs to tell a story, no matter how contrived, and illustrate his narrative with the changing troublewit patterns.

It is sometimes claimed that troublewit was invented in ancient China. That may be so, but it is no less likely that it was invented by an Englishman (who gave it a Chinese ancestry to add to its mystery). It is a form of entertainment that became enormously popular throughout Europe in the eighteenth century – and news of it travelled eastwards.

It was first mentioned in a treatise called *Sports and Pastimes: or, Hocus Pocus Improved ... A sheet of Paper called Trouble-Wit, with divers other Legerdemain Curiosities,* published by G. Conyers in London, in about 1710. It was next recorded in a Spanish book of amusements, *Enganos a Ojos Vistas ...* by Pablo Minguet, published in 1733. It appeared for the first time in France two years later, in *Récréations Mathématiques et Physiques* by Jacques Ozanam, and then in Italy, where *I Giuochi Numerici* by Giuseppe Alberti was published in 1747.

Troublewit enjoyed renewed popularity in the Victorian era. It was adopted by the famous magician David Devant as part of his stage act, and he revealed his method for making troublewit, and performing it, in an article by L. S. Lewis in *The*

Strand Magazine in 1896. Devant's method, simpler than earlier versions, continues to be used by such entertainers as Steve Biddle for children's shows. Some related ideas for performing with pleated paper were introduced by Eric Hawkesworth in his *Pleated Paper Folding,* Faber, 1975.

Troublewit seems to be no more than a sheet of paper with pleats across it, but in fact there are pleats which lie across the visible pleats, and there are 'reverse fold' crease lines where the pleats cross which enable parts of the paper to be raised at right-angles to each other. In Ozanam's version, the sheet of paper is first divided into eight equal panels which are then pleated; in Devant's version, the primary pleats divide six equal panels and a narrow central strip.

Here are instructions for both making and manipulating troublewit, based on David Devant's method.

How to make
troublewit ★★★★

If you wish to perform troublewit in front of an audience, you will need to use a very large sheet of strong cartridge or watercolour paper. For a first attempt, or for private amusement, it is better to use a sheet of A4 (8×11in) writing paper and trim it into a rectangle measuring 19×28cm if you intend to work in centimetres. The following measurements assume these proportions

Construction

Divide the paper so that there are three 3cm wide (1¼in) panels at either side of a 1cm wide (⅓in) strip in the centre.

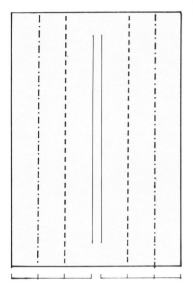

1

Make valley and mountain folds between the panels.

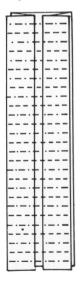

2

Pleat the paper accordingly then divide the length into 1cm wide (½in) bands and valley and mountain fold into pleats.

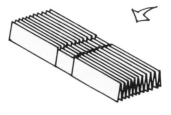
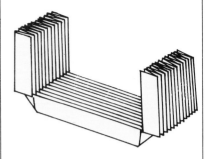

3

It is now necessary to make reverse folds at each corner where the pleats cross. Take one of the folded edges that lies across the centre of the structure and gradually ease it up until it stands at a 90° angle from the main part.

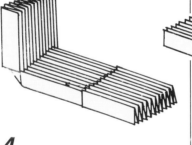

4

Pinch the corners to establish the reverse folds which this action has created. Now take the other central folded edge and gradually ease this up in the same way.

5

Once again pinch the corners firmly to establish the new reverse folds. Now take the raw edges on the left and right, in turn, and ease them up gradually to form reverse folds where the pleats cross.

6

Again pinch firmly. You now have all the creases you need for the final manipulations.

Steps 3, 4, 5 and 6 show four basic positions. You can readily see that by 'closing' one of the horizontal panels in step 6, so that one end resembles one of the ends as shown in step 5, you can create a fifth basic position – and by closing both panels, so that one end resembles one of the ends in step 3, you can create a sixth basic position.

Indeed, you should open and close these panels many times, not only to familiarize yourself with all the basic positions, but so that the corners become very flexible. Then you will be ready to perform troublewit. ▶

troublewit continued

Manipulation

There are thirty-six shapes which can be achieved by troublewit – and each of these serves to represent more than one object. Twelve manipulations are shown below; you may like to experiment and discover the remaining possibilities for yourself.

First basic position

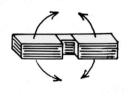

1

With the troublewit closed, as shown in step 3 on page 175, bring the top and bottom of each side panel together.

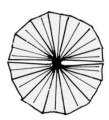

2

Hold it at the outer edges to form a circle. This is the rosette.

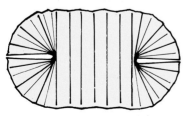

3

Pull the sides apart and the rosette will stretch into a bath mat.

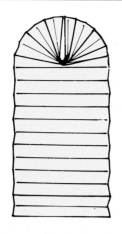

4

Release one end and let it hang to represent a church window.

Second basic position

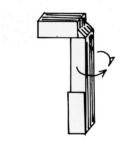

1

Start with the troublewit as shown in step 4 on page 175. Bring the front and back panels together on the right side.

2

This will form a toadstool or, if the upright section is held at the base, an umbrella.

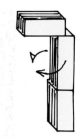

3

With the troublewit returned to its position in step 1, bring the front and back panels together on the left.

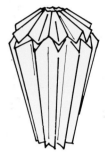

4

This will produce a vase.

Third basic position

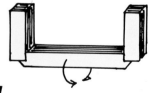

1

Start with the troublewit as shown in step 5 on page 175. Bring the front and back horizontal panels together underneath.

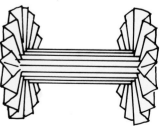

2

The result resembles a pair of dumb-bells.

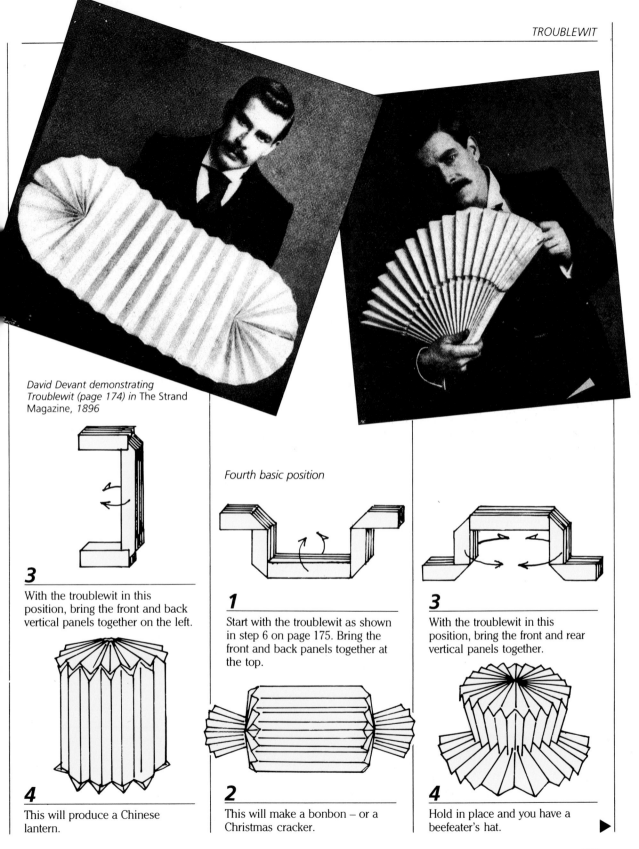

*David Devant demonstrating
Troublewit (page 174) in* The Strand
Magazine, *1896*

3

With the troublewit in this
position, bring the front and back
vertical panels together on the left.

4

This will produce a Chinese
lantern.

Fourth basic position

1

Start with the troublewit as shown
in step 6 on page 175. Bring the
front and back panels together at
the top.

2

This will make a bonbon – or a
Christmas cracker.

3

With the troublewit in this
position, bring the front and rear
vertical panels together.

4

Hold in place and you have a
beefeater's hat.

177

troublewit continued

Performance

Once you have explored the possibilities of troublewit for your own amusement, you may wish to construct one on a larger scale and try it out on an audience of a few friends. Here is some advice on making preparations for a performance.

Consider all the possible things that the shapes shown, and others which you will discover for yourself, may represent (it is a good idea to jot them down in the form of a list); then build a story, no matter how improbable, around these representations.

Try to manipulate the paper quickly and with confidence, but without looking at it. Keep the story flowing and do not give your audience too much time to look at one shape before either moving onto the next or returning to the first basic position.

As a general rule, the plain side of the troublewit, the one without the cross pleats showing, should be turned towards the audience. It will then appear as a plain sheet of pleated paper and your ability to produce so many different shapes from it will seem all the more mysterious.

TWIST FOLDING

A few traditional models are constructed by laying a number of crease lines into a square of paper and then collapsing it with a twist to raise the form. Japanese chemistry teacher Shuzo Fujimoto has developed this technique into an original and individual style which he calls *nejiri-ori:* twist folding.

By laying pleats across each other in a sheet of paper and then 'twisting' the paper where the pleats cross, he creates many repeat patterns. He also uses the technique to make decorative boxes such as the one described below. You may be able to see that the folding method can be adapted to make a box with any number of sides.

It was through his work as a chemistry teacher that Fujimoto first became interested in origami, seeing it as a potential method of making regular geometrical shapes and solids for display in his classroom. A complete guide to his technique appears in *Sozo Suru Origami Asobi e no Shotai* (Invitation to Creative Origami Play) by Shuzo Fujimoto and Masami Nishiwaki, published by the Asahi Culture Centre, Osaka, in 1982.

How to make a
six-sided box ★★★
(Shuzo Fujimoto)

Use a rectangle of paper about A4 (8×11in) in size.

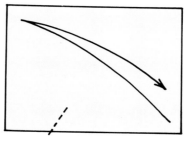

1

Fold the bottom right corner to the top left corner. Crease the bottom of the fold only, to mark the edge of the paper, and return.

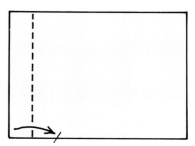

2

Fold the bottom left corner to the crease mark just made.

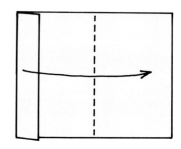

3

Now fold the paper in half, taking the folded edge on the left to the right, raw edge.

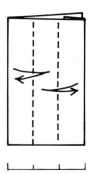

4

Divide the folded paper into thirds; open it up.

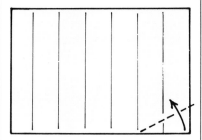

5

Make sure that the six panels of equal width are on the right. Fold the bottom right corner into the nearest crease line.

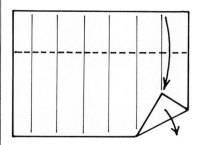

6

Fold the top edge down to meet the raised corner; then return the corner.

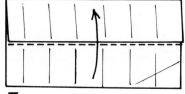

7

Fold the bottom part over the raw edge.

8

Make diagonal mountain folds across the six panels of equal width. Make a mountain fold parallel with these in the remaining panel. Make valley folds of all the vertical creases. Then bring the two ends together.

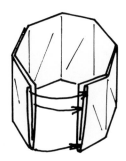

9

Tuck the layers of the left-hand panel between the layers of the right-hand panel to make a six-sided tube.

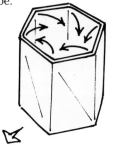

10

Now take the top edge of the inner layer and push it down, twisting it in a clockwise direction.

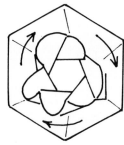

11

(Top view) It is probable that you will find this difficult on a first attempt – do not be discouraged, continue twisting.

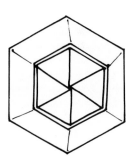

12

The paper should suddenly collapse into this form.

13

The completed box upturned. Make a second box to form a lid. Try making more boxes from other shapes and sizes of paper.

UMBRELLAS

Perhaps the most widely used practical application of paperfolding is in making umbrellas – or it was in Japan until after World War II, when cloth umbrellas finally replaced the traditional paper ones (these were made by pleating tough varnished paper onto bamboo frames).

Invented in China and introduced into Japan in the sixth century, the pleated paper umbrella was at first used only ceremonially; it is said that the emperor never appeared in public without his umbrella bearer. By the seventeenth century it had become an accessory to female dress, and Japanese prints from this period show fashionably kimonoed ladies escorted by maids with their umbrellas. The use of umbrellas later spread to the whole population. By the 1930s it was customary for even the poorest rural household to have several paper umbrellas and for these to be freely lent to passers-by caught in the rain.

A method of making an attractive paper umbrella for decorative purposes – one which has a secondary pleated paper frame instead of bamboo strips – is described below. It appeared in Toshie Takahama's *Creative Life with Creative Origami, Vol. 1,* published by Makō-sha, Tokyo, in 1969.

How to make a

Japanese umbrella ★★★★

(Toshie Takahama)

You will need two 25cm (10in) squares of tough, patterned or coloured paper (not necessarily similar), one 5cm (2in) square of paper, a thin dowel, a little sticky tape (or coloured paper scraps and glue), string or thread and a cutter or scissors.

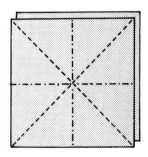

1

Prepare one of the 25cm (10in) squares by folding it into a preliminary base (page 20).

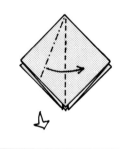

2

This has two pairs of triangular flaps. Squash fold one flap to the right, and repeat on the other three sides.

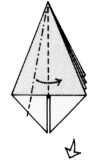

3

You should now have four flaps on either side of the axis. Squash fold one flap again to the right, and repeat on the other seven sides.

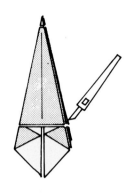

4

You should now have eight flaps on both sides of the axis. Cut through all the layers just below the horizontal edge; then cut off just the tip. Repeat steps 1–4 on the other 25cm (10in) square.

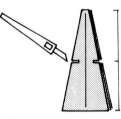

5

On one of these pleated forms only, find the halfway mark and cut a slit through all the layers at either side, each slit being equal in length to a quarter of the total width.

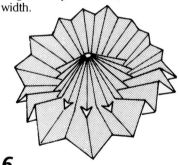

6

Open up the paper. Change the creases radiating out from the slits from valley folds into mountain folds and vice versa. Then raise this form. It will become the opening mechanism of the umbrella. ▶

Japanese umbrella (left)

umbrellas continued

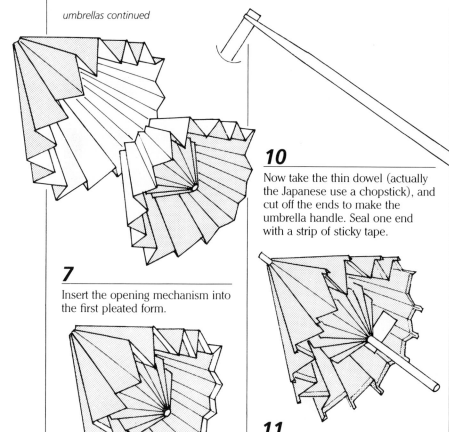

10

Now take the thin dowel (actually the Japanese use a chopstick), and cut off the ends to make the umbrella handle. Seal one end with a strip of sticky tape.

7

Insert the opening mechanism into the first pleated form.

8

When properly positioned, hold it in place by applying a little glue around the edges.

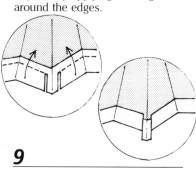

9

(Detail: inside view of pleated edge) Make a cut about 2mm (²⁄₂₅in) on both sides of each valley fold crease. Fold up the edges between the cuts into a hem and glue into place.

11

Insert the handle through the umbrella. Wrap a scrap of coloured paper around the base of the opening mechanism. Glue one end only to the mechanism so that it can pass freely up the handle.

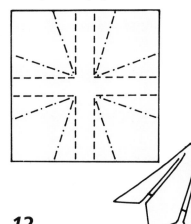

12

Take the 5cm (2in) square of paper and raise the four corners.

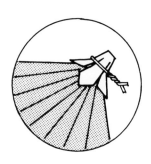

13

(Detail) Fit this shape to the top of the umbrella.

14

Tie it in place with thread or string.

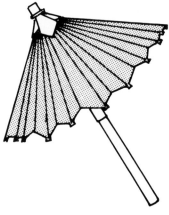

15

The completed Japanese umbrella.

UNBASIC FORM

Some time in the 1960s, the late Robert Harbin devised, or discovered, a development of a blintzed waterbomb base which seemed to him to have the attributes of a base. It had a cluster of points which invited manipulation, but although Harbin tried to develop the form further, he could not. For this reason he called it an 'unbasic form' – a base which was not a base.

Later Rae Cooker folded several of the forms, from graded sizes of paper, to construct a multi-piece Christmas tree.

How to make an

unbasic form ★★

(Robert Harbin)

Use a square of paper. Start by folding a blintz (page 27).

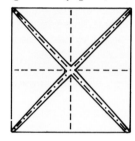

1

Fold the opposite edges together in turn and open up. Mountain fold the opposite corners together in turn and open up. Then collapse the paper to resemble a waterbomb base.

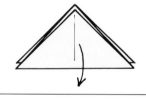

2

Bring down the front flap.

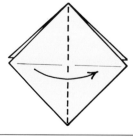

3

Fold from left to right, in a valley fold.

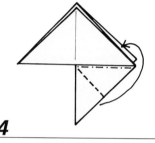

4

Make a valley fold crease in the bottom flap, then bring it up in a crimp behind the front flap.

5

Repeat step 4 on the remaining three sides.

6

The completed unbasic form.

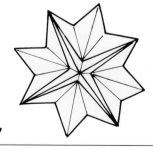

7

The unbasic form seen from above.

VALENTINE

The method of folding the valentine or heart, described below, contains a particularly interesting passage in which the form is brought into relief.

How to make a

heart ★★

(Makoto Yamaguchi)

Use a square of red paper. Start by marking the diagonal creases.

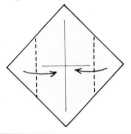

1

Fold opposite corners in so that they meet at the centre.

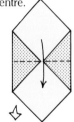

2

Fold the paper in half, taking the top corner down to the bottom.

3

Fold the paper in half again, taking the right edge over to meet the left.

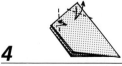

4

Fold the top corners down in turn; crease and return. Open up the paper. ▶

heart continued

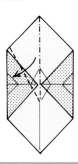

5

Note the diamond pattern of creases in the centre. Form the bottom left edge of the diamond into a valley fold and extend it to the top edge. Form the vertical mountain fold at the centre.

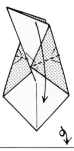

6

Then use these creases to swivel fold the paper like this to raise the form. Now bring down the front layer of the top flap, flattening the ridge behind it and allowing it to become concave. Turn the paper over.

7

Inside reverse fold the two top corners on the existing creases.

8

The completed heart. Slip a loop of coloured string or embroidery thread between the two layers to make a pendant decoration.

VISITING CARDS

*I*n the days when it was the custom to carry visiting cards to hand to a servant at the door of the house one was visiting, it was also customary to convey a message, other than the fact of one's presence, by creasing the card in one of several ways.

According to an etiquette book called *Manners and Rules of Good Society,* by a member of the aristocracy, which was current in the 1920s, the following code was in vogue.

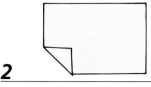

1

Fold the upper left-hand corner to signify 'Congratulations'.

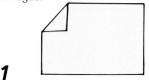

2

Fold the bottom left-hand corner as a message of condolence.

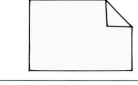

3

Fold the upper right-hand corner to denote a personal visit.

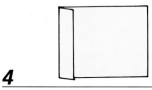

4

Fold the entire left edge to signify a call on the family as a whole.

WATERBOMB

*T*his closed box shape is believed to be one of the oldest traditional models in the world; it may have originated in ancient China.

Among Chinese children it was the practice to stretch the little hole at the top and to try to tempt a fly inside. They would allow the hole to close so that the fly was trapped, and then put the box to their ears and listen to the greatly amplified sound of the fly buzzing.

The Japanese use the boxes as balls or balloons to throw to each other; they also make them in coloured papers to serve as decorations. In America it has been known for children to draw a little picture in the centre of the paper before folding it to make a peep-show. By holding the box against the light and looking through the little hole, the picture can be clearly seen.

But most people know this structure as the waterbomb and can recall, at some time in their life, filling one with water and dropping it from an upper window with devastating effect.

How to make a waterbomb ★★

Use a square of paper. Start by completing the waterbomb base, page 22. ▶

Irises (page 62) with twig stems

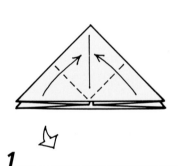

1

Fold the two bottom corners up to the top so that they meet at the centre. Repeat behind.

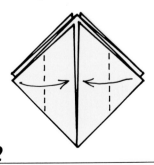

2

Fold the left and right sides in to meet at the centre. Repeat behind.

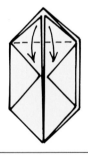

3

Fold the two top points of the front flap down to the centre on a line between the two upper corners. Repeat behind.

4

Fold the two little triangular flaps and tuck them into the adjacent pockets. Repeat behind. Fold the bottom point up to the centre, and return.

5

Apply pressure at top and bottom and blow into the little hole to raise the form.

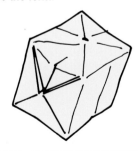

6

The completed waterbomb.

WASHI

Japan is the third largest paper-manufacturing nation in the world. Most paper from Japan is machine-made nowadays, but a certain amount is still made by hand, using methods which go back to the eighth century. Handmade paper is called *washi* or Japanese paper. Made from a pulp which contains bark stripped from the mulberry and other trees, its lightness and agreeable softness to the touch make the difference from other papers immediately apparent.

Furthermore, it is remarkably strong and durable. Folding tests have shown that *washi* can withstand several thousand vertical folds compared to mere hundreds in the case of other paper. Because of this, it is used throughout the world for important documents: it was used, for example, in the Treaty of Versailles which followed World War I.

In addition to its toughness, its translucence makes certain types of *washi* suitable for windows and room dividers in Japanese houses. Other *washi* is used rather like a fabric to make purses and similar dress accessories. The doll in the accompanying photograph, which is made entirely from *washi*, gives some idea of its appearance.

Washi: The World of Japanese Paper by Sukey Hughes, published by Kodansha International, Tokyo, in 1978, gives one of the fullest accounts of the subject.

WAXING MODELS

Waxing is an old method of making artificial flowers permanent. It can also be used to preserve origami models, but it will not be to every paperfolder's taste because much of the characteristic crispness of folded paper is lost in the waxing process.

If you want to try waxing an origami model, you will need a saucepan, a tin can, three or four household candles and a pair of tweezers. Put the candles in the can and place this in the saucepan half full of boiling water. Simmer until the candles have melted; the candle-wicks will sink to the bottom. Do not let the wax boil and do not attempt to melt the candles without water.

Take hold of the model with the tweezers and dip it into the molten wax so that it is completely covered. Remove almost immediately and shake off any surplus wax. Do not allow too much wax to penetrate the corners and crevices of the model where it might gather and distort its form. If you want a shiny surface, dip it straight away into cold water. Accidental cracks can be recoved by warming the model or, if the cracking is too severe, redipping it.

Three-dimensional models of flowers, such as the traditional iris (page 52), make successful subjects for waxing. When dipping them, hold them with the tweezers at the centre of the base.

WESTERN TRADITION

Whereas traditional Japanese methods of folding paper can, in some instances, be traced back for many hundreds of years, there is little from the West, with a few notable exceptions such as the PAJARITA (page 133) and TROUBLE-WIT (page 174) perhaps, which appear to predate the middle of the last century.

The development of Western paperfolding can be traced to a single event: the visit of a troupe of Japanese jugglers to Europe in the 1860s at a time soon after Japan's long period of isolation ended with the Meiji restoration. The jugglers brought with them knowledge of the FLAPPING BIRD (page 11) and soon instructions for this and other models were appearing in English and European periodicals.

Making flapping birds and jumping frogs is a kind of parlour magic. Indeed, turning a sheet of paper into a series of delightful things is rather like transforming base metal into gold. Origami *is* a form of magic and although the educational ideas of Friedrich Froebel, which encouraged paperfolding because of its value in developing manual dexterity, began to have a wide influence towards the end of the nineteenth century, it was the magicians and lovers of magic (which naturally included children) who became the real custodians of the paperfolding tradition until after World War II. The titles of two books which include some examples of paperfolding – Will Blyth's *Paper Magic* (London, 1920) and the ghost-written *Houdini's Paper Magic* (NY, 1922) – demonstrate the continuing association between paperfolding and magic.

A book which was to have a greater influence was Margaret Campbell's *Paper Toy Making,* first published by Pitman, London, in 1937. Margaret Campbell was a widely travelled member of a distinguished family (which included Sir Patrick Campbell and Donald Campbell, the racing driver). Having learned her paperfolding in the Far East, she was able to introduce several new models into the limited repertoire of Western folders. Her book remained in print for many years; and her son, the poet Roy Campbell, later said ruefully that his mother's book on paperfolding had sold more copies than all of his more literary books put together. Copies of *Paper Toy Making* were to be found in school staffroom libraries and other institutions well into the 1950s.

This was fortunate because when the stage magician Robert Harbin went to visit his wife, who was being treated for severe burns at East Grinstead Hospital in 1953, he met some airmen there, fellow patients, who were folding models from Margaret Campbell's book as therapy after plastic surgery to their hands. Harbin's childhood interest in paperfolding, which he had discovered in the *Boy's*

Own Paper, was immediately revived. He embarked on research to find out all he could about paperfolding and produced his own book with a familiar title: *Paper Magic.* When this was published by Oldbourne Books, London, in 1956, Harbin thought that this would be the definitive work, that there was nothing more to be said. In fact it stimulated so much interest that it opened a new career for its author as a publicist for origami. Harbin's second book, *Secrets of Origami,* appeared in 1963 and this was followed by several more titles. He appeared in a series of television programmes on origami which were broadcast for a three-year period during the mid 60s. When the British Origami Society was founded in 1967, largely through the interest he had created, Robert Harbin became its first president.

In America, paperfolders had already found a champion in the diminutive form of Lillian Oppenheimer. She turned her New York apartment into the Origami Center in 1958 where people who shared an interest in paperfolding could meet and exchange information. An attempt was also made to keep a record of the many new origami designs which were being created. Through such associations, formal and informal, the tradition continues in England and America and now throughout the world.

See also SOCIETIES (page 161).

*W*ET FOLDING

*I*f a sheet of paper is made moist it can be moulded as well as folded, and the folds placed in it can be given various qualities – sharp creases can be interspersed with softer changes of plane, for example. Immediately before you start to fold your paper, try moistening it either by lightly wiping both surfaces with a dampened muslin cloth or sponge, or by covering it with a fine mist from a spray bottle containing water. You can remoisten the paper, if necessary, while folding. When the folded structure dries, you will probably find that it will hold its shape better than models folded from untreated paper.

Try laminating two sheets of dampened paper with a flour-and-water paste (see LAMINATING PAPER, page 99) and use this as your folding material. The paste should permeate through both layers of paper so that when it is folded, after being moistened once more in the above way, it will produce a structure remarkably rigid and one incapable of being unfolded.

WRAPPING

'*J*ust as one helps a friend into a coat carefully and courteously, a gift should be wrapped tenderly and conscientiously,' says Kunio Ekiguchi in his *Gift Wrapping* (Kodansha International, Tokyo, 1985). In Japan, different methods of wrapping gifts are considered suitable for different occasions; Westerners are generally less fastidious about the wrapping but make much of the opportunity to utilize decorative ribbons and bows. For comprehensive advice on wrapping gifts in ways which are both decorative and suitable for posting, see manuals such as Adelaide and Josephine Shaw's *Gift Wrapping*, Arco, NY, reprinted in 1974.

It is worth recording one way of wrapping which requires no extras such as sticky tape or string. This is a popular method with paperfolders and is taught by the Origami Center of America.

The seed packet which follows is a traditional model which Marlene Stroud learned as a schoolchild in Germany. You will find it a useful method of containing all sorts of small, loose objects.

How to make an unsealed wrapper ★★

Select a piece of paper three times as wide as the gift box and with an overlap at the ends a little greater than the thickness of the box.

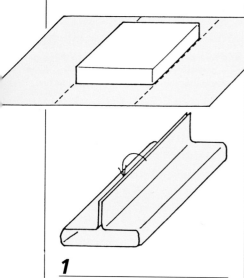

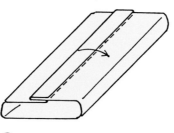

1

Place the box in the centre of the paper and bring the two edges of the paper together. With the two raw edges of the vertical layers held firmly together, fold backwards and forwards to make creases where the vertical layers meet the horizontal; then fold flat.

2

Fold the pair of raw edges into the crease made in step 1.

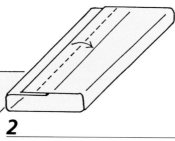

3

Then fold them again. This should stretch the wrapping paper tightly around the box.

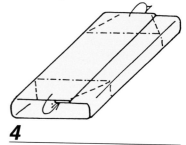

4

Tuck the upper layers of the two ends neatly under the box.

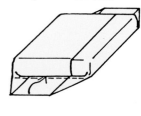

5

Tuck in the remaining bottom layers.

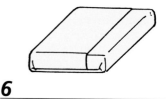

6

The completed wrapper.

How to make a seed packet ★

Use a rectangle of paper of any proportion.

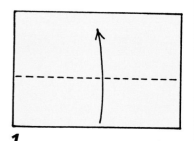

1

Fold up the bottom edge to within a couple of centimetres (about an inch) of the top edge.

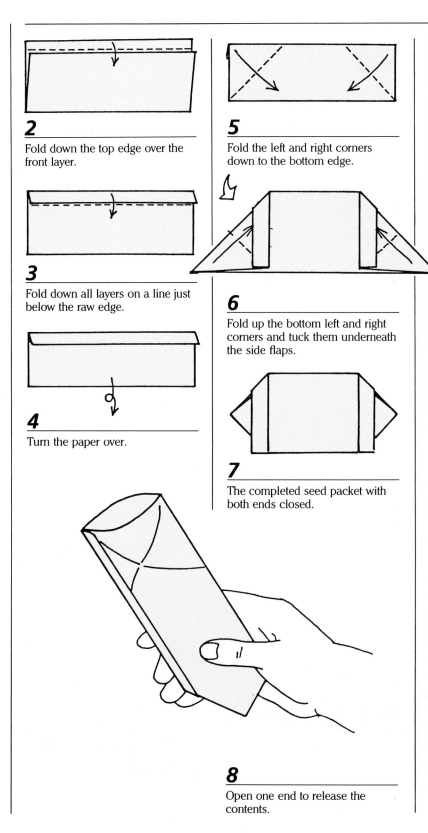

2

Fold down the top edge over the front layer.

3

Fold down all layers on a line just below the raw edge.

4

Turn the paper over.

5

Fold the left and right corners down to the bottom edge.

6

Fold up the bottom left and right corners and tuck them underneath the side flaps.

7

The completed seed packet with both ends closed.

8

Open one end to release the contents.

X-RAY COVER SHEETS

*A*merican paperfolder Ed Sullivan offers the suggestion that the cover sheets which protect X-ray films make suitable material for some kinds of origami, being white on one side and silver on the reverse.

It is a good idea to keep on the look-out for unusual papers which you might encounter unexpectedly. One paperfolder habitually uses powdered-soup packets since he discovered that the inside surface has a matt silver appearance, which appeals to him.

YAKKO-SAN

Yakko-san is the name of a traditional Japanese clown. He is a kimono-clad figure of fun, generally shown as squat-bodied and large-headed. His painted face can be seen on kites and he is a popular subject for Japanese children to fold from paper.

Indeed, Yakko-san may be one of the oldest designs in origami. Japanese mothers have traditionally taught their children how to fold him. Indeed, according to one source, the folding method may have originated in the Muromachi period (1394–1572). Peter Van Note suggests one reason why this stylized and not immediately attractive, figure has survived the centuries: there is a surprise waiting for the child who folds him – lift the edges of his kimono sleeves and you will find his little pointed hands.

The folding method is simple and easy to remember. It is also related to other traditional models such as the salt cellar (page 153), and you may be surprised to find that, with a little experimentation, it can be developed into many other shapes. Japanese paperfolder Kunihiko Kasahara has published a book of models, every one of which is a development of Yakko-san.

How to make a
Yakko-san ★★

Use a square of paper. Start by completing steps 1-4 of the Salt Cellar (page 153).

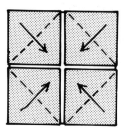

1

Fold the four corners into the centre once more.

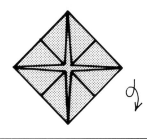

2

Turn the paper over.

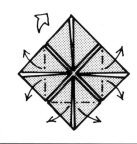

3

Separate the raw edges at the centre of three of the little corner squares, and squash fold.

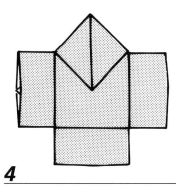

4

The completed Yakko-san. See his skirt, sleeves and diamond-shaped head. Some people like to draw in the features.

ZEN

Is origami just a form of creative play, a pursuit of decorative forms, or is it something more? To a few paperfolders the oneness of the square of paper (which has the capacity to become all creatures, interdependent because the square always remains a square) symbolizes their belief in the harmony of the universe and the presence of the Buddha-nature in all things.

Just as the influence of Zen – that Japanese approach to self-awareness through meditation and the development of intuitive knowledge, which is characterized by a preference for simplicity over complexity – can be seen in other traditional Japanese activities, so it is apparent, to a degree, in origami.

For example, Italian origami teacher Vittorio-Maria Brandoni, who has founded a school of origami in Turin based on Zen principles, believes that origami should not just express what he calls an 'empty aestheticism' but rather an attitude to life and nature. Just as the practice of contemplation in Zen leads to enlightenment, so folding paper in the right way should lead to a 'waking up' of our minds and hearts, he says. 'But', he adds, 'origami is only folding paper – he who wants to understand it, just has to start.'

INDEX

Numbers in italics refer to photographs